MSU LIBRARIES
3 2109 00135 5040

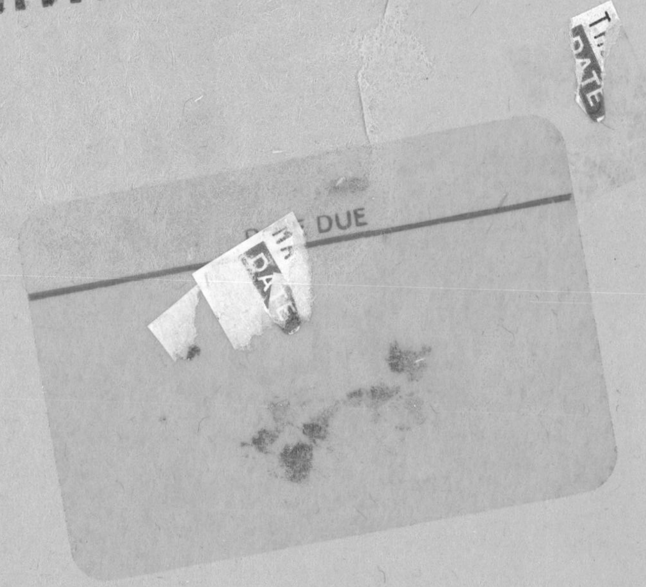
DATE DUE

D1248768

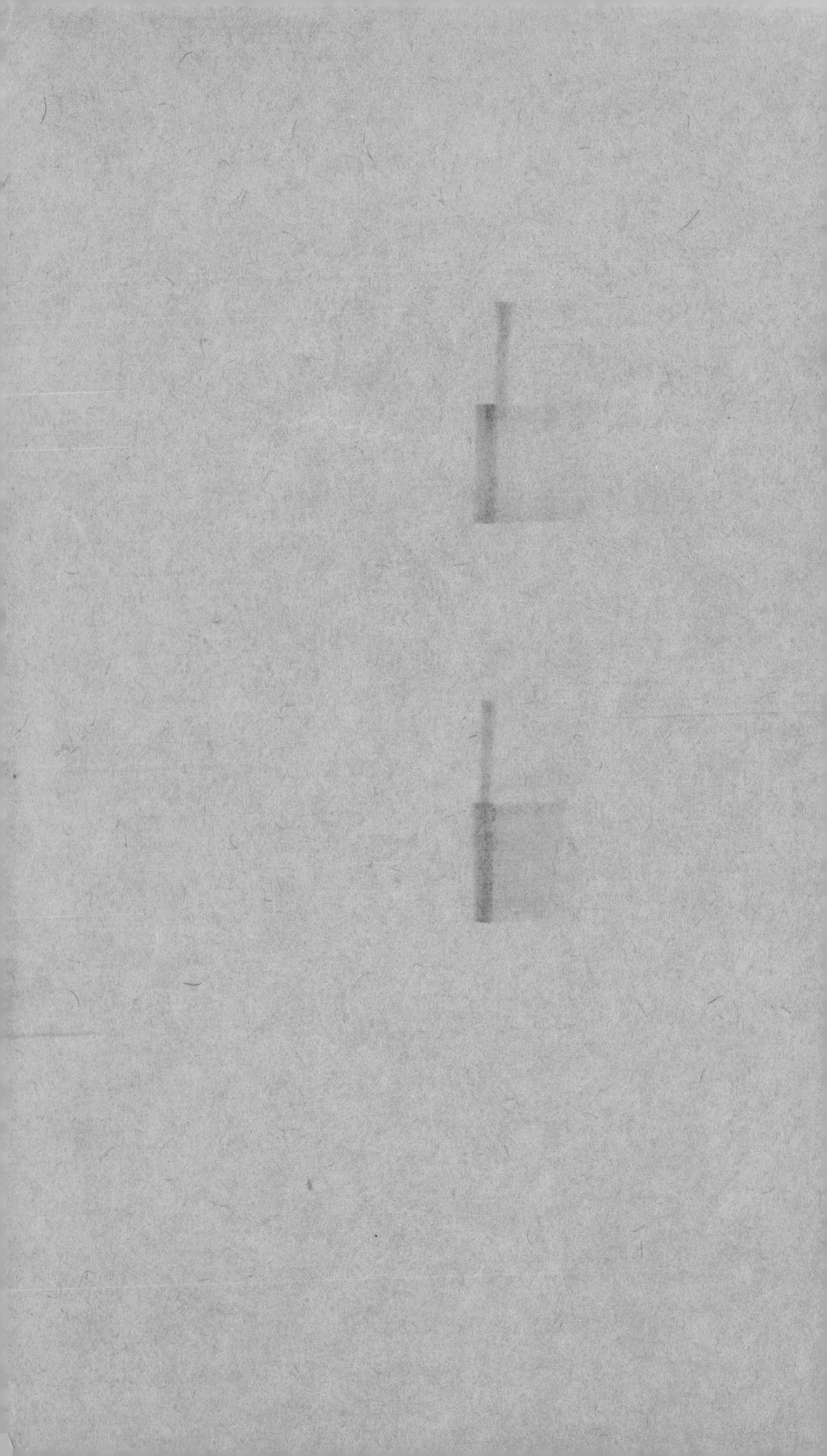

DEEP DELTA COUNTRY

AMERICAN FOLKWAYS

EDITED BY ERSKINE CALDWELL

DESERT COUNTRY by Edwin Corle

DEEP DELTA COUNTRY by Harnett T. Kane

PALMETTO COUNTRY by Stetson Kennedy

PIÑON COUNTRY by Haniel Long

OZARK COUNTRY by Otto Ernest Rayburn

MORMON COUNTRY by Wallace Stegner

HIGH BORDER COUNTRY by Eric Thane

BLUE RIDGE COUNTRY by Jean Thomas

SHORT GRASS COUNTRY by Stanley Vestal

FAR NORTH COUNTRY by Thames Williamson

In Preparation

GOLDEN GATE COUNTRY by Gertrude Atherton

BUCKEYE COUNTRY by Louis Bromfield

PINEY WOODS COUNTRY by John Faulkner

CUTOVER COUNTRY by John T. Frederick

NORTH STAR COUNTRY by Meridel Le Sueur

MISSION COUNTRY by Carey McWilliams

BLACK JACK COUNTRY by George Milburn

TIDEWATER COUNTRY by Elswyth Thane

TOWN MEETING COUNTRY by Clarence M. Webster

Other Books by HARNETT T. KANE

THE BAYOUS OF LOUISIANA

LOUISIANA HAYRIDE

EDITED BY ERSKINE CALDWELL

DEEP DELTA COUNTRY

by

HARNETT T. KANE

DUELL, SLOAN & PEARCE • NEW YORK

5

PRINTED IN THE UNITED STATES OF AMERICA

Contents

INTRODUCTION

Paradise Incomplete

POURING down out of North America's heart, the Mississippi nears the end of its long travels; and suddenly it finds itself in a new land, a region in some ways like no other in the world. From New Orleans to the Gulf of Mexico, for one hundred and fifteen miles or so, spreads the river's Deep Delta. Those who are arrogant in their definitions have asserted with a smile that the great waterway has now "left the States;" and it can be admitted that the terrain and the population alter before the eye. For that matter, in this locale where many things are not what they seem, the Mississippi itself becomes a changed stream.

The great Delta is a favored scene and a tormented one, of alternate felicity and frowning hazard and mystery. For centuries men have speculated about it, settled upon it or tried to do so, and cursed it and loved it. To some it has a sodden, almost terrifying aspect. Colonel James Creecy was haunted by its strangeness ten years afterward: "The wildness and desolation will ever remain deeply engraved in my memory . . . so waste, so uninhabitable, so lonely, so like the Great Desert of the Sahara, in monotony and dreamy stillness—a dreary home for alligators, mud turtles, catfish and sea birds." Mrs. Frances Trollope, on her way to scan the "domestic manners" of Americans, looked hard and informed her readers that its horrors would have given Dante superb materials for another Inferno. Others have observed more closely and more accurately, to discover here a rare and untamed quality, beauty in rich profusion and turbulence.

A philosophic friend, who digs oysters for a living, tells about it in this way: Le Dieu Seigneur, the Lord God, had a light mood and decided to create a new paradise on earth. Not with a wave of the hand as He did in the case of the Garden of Eden, but after a more delicate fashion, setting up something that would extend itself over the ages. By design or through forgetfulness—or perhaps because He chose the undependable Mississippi for the purpose—the task was never quite finished. So it remains, a disturbing, ever-changing place, no nearer completion today than it ever was.

A glance at the map that forms the end papers of this book may help the reader understand something of this uniqueness. Between city and Gulf the soil is strung along the river like tattered bits of cloth hanging from a double line. Many Americans visualize New Orleans as located directly on the sea. Had such a feat been possible, parts of the nation's history might have been different. Nowhere in this expanse of the Delta have men felt that there was sufficient dry, dependable space for the creation of a large city. After preliminary hesitation settlers moved here, and prospered; but they lived as the shape of the land dictated, fitting themselves to it, not it to them.

In real and direct fashion, the Father of Waters has engendered everything in sight. Long after the rest of the continent had emerged from prehistoric gloom, this was a heavy, pounding sea. The coast ended many miles to the north; but downward through the centuries the inland passage was forcing itself, one river digging and depositing as it went. In its lower reaches the Mississippi was erratic, vacillating; it has shifted over five or six courses through the present limits of Louisiana. A few thousand years ago—not a long time as geologists reckon—it picked what is roughly its present route below the site of New Orleans. With it the river brought the richest soil that the world knows, its choice of all the teeming land between the Rockies and the Alleghenies. Daily it has dropped an almost incalculable tonnage of silt to the sides and at its farthest reaches to the south. Especially in flood stage it has thrown thick coverings of new earth along its course. Bit by bit, from the silt, from weed fragments, from mineral remains, the ground has built until it lifted above the waves into the sunshine, and higher by slow degree.

It has not been an easy process. This is a locale of endless conflict between brown river and blue Gulf. At times victory has been with the sea; its waters—lapping, sucking—pull at the river's creations, and the wild, cyclonic sea winds rip off heavy masses of the new earth. But the Mississippi fights without letup.

Like a tawny hand it has reached its way into the deep, and a thickening, widening arm has followed. The stoic wife of a shrimper today stands in the door of her palmetto-thatched cabin and points a few feet away: "This was where shore end' when I was a girl." The tan earth has advanced ten miles outward, surrounding, absorbing old islands until they are part of it.

Meanwhile the Delta is never fully in balance. Where the soft soil fails to receive a regular renewal from the river, it begins gradually to drop away, dissolving into uncertain marshes, into water-ringed ridges and then into nothing; and the Gulf slips inland, to swallow everything in sight. I have rowed over a shallow lake among the gray-hung trees of a ghostlike forest. Everything is sagging; inch by inch the water has slipped up the rotted bark. The sea is taking back what it gave up. One observer, surveying the changes, put it succinctly, "Nature is here, as at Niagara, caught in the act . . . geology transacting before men's eyes."

All seems endless lowland; yet there are differences of which the Delta people take advantage. In most parts of America, land sinks to the river's edge. Here the opposite is true; it is highest at the "front," where the Mississippi has made its first, heaviest deposits, and it thins to the rear. The river's banks are the backbone of all this country—a double ridge on which most of the Deltans live.

As the Deltans tell you, "The groun', she begin way down and keep getting further down." Near New Orleans the highest natural elevation is about fifteen feet above sea level. This declines to ten, to eight, to four feet and eventually into the blue waters themselves. In the vicinity of the city the dry ground is several miles wide on each side of the Mississippi. As the Delta reaches toward the Gulf, this tapers to a half mile, to a few hundred yards and then to a line that disappears in the sea.

A short distance from the ridge of the river the land falls and soon it is marsh, the vast plains of unending green and gold variations that make up most of the Delta. Parts of the marsh stay dry, or nearly so; much of it remains a few feet above the sea, and is regularly invaded by wind-driven waters. Toward the shore it is continually covered by a slow-moving salinity. Everywhere the surface is broken by curving rivulets, inlets, bayous, and green-fringed canals in which the skies are always to be seen in silver reflection. From almost any point to the other, the Deltan can find a route by boat among the weblike turnings.

Thus encircled, the Delta overflows with a life that seems frantic in its exuberance. Here is growth as close to the tropic as can be found in the United States. Along the river lift the tall willows, the soft cottonwoods and the hackberries with their purple dots against the bank; the oaks that are always grotesquely twisted, and about them the crawling vines and creepers, some as thick as a man's wrist. Banana plants wave heavy emerald leaves in the wind; the sun throws a finger of light across the bristling fan of a palmetto, to be caught by its long points and by the high white blossoming of the Spanish dagger.

At varying distances from the river spread the freshwater swamps, their shadowed liquid stained by the slowly dissolving vegetation, the feather-leafed cypresses planting firm bases in the green-black moisture. Farther to the rear stand the wild canebrakes, reeds and sedges and bulrushes, some of them higher than a man's head: lances of green that are fragile or cruel—the sawgrass that cuts the flesh like a razor, the salt cane or "oyster grass," cattail, alligator weed, and hundreds of others. And among them hide the soft hues of the mallows, the slender thrusts of the water lilies and the unexpected flare of the purple iris, the lost flowers of the backwaters.

The scene offers little of the trim prettiness of temperate places. Everything blooms flamboyantly, insistently, with a sped-up, shorter span than in the country above: early birth, quick maturity, abrupt death. Dying, the growths are succeeded by others, rivals or members of the same family, to ripen and give way in turn. This teeming fecundity has almost a sinister quality. Those who cultivate their fields must fight dozens of other offshoots of the soil that seek dominance. I have heard Deltans, stabbing at encroaching weeds and grasses, tell the ground "Stop growing for a while, damn you!" Beneath their feet, in the moist earth, stir millions of minute forms, creeping animals and insects that are at ease on land, in water, and in the air. Parasites abound—thick spiders, ants, lizards, chameleons; every blade, every drop of water, every crevice in the earth harbors swarming, microscopic creatures; and before the eyes whir hordes of insects of bright and tormenting coloration.

The Seigneur, says my friend as he slaps at a persistent mosquito, made this all too inviting a spot for every kind of growing thing.

As in the old days, the best introduction is by the river, from a steamer in the spring. This country does not sleep through the winter—it merely drowses; now it is vibrantly awake. The gray-black industrialism of New Orleans' wharves and factories slowly disappears. With every mile or so the surroundings are more open, and the green-topped levees slip lower. The living places to both sides come into greater relief—a shining roof, then a house to its window tops, then part of its gallery. The eye is drawn by the generous outlines of a few once-superb houses, last of a procession of plantation establishments that studded these acres. Now the land lies fallow, or it has been turned to truck gardens that pour forth an enormous yield, a crop every three months, harvest upon harvest from the almost inexhaustible, mealy black ground.

All is greenness—an ever-present verdancy of grass and tree and bush. Along the river extends a line of cottages with big porches and big families on or about them; and the numbers increase until they become an unending file anchored to the bank. Sharp spots of blue and pink and yellow shine in the sun, but generally the houses are weather-worn and unornamented; huddling among the many plants, they seem almost like natural outgrowths of their background. In front of many of the houses family wharves on spindly legs reach into the river, draped with drying nets, flanked by skiffs and pirogues, the frail Louisiana dugout canoes. Canals with worn locks open at intervals, and bobbing fleets of motored vessels join us in our downward passage.

With us move others: low-hung, cocky tugs, impudent of anything that rides more slowly; a small white paddle-wheeler loaded with cattle, an armored vessel whose gray is grim and utilitarian, and ponderous black tankers. Around us, little concerned, people of the Delta paddle or chug across the river, calling to friends on shore, sometimes veering out of our path in the nick of time to avoid collision. Edging the banks, among the overhanging willow branches, cling masses of plants, the thickly-matted water hyacinths, bulbous, waxen leaves upholding lavender flowers over the water. At the levee, statue-like, a snowy heron stands, the pure outlines of its silken body supported by gleaming black legs. A quick gesture, and it takes lightly off, to disappear over the embankment.

The Mississippi has changed about us. Gone are the torrent-like stretches, the swift and roaring turns. The stream has deepened into a great trough, a serene expanse nearly a mile wide. The river becomes a more stable waterway, resting, perhaps, after its hard labors above. Yet its flow is more powerful than ever, an unhurried surge that has the enormous force of the continent's central waters. For a time it is difficult, watching this yellow-tinted placidity, to shake off the impression that we are riding the waves of some protected lake.

A cool fragrance, hard at first to identify, lifts from the west bank. Close behind the low levee, for uninterrupted miles, extends a line of squat, bushlike trees. Over them hover hundreds of blackbirds; and against the dark foliage shine thousands of small orange blossoms. This is the great citrus center of Louisiana; the soft air and the rich soil produce fruit of a peculiar lusciousness. (Within a month or so, among the trees will stand Creole Easter lilies, creamy flowers that flourish in the Delta as they do in few parts of the hemisphere.)

The large trees have thinned out. This land is rapidly falling and narrowing as well; now only about five hundred yards of dry earth are available, and there is little dependable base into which the oaks and other heavy growths can sink their roots. The willows and cottonwoods hold for a time, but even they disappear. Beside the pilot atop the boat, we can catch a glint of water among the reeds in the distance. These green reaches seem merely pleasant, spreading meadows; but the Gulf washes not far to the back, and the marshes are advancing toward the river edges. Yet a few houses still hug the banks. Places so situated appear to invite ruin; the Delta dwellers will take the risk.

Soon, too, we realize that the sea is not far ahead. The air fills with a tang, a thin spray ascends with the freshening breeze. Into the winds beat many birds, screeching gulls with wide, dark-tipped wings, a slow and indolent crane, a flapping group of heavy, pouch-billed brown pelicans. From the nearby marshes rises a combination of brine and musk and the smell of wetted grasses—a breath of moist fecundity. What land remains is in thin strips, and some have called it "floating," so insubstantial does it appear in the all-encompassing waters.

The tranquil river has been widening; in a moment it is more than two miles across—the Head of Passes. From here the stream breaks into three main branches that reach toward the Gulf like the webbed toes of a duck. Each is large enough to be classified in most places as a good-sized river, and each builds a minor delta of its own. The lines of earth grow yet thinner until they look almost like green ribbons; yet they keep the waters distinct, the mud-tan in the center, the wider, foam-edged blue to each side. For miles the passes hold firm, and then they taper downward into the Gulf.

But even now the Mississippi, so long the master, has not surrendered. Into the sea it asserts itself. A sharp line separates the silt-freighted liquid from the brine. The fresh overlies the salt; at the edges the waves beat against the river water to little avail. At the point where sea meets river the waters boil; into the air dart mullet, shrimp, and silver eel. Small forms feed on microscopic ones, great on small; from the skies the birds wheel down, to steal from their scaled rivals. Then the prow of our ship, cutting through the water's brown top, brings up a blue-white mixture. The last shreds of the river scatter, and we are in a southern sea.

Over the waves leap flying fish, like magnified butterflies reflecting in the air, beings that speak of another age when many creatures of one element were equally at home in another. Rolling and leaping about us are the porpoises, fat and friendly whales whose name the Latins devised well from their words for fish and hog. The deep blues of the Gulf skies hang low; the sun beats with a painful fervor, and there is a somnolence that hints of spiced islands. From the shelving bottom rise reefs and contorted archipelagoes of a thousand shapes, bathed by the sea and piled with its drift. Against the sandy shores, in the almost transparent waters, clusters of purple sea flowers wave, and mottled crabs scurry furtively about the bright white shells.

Strangely, the Gulf also invades the Mississippi. During the "dry" months when the river flow is at its lightest, a bottom layer of blue creeps up the channels. The water takes a new tinge, and often it seems as if this were the ocean itself. When the Deltan casts his bait in the stream, he may bring up a redfish or a mackerel. One child shrieked when he discovered an octopus a few yards from his home. Others have dropped lines, taken a fresh-water fish, then sunk them lower and caught one of salt variety. Eventually the Old Man has reasserted himself, trapping the intruders from the brine, sending them below with the rest of his debris.

The newcomer decides that the Delta is a place of unending waters—to the front, to the back, to the sides and from above. Quasi-tropic, the region receives as much as 60 to 65 inches of rain a year. Thankful residents smile at the heavens that help their crops, then frown as deluges sweep down, fill canals to overflowing and threaten to cover their plantings. Nowhere have I felt the beat of rains like those of the Delta's wet season. Thrust about by the wind, the water pours from all directions with the rage of an animate thing. And meanwhile moisture seeps and filters everywhere. The country is humid beyond the belief of most outsiders. Roofs drip heavily; doors and chairs are damp to the touch. Housewives complain that their bread molds in the night; walls sweat; chickens scratch dispiritedly in moist ground. From the north the river bears the chill of mountain and hill and plateau; from the south comes the bland air of the Gulf. The two meet, and for months thick fogs hang over the Delta. During such periods, the residents spend hours of every day in the prowling gray envelopment.*

At other times the fogs form only above the river, leveling off a short distance in the air. On the bridges of the ships, river pilots

* This heavy humidity makes the brief Delta winter sometimes hard to bear. The region normally has only two months or so of cold; January 1 may seem like the May 1 of other places. But during the short period of cold, unprotected men and animals can suffer.

sight ahead in clear air, but the decks below are out of sight to them—a peculiar, often an eerie sensation. So trapped, a vessel can only drop anchor and maintain vigil. Through night and morning the Deltans have heard the mournful, monotonous blowing of horns and thought about the unseen people who waited on the decks or in the cabins near them. Again they have caught the sound of something else—a dull crash, a red-tongued explosion; and they have rushed to the river to find disaster in their front yards.

These river people are familiar with death from other sources. Through many years the Mississippi's mouths have served as a kind of magnet for brutal manifestations of wind and water. Again and again they have felt the fury of tropical hurricanes. Up the stream rush ominous tidal waves, eight and ten feet high or higher, grim billows that smash boats and homes and dissolve the earth in their path. From the "back," from lakes and marshes to the east and west, comes more water, lifting quickly, "drowning" canals and small streams, leaving only the tops of the highest reeds to bow madly in the air. Men and women make signs of the cross and cry aloud, then die in a moment. Those who live, sigh and go back to their tasks; they know that such ruin has come periodically in the past and that it will come periodically in the future.

"Le Bon Dieu," say the devout, "sometime' he treat' us bad. But then he been kin', too, ain' he?"

For this was, and to a great extent continues, a district of lavish wealth in many guises—one of the last of American frontiers. The settlers took the best available dry spots and some of the wet, and they fought heat, moisture and insects to bring rich crops out of the earth. Then they looked about them and beheld a bewildering, untouched abundance of fish and game: thick oyster reefs, heavy concentrations of shrimp; deer, turtles, furred animals; alligators, wild fruits, great flocks of birds—for the Delta has always been one of the greatest gathering places of the birds of the New World. The Deltans lived with the seasons, skimming the cream of each of nature's offerings, moving between shallow lagoons and silvered lakes, from slow-moving river to beaches pounded by the sea.

A light-hearted visitor of the last century described them as "aquatic men, with fins like fishes, noses like alligators, feet like ducks." The Deltans lack these picturesque attributes, of course; but to watch one of them scurry without accident over a gluelike half-marsh is to conclude that they do not need them, or have developed good substitutes. And I have met some whose nails have been so stained with the dyes in the waters about them that they will never be restored to their natural hue.

In 1872 the Reverend Mr. Edward Fontaine reported the Delta populated by "a greater variety of races than can be found anywhere else on this continent who are not congregated in cities." The variety has not grown less. First arrived the French, largely the less well-to-do, the simpler and hardier ones. Not long afterward came the Spanish, to give a warmer coloration; then infusions of South European Slavs; Germans, Italians and Irishmen; Spanish-speaking Filipinos; Chinese, Malays; Portuguese, English, Danes, Greeks, and Swedes. Beside them settled the Negroes and also colonies of mulattoes and quadroons, with a separate status which they maintained with determination.

Largely without cities or towns as others recognize the terms (there is no single incorporated community), many of the Deltans yet stay closer to each other than do most farmers. The clusters of houses along the river might be the progression of hamlets of some European border territory. Every few miles introduces another element, another language or tint of complexion. A group of families who seem unquestionably Castilian gives way to a settlement that is French in inflexion, in eye and in gesture. On a connecting canal is set a group of homes whose stolid occupants could be transported easily to a warm Adriatic beach. Toward the Gulf, among the sands and reeds, rests a tropic colony whose houses, roofed with yellowed palmetto fans that flap in the wind, differ little from those of dwellers along the mud flats of China. Over all hangs a sun-shot dreaminess that some would call Old World in character. Yet these people are children of the Mississippi as truly as any redneck or shanty-boat resident above.

This Deep Delta remains a country of many tolerances. One of Spanish descent, who is most comfortable when using the language of his fathers, caulks a boat on a bank with another who talks to him in sing-song French. A thickset Dalmatian runs a store with his wife, a plump woman of Italian extraction. In an oval face that is vaguely Oriental, the blue-gray eyes of the West gaze forth. Yet the Gallic note is prevalent. The French pioneered and they stayed, to dominate and yet to undergo a Delta sea-change.

In a region born of conflict, surrounded by uncertainties, the Deltans have fitted themselves to the rhythms of their background. They have battled the elements and sometimes other men for survival; their ways have tended to harden with their muscles. Here and there, in the farthest reaches, they take on something of the sadness of their lonely grasses and waters. Like the land in which they live, they alternate violence with placidity. They enjoy long periods of rest in the shadows, followed by bursts of sharp excitement; and when they are stirred, they become a furiously positive people, with a gift for riproaring action. Since they are largely Latins, they possess also a capacity for release in gaiety, and they have retained their zest for gusty humors: tall stories, the hairy traditions of hale men, the elemental joke that calls for a dousing in the Mississippi or a kick in the backside.

Fatalists, they reconcile themselves to what the seasons will bring, bowing their wills to the river, or the winds, or the changes in the water table. Life can be hard, yes; but a man cannot always count his sorrows. He will go to the store at the levee to "pass a good time." He will play cards with his friends and he will cry a bit into his strong orange wine. In the morning he will rise to the first honk of wild geese over the lakes, he will sniff the brisk air and, damn it, he will tell his son, but this will be a fine day for a hunt! Le's go.

In their demi-paradise, most of the Deltans have lived simply, humbly, garnering their sustenance from the storehouse about them. Some have turned to quicker ways of reward. This traffic route—one of the great ones of the Western World—has been equipped with all too many side alleys, water cuts that seemed created for devious dealings. From early days the region caused concern to officials as a district of smuggling and related operations. Corsairs made this their harborage during many generations. In the last century the Delta nourished a number of hell-spots, brawling hangouts of underworld figures of all hues and assortments. And almost to the present day it has provided a well-trodden pathway for forbidden cargoes.

Most strangers who know about the Delta have heard of it in connection with troubles: disasters, irregularities, and flaring violences. They have laughed at reports reaching the outer world, have shaken their heads, or grown red in the face. They tell each other, half in joke, half in earnest: That's *some* place down there. But generally they understand little of the country's real nature. So close and yet so remote, it is as unknown to most Louisianians as to the natives of Brooklyn or Chicago.

Today, the Delta and its ways remain remarkably unchanged. Men live by their waters and do not understand why outsiders should wonder at a world in which cats learn to swim and chickens scratch warily at the shallow water edges, lest the watching crabs nip off a claw. In springtime, a family looks in its backyard or in one of the wet spots under its house for red crawfish to boil for the table. Fathers and sons wrestle alligators with their hands or fix traps for them, baited with dead birds held just above the water. Many catch extra sacks of fish, to feed their hogs. When the boys come in with a neat batch of frogs, Maman hangs the amphibians on a line in the yard with clothes pins, to drip. To the rear of the house devices are set for muskrats in the marsh; into the Mississippi, in front, the girls drop containers filled with cornmeal, to catch the gray river shrimp. And some move their cattle by boat for pasture close to the river's meeting with the Gulf. The stock will stay there, on the thin edges of green, because they have nowhere else to go.

At the "back," on small ridges along canals and lakes, other families erect houses on tall posts, then set to work to create ground beneath them, with oyster shells and earth scratched up from near by—man-made islands in the wet expanse. Nearly everybody has a boat at the wharf or under the house for an emergency. A push-pole, for achieving a quick passage through shallow water, is as much a necessity as a pair of boots in the treacherous marsh. Petroleum is the fuel of life, to maintain the "gazzoleen"—the Delta's motored vessel.

In far-down settlements, children grow up away from the

sight of anything that has the properties of land; their "road" is a line of boards twisting between a collection of houses over the limitless grasses. They and their parents lead a hidden life, their only means of communication with the world an occasional passerby upon their slow waters. Of New Orleans, the prideful, careless metropolis that might seem so near, they know little. They may live and die without having approached it; or, after a one-day visit, they see no reason to return. Others make regular trips there with their produce; they head directly for the markets, get their money and leave without a side glance. New Orlean'—you can have it!

At the river mouths, the bays and quaking surfaces have been found to overlap deep pools of oil in the alluvium—a startling discovery of the present century. Derricks rise out of the soft base, and a chug and a hiss sound over stretches that formerly knew only the splash of fish and the whirrings of birds. Just a short distance off a few patient oxen pull at their tasks as they did when France ruled Louisiana. An elaborate speedboat, utilizing the newest findings of hydraulic engineers, slips past a fisherman who paddles a pirogue that his father hollowed sixty years ago. Between them a muddy shape lifts itself—the alligator gar, the poison armé or armed fish which early colonials described to amazed countrymen across the sea. Half reptile, often more than six feet long, covered with a bonelike coat that is almost impenetrable, this survivor of an earlier age has become a major predator of the Delta. When men are sending space ships across the Gulf, I suspect that this villain will still be killing smaller fish and wrecking the fishing lines of the Deltans. Above, a mechanized hawk of a plane sweeps from the southward, bringing momentary excitement to a group of children in a rice field. They stand on crude wooden elevations, popping cloths to scare away the birds; and the methods of rice culture are those that were followed centuries ago in any Asiatic backland.

Meanwhile, as our oysterman-philosopher points out, the Delta stays unfinished, rising in some places, lowering in others; and for part of the sinkage he blames man, who tinkered and altered the original plans. As he built levees, small or large ones, he prevented the annual rises of the river over the land to each side—the regular floods and deposits of silt that built up the area. Had man waited before moving here, or at least delayed the building of the artificial mounds, it might all be many feet higher—a dry, even-more-fertile plain reaching to east and west. "That," says my friend, " must have been the way Dieu Seigneur intended it."

In any case the Deltans must take additional precautions. The usual man of the Mississippi has to concern himself only with the danger of water from the river itself. The Deep Deltan must watch to the back as well. He raises rear levees to keep the water from creeping out of the marshes. He installs heavy, Diesel-powered drainage machines, half lost in the junglelike foliage. After a heavy rain, or when the wind has forced a rush of water from the Gulf, the pumps run at full capacity, to draw every possible gallon out of the too-receptive soil. Staying in the Delta, I have, like others, come to accept the endless chug of the equipment. On these long, jagged peninsulas thrust into the sea, it is a sound that all expect and welcome, unless they prefer to find their yards covered by a small lake in the morning. When it stops in the night, the Deltans wake at once, and inquire what the trouble is.

My curiosity about such subjects was a matter of surprise to the children. "Don't they got back levees around your house?" one inquired. When I answered in the negative, she asked: "Well, you got a pow'ful drain machine, then?" When I again said no, her eyes widened at the thought of a strange world in which people could let water come and go around them without having to do something about it.

PART I

THE "GLORY DAYS"

CHAPTER 1

Corridor to a Treasure House

FROM the first time that they saw or heard of the Deep Delta, red men and white-skinned ones have told tales about it, their originals born of terror or of wonder, their later versions of other and mixed motives. The Indians generally avoided the place, especially its farthest reaches. The steams and mists were treacherous obstacles. Few barks could withstand the storms that roared about the low yellow earth; fantastic brown accumulations loomed to snatch at unwary vessels. And strange things happened before the eyes of intruders, when the ground groaned and shifted and the bottom of the river rose suddenly high into the air. It was indeed a region that hostile gods might have frequented. Only at the edges of this wet uncertainty did the Indians occasionally set up their homes, to leave behind shell mounds that gleamed in ghostly whiteness over the miles of grasses. So the Delta remained to itself through the centuries of prehistory, an unsettled luxuriance of forest and marsh and flower, cleaved by the unpredictable power of the Mississippi.

For long years after the New World was discovered, the region eluded the conquerors. Europeans settled the Caribbean, Mexico, Florida, and prowled about the eastern and western Gulf; they seemed always to miss or pass by this entry-place to an unguessed empire. Drawn by their visions of the golden East, countless others followed Christopher Columbus in obscure, unrecorded expeditions. One day the first white man stood in the prow of a sailing vessel and gazed in awe at the might of the river. A map, published in 1513 but bearing an earlier date, shows clearly a three-clawed extension of a stream into the sea. Yet there is a mystery here; who saw it and set it down, or told the chart-makers of it, will almost certainly never be determined.

The year 1519 saw Alvarez de Pineda hastening along the

Gulf coast. He reached a stream, "very large and very deep," which he called the River of the Holy Ghost; and early historians thought that he had come upon the Mississippi's Delta. But he and his men, alas, told too much. At the point of discharge, they said, they came upon a sizable Indian town; friendly redskins escorted them along the river to forty villages, with gold-filled houses and people of assorted shapes and sizes, monstrously tall or dwarfs, their ears and noses decorated with fascinating metals. Clearly this could not have been the Mississippi's mouths—a marshy terrain barren of Indians with or without gold upon their faces. Further study of the descriptions indicates that the party probably went to the site of Mobile Bay.

A year later Pineda was back. Again the river mouth escaped him. He found more Indians and, with them, death. Yet his falsehoods, or his embellishments, went marching on. Men remembered those delightful phrases, those stories of a vast river, wherever it might be; and their fingers itched to touch the gleaming metals. Spanish eyes fixed themselves on the northern Gulf; Spanish avarice organized; within a decade Pamphilo de Narváez reached Florida and struck inland. But all that gleamed was the water of the lagoons; "great cities" turned out to be mud huts. Hopelessly lost, without vessels, the desperate men fashioned a crude fleet and sailed westward along the shore. A month later they discovered that, though they were some distance from the coast, they floated in gray-brown water. They let down water containers; it was fresh.

The Spaniards ventured toward the river, to find themselves in a current of frightening strength, buffeted by a wind from land. For two days they tried to fight their way northward. The ships separated. The commander gave a last order: Each should do what he thought best to save his vessel. Most of the party drowned. Eventually, of the several hundred members, four furtive wretches remained, to wander eight years before they reached a Spanish settlement on the far Pacific shores. The Mississippi had spurned the first whites known definitely to have felt its might.

Yet others still visioned easy reward above the Gulf. De Soto, plunderer of Peru, aimed at bigger things. He brought to Florida the most glittering cavalcade of American colonial history. If pomp could conquer, it would be a glorious venture. Instead, it became an exercise in mass cruelty, and one of the great fiascoes of Spanish memory. For the Indians the conquistadores had harsh demands, the whip and the faggot. Where was the treasure? Where? Tell, you vermin. Gold was all that the invaders wanted, that and the occasional use of the more comely women. (For high De Soto himself, says the record, a pair of the best at each stopping place.) When one obstinate heathen dared say he knew of no treasure, he was burned alive.

The Indians retaliated with imagination, tearing out eyes and other organs of the white men, torturing, murdering from ambush. Through most of the present Southern states ranged the despoilers. They lost first their plumes, then their composure, then their courage. Passing a majestic stream, they crossed; but soon they saw that they must make haste to escape this country alive. De Soto died on the river shore; his men improvised boats to follow the stream southward. For five hundred miles they moved with the Mississippi's surge, fighting red men on the way. Through the Deep Delta, they reached the Gulf, caring little for the scenes about them. Four years after their gallant departure, the haggard wrecks reached Tampico, to kiss the ground and cry.

Now they told what they had seen. They might have pictured the vast interior of fertile America, and the magnificence of the stream leading to its center. That was not what the valley of the Mississippi meant to them. They described a hell upon a hostile earth; and they added that they had not reached a single mine, or one gem-encrusted city. Spain abruptly lost interest; it would concentrate on Mexico and places farther south, where it was certain there was booty. Men knew definitely, at last, that the three-pronged entry was a doorway to a continent; and men did not care. The Delta had to be discovered all over again; but the Mississippi was to flood many times and nourish and build up many more miles of soft, green-crowned soil before this could happen. For nearly a century and a half the Delta was ignored by "civilization."

Far to the north the French advanced along the St. Lawrence into the chill wilderness. The Indians told them of a "great

western water," and the French, too, dreamed foolishly and fervently of a central thoroughfare to the Orient. To be sure, the Spaniards had clearly established that the great stream reached from north to south. But few heeded, and few knew of a certainty what the Spainards had found. Dogs in the New World manger, the Spanish did not want the valley, and did not want any others to take it. The river was left off many maps. The Gulf was a Spanish lake; let all foreign curs keep away. But the French came to the Delta from the north. Laboriously they fought downward through connecting waters; and then in April of 1682, the grand seigneur La Salle and his men glided through the diminishing land.

Hearts quickening, the Frenchmen saw the river break into three outlets. Soon they stood in their vessels, lips parted, and beheld the ageless blue of the Gulf, empty as if a Spaniard had never beheld it. Turning to mundane things, one party came upon a supply of dried food, left by venturesome Indians. They quickly gulped large mouthfuls, until one, looking hard, announced that it was human flesh. The chronicle of Father Zenobius Membré adds, in a note of gentle observation, "It was very good and delicate."

A day later La Salle, the priest, and others gathered on a brief skirt of shore a few miles above the Head of Passes to take formal possession of all of the Mississippi, its tributaries and their lands. The men lifted their muskets above the grasses and wild canes. A sudden volley sent into the air thousands of white and brown birds that heard such sounds for the first time. An alligator slipped heavily into the water near them; a lone pelican, long-beaked and curious, wheeled low, to start away at the cry: "Vive le Roi! Vive le Roi!" "La Louisiane" was claimed and named for Louis the Great.

At court, La Salle won support for a second trip to make a permanent settlement. This time the Delta would be reached from below. Using his astrolabe, La Salle had found the latitude; but he did not know the longitude. How far west should he go? He guessed, passed the low Delta coast, and landed at Matagorda Bay in Texas. For two years the party remained in a small fort, dying of disease and deprivation. One group beat its way toward Canada, to bring help, and on the journey La Salle fell at the hands of his men. Indians captured or killed the last woman and child. And the river still flowed unceasingly to the Gulf.

La Salle's idea languished, but did not die. France was occupied for years in war with England. With peace came respite for conquest, and also rumors. The British were now claiming the Delta. Daniel Coxe, a New Jersey merchant, had letters patent to an "English Province of Carolana," about and above the river mouth. A trading company organized rapidly, and an expedition with settlers moved toward the New World. Waking suddenly, the French also set to work. They chose Pierre Le Moyne d'Iberville of Canada, as ambitious as he was skilled, to head their own party. In 1698, a race was on.

A quick trip to the West Indies brought advice from the Spaniards: The French were foolish; everybody knew it was impossible to ascend that terrible river mouth; the great rocks meant death. That, Señores, was why it was called the River of the Palisades. Iberville nodded and pursued his course, guarding against storms and Englishmen. Weeks later the party appeared near its goal. Small islands came into view; cruising about, the Frenchmen named them, sometimes with a grin: Horn, because a sailor dropped one there; the Chandeleur chain, for the feast of Candelmas; Cat, for the furry little beasts found on it—raccoons; Pea Island, because the mosquitoes attacked them and they fled it, leaving behind a bag of the plants. At Ship Island they found a secure anchorage. The men watched the magnificent flights of wild fowl, and laughed over the playful porpoises. It seemed a paradise of gleaming water and soft sand, of delicate-fleshed fish, and everywhere the birds, grotesqueries in feathers that they could not name.

Wherever they turned they met deceptive alternations of islands, spits and reefs. They entered bays, they towed their small boats over shallows, and they watched the skies. Winds mounted, and high fogs crawled about them. A succession of gusts ripped their sails, and bore them steadily inward against every effort. Night approached, and they looked ahead to find—just as the Spaniards had predicted—a frowning barrier of rocks. But the waters beneath them became more agitated than ever. Disaster in the sea was at least as certain as wreckage ahead. Iberville gave the signal: To the rocks.

In the gloom, they held tightly for the crash. A slight jolt, and they went through! For these were not rocks at all, but accumulations of timbers and mud, dried so that they had the appearance of boulders. The French had defeated the river in one of its tricks. Now they dodged floating timbers that could smash their craft in a moment. Without warning, the river bottom reached at them; their boats struck hard, almost capsized. But they kept onward, and won.

One day the rivals came. Six months after the arrival of the party, Iberville's brother Bienville was paddling downstream with a group of Canadians when he rounded a certain large bend in the Deep Delta. Anchored in midstream lay a twelve-gunned British man-of-war. Boarding it, Bienville met a Captain Banks. The vessel was part of the expedition that had left England the previous year. (Fortunately for the French, it had stopped on the Atlantic coast for the winter.) Now, after cruising all about the Gulf, Banks "congratulated himself" on his finding of the river entry.

The two men eyed each other. Bienville informed his enemy that the river was possessed by France, that she had a large force with which to make her claim good. He told Banks to leave voluntarily, lest he be forced to do so. The French were outnumbered; their nearest ships were miles away to the east in the Gulf. But the river made an almost complete circle here, and there might well have been men and guns upstream. Banks announced that he would return with a fleet of warships light enough to enter the Mississippi and take it. Then his vessel turned about and sailed back. This point on the river, at which an exercise of bloodless diplomacy may well have prevented the British from making the valley their colony, has ever since been known, rather unkindly, as "English Turn."

The incident alarmed the French. Within four months they were at work on the first fort in the lower Mississippi, at a spot fifty miles from the mouth, "the nearest to the sea that was not swampy," which Indians said was "never covered with water." A Jesuit missionary, Father Paul du Ru, arrived at this early period to find the French adapting themselves to Delta materials and ways. A house was built of wild cane walls with a palmetto roof. The priest fashioned an altar of the cane, a novelty in ecclesiastical construction. Among the light-leafed willows, he noted cocoons of silkworms. Iberville sent some to France, and armchair planners decided that great silkworm factories would soon be ornamenting the Mississippi. A Mougoulacha chief showed dresses of buffalo skin; Iberville took samples, and for a time it was thought that Louisiana would be a vast buffalo farm. The Indians offered a few pearls which the priest thought of "rather bad water," not improved by their red paint. The courtiers' eyes glowed at talk of pearls; might this be their Louisiana's answer to Mexico's gold mines? When the first handfuls arrived, they changed the subject.

Everywhere about the Delta crawled the alligators, and Father du Ru observed, "This beast, which in Europe is considered quite a terrible creature, is regarded here as merely one of the fish, and the savages play with them while bathing without suffering any harm." Once, when a Frenchman raised his gun at an enormous specimen, sunning itself, an Indian stopped him and dived into the water. Creeping up, he slipped one hand under the reptile and caught its jaw with the other. Holding the creature firmly to his breast, the Indian dragged it to a tree and killed it with a few blows. In due time the French would be imitating him.

As early as February the pale lilies and the creeping flowers were already blooming. Everything waxed so enthusiastically fertile that the priest tried his hand. Believing that whatever thrived on the Caribbean Islands should thrive here, he set up a garden at the river edge, with citrus fruits and sugar cane. He knew nothing of proper seasons or methods, he admitted, and he failed. Years later the Delta was to become celebrated for these two crops. But men had first to learn the secrets of the land.

For a time it seemed that the only thing that would grow here was the long line of crosses in the cemetery beside the fort. The place was one of the most remote spots in a colony of many remotes ones. Officials, maintaining headquarters along the Gulf beaches, had troubles of their own. For long months the soldiers at the fort had to live as best they could, depending on rifle or plow or good relations with the Indians to stave off starvation. The red men who promised that this "high ridge of land" would be ever dry had proved wrong. A visitor in December of 1700 found that for four months there had been an overflow, often knee deep. It was not a matter of river flood, but of heavy swells from the Gulf at the back. The gardens failed; the waters deposited "a great quantity of black snakes that eat the lettuce and other vegetables off to the root."

For a decade or longer, the fort sagged slowly into oblivion. Eventually and quietly the French abandoned the moist stronghold.* The colonists, as a matter of fact, had little idea what to do with or about the Deep Delta. The officials had many problems—lack of settlers for Louisiana, the King, the courtiers; not the least of their difficulties were those growing out of the geography of the Mississippi's final miles.

Up the river, some of the leaders came to realize, waited the true treasure of the territory, the products of the fertile soil. But it was not always easy to get in or out of the river mouth, to approach these upper sections and bring out their goods. Just where the Mississippi reached the Gulf, it quickly dropped its heaviest deposits of silt, to form "bars" of sand squarely in the passes. One of the first reports of Iberville to the Minister of Marine was that in using the eastern route he found only eleven feet of water. The other two passages were even more shallow. As the years passed, the bars changed, and vessels met varying fortunes. Men sweated and cursed; sometimes they scraped through, again they were caught. Gradually only smaller boats attempted this route.

From the early days it had been proposed that the colony have its capital on the Mississippi itself. But the settlers had looked over the soggy "wastes" of the Delta, considered that awkward river entry, and shaken their heads. The capital instead went at various times to several shifting points along the Gulf to the east —sandy, disadvantageous places in every case. Many of the supplies from up the river—indigo, rice, corn, pelts, and the rest—were taken to the shore settlements of Biloxi and Mobile, but not through the Deep Delta. In a curious chapter of the story

* Even the site was lost, until in 1936, a group of Orleanians surveyed the scene with rod, shovel, and airplane, to locate a forgotten ridge, a rotting section or two of wood, and a cannonball. The roots, the waters, and the silts had devoured everything else. The French government decorated the discoverers; the natives of the nearby settlement of Phoenix grinned when told of the way the water had rolled up over this pioneer place. Eh, it still do that!

of American transportation, this place that was to become a world highway was now by-passed.

During his first months in Louisiana, Iberville had stopped with Indian guides at a point about a hundred and fifteen miles from the Gulf. Here the Mississippi made a semicircle; a small bayou led to Lake Pontchartrain, and the Lake to the Gulf. Across a short reach of earth the Indians had created a portage, along which they moved their goods and saved themselves the long trip to the river mouths. Soon the white men were following this example, with vessels at the lake awaiting goods carried from the river. It was an inconvenient method, but everyone was certain that the other offered even greater problems.

Iberville's brother, Bienville, became governor, and remembered that spot up the river. He saw it as something else: the capital of Louisiana, on the first moderately dry land, yet fairly near the sea at that. Others, snickering, called the place the governor's frog pond. Bienville shrugged, but lost no opportunity to urge his project. He fell from power, he stayed on, he came back to authority. He persisted; he dispatched men up the river to start a town on the spot, and he pounded tables.

The superior council opposed him; so did the chief councilor, the chief engineer and others. Why did Monsieur le Gouverneur talk that way? If a city did grow up at that mosquito-and-alligator-infested point, certainly that little portage would not support the trade, would it? And then what would he do, with the river entries closed? But were they closed? Bienville asked back.

Chance came to his aid. The unfriendly chief engineer Latour became ill. His assistant, Pauger, had a more open mind. Pauger went to the Gulf, made soundings, and drew up a report that ships drawing fourteen, fifteen, or more feet could now pass. Also, with certain engineering operations, the depths could be increased.

The council had not received the news. To it Bienville proposed a test. Let the vessel *Dromedaire,* already loaded in the Gulf, be sent at once through the river. The council hesitated; suppose it were lost? Then he would be responsible to the last penny. Bienville nodded briskly. Both sides waited nervously. The *Dromedaire* went through without delay. Bienville suspected that the chief councilor and chief engineer would table the assistant engineer's reports. He ordered secret copies, sent them to France, and the results were several. In 1722 the capital of Louisiana was moved up to the place that was now called New Orleans. The Delta entrance was to be used henceforth. And the individual who had so much to do with it, the assistant engineer Pauger, received a rebuke from home. He had taken entirely too much upon himself!

To Pauger the Mississippi Valley might owe a greater debt had the court heeded him in full. He proposed that the river's flow be controlled so that it would wash away all the sand bar at the Gulf edge. He would sink old ships or debris in all but one pass; then he would build "dikes or stockades" into the Gulf, constricting the flow so that it would cut directly across the impediment. France delayed and did nothing. A full century and a half later the valley was to find a commercial catastrophe upon it, and turn to a project much like Pauger's to save it.

Other suggestions of the assistant engineer were accepted. He recommended a harbor at the entrance, to guide vessels in and out, and he was assigned to create an outpost of France at this spot. Along the east passage, a small island of river deposits raised itself above the waters. Out of almost nothing, Pauger and his men proceeded to build their place. They dredged the pass and piled mud up for a higher base; they caught at floating logs to erect a barracks. Eventually there rose a chapel, with a steeple doing double service as a lighthouse. From the river the men scooped more soil for a garden—the first such sight for those who came long miles across the ocean.

This was "the Balize." The word signifies a beacon; and it was a happy sign for thousands who arrived there each year. Here stood the small outer gate of Louisiana, through which all must pass. The men rose to brilliant dawns that crimsoned the slow waves and the bent grasses alike, and went back to their huts to long sunsets of bronze and purple. The gulls and the terns lifted and fell above them, and others nested by the thousands in the marsh or on the dots of white islands lost in the Gulf beyond. Yet it would be a less peaceful spot than it seemed. The Balize would know more than its share of terrors and tragedies.

Meanwhile the Delta was being settled not only at the Balize but from above as well. A semi-feudal design was fixing itself upon much of Louisiana. Spreading land grants were the order; the recipients took mile after mile of flat, potent soil and considered ways to obtain fullest returns from it. Vessels moved back and forth from Africa, their holds packed with human prey. Up from New Orleans the thick Mississippi banks became the locale of great estates. Below the city, in the Delta, was equal fertility, but also uncertainty. For some years the plantations would remain only upon the upper borders. The high landlords would not run the risks of this terrain; but others were willing.

These were the lesser people, whose names do not appear in the history books, who moved out of the capital city in a tentative, varying file, taking what they could. The region was not all the "waste" that the first arrivals had termed it. The edges along the river and along the smaller streams leading from it provided dry strips of varying sizes, and on these the first settlers took their places. They had been farmers in the old country, or fishermen and small townsmen. Here they found themselves in a territory that called for pioneer qualities. Wherever they discovered a patch of fairly certain land, they set up small, peasant-type houses with their chickens and hogs in easy reach. In the upper limits they were year-round growers of crops, yeomen occupying the best land that they could obtain. Sometimes they might prosper sufficiently to acquire a slave or two, but almost always they had only the labor of their own families. They watched the waters and the winds and they learned not to be over ambitious.

Eventually many of the Deltans turned to their surroundings to find wealth equal to or greater than that of their soil. They fished, they hunted, they trapped animals, they dropped nets. Their water trails, fresh at the start, became briny passages leading to the silver Gulf. There they searched the waters for the rich pompano, the lively red snapper, and the mackerel. On the sandy islands along the shore they rested in the late afternoon to watch the glow that lingered for hours over the warm horizon. Well rewarded for their work in the water, they turn homeward to replenish the family's supplies.

This land lost its oddness for them. In time its prevailing lowness offered many variations to the experienced eye; they learned that a difference of six inches in elevation could mean success or failure to a crop or a home.

As a stream moved through the slowly forming soil, it spread ridges to both sides. A wise man followed these waters and soil borders, with their willows and myrtles and thick shrubs. Only when necessity demanded did he advance into the less dependable places. The marsh was of several kinds, ranging from the firm "roseau," with its thick reed-grass, sometimes twelve feet high, to the "floating prairie," a growth out of a matted base suspended over water or liquid mud. In time they mastered the secrets of the region, acquiring nimbleness in stepping quickly from one spot of soft ground to another, leaping again before they sank in.

Too, they understood the appeal of the open lands, stretching unbroken to the horizon, and the massed clouds flowing across the sky's infinity. They came to appreciate the beauty of the Delta: the pale blossoming of the couch grass; the wild mallow or hibiscus, its white and rose shadings covering miles of the green; the thick rich leaves of the lotus, and the delicate spider lilies. Fruit trees, soon to bear thick brown figs and flamboyant persimmons, oranges, and pears, threw heavy flowerings into the soft air along the river. And through every month of the year the land was heavily verdant.

Some lived, as they have said, with one foot on the ground, the other in the water. At the lower fringes, many might go for months, perhaps for years, without the feel of truly firm land beneath their feet. They knew only the spongy, semi-liquid marsh and the water, and their small shacks like matchboxes on stilts. But the Deltans wanted no pity from their rare city visitors nor from anyone else, s'il vous plaît. They would manage; and they did. Their numbers increased. Some were sharpwitted Gascons, others Normans, Picards and the men and women of Provence. A number of Germans arrived, members or descendants of those families brought to Louisiana when John Law's Mississippi Bubble hung over the French colony. As time went by, they were joined by people of Nova Scotia, the ill-fated Acadians expelled in the clash between France and England. Despite its drawbacks, the Delta presented to all of them a chance that would not have been theirs in the plantation territory above.

Scattered men were drawn because it was largely a wilderness. These were hunters and woodsmen, an important element among the first settlers of the colony. Restless individuals, dissatisfied with the pallid ways of others, they paddled about the swamps and pushed their paths along sedge-fringed lakes to inhale the breath of freedom. A man was his own master here. For the city toilers with bent backs and humble shoulders such men had only contempt; they preferred death to that worm's-eye view of life. And some came for the reason that has always drawn men seeking escape from civilization: they had broken a law of their fellows, a major or a minor one, and here was silence and also refuge.

Before the Deltans passed the commerce of the valley. For most, the sight of a ship moving with the wind was their main contact with the world beyond. They wondered at the size of the sails and speculated on the lives of the elegant ones who leaned over the rails and looked with curiosity about them. Eventually some Deltans knew a source of income from this movement. Vessels moving up the river found themselves at short rations. For weeks the passengers had not tasted fresh foods. Would the Deltans trade? The Deltans laid out extra rows of greens along their narrow edges, penned in extra chickens or hogs. The vessels tied up, and exchanges were made.

The seamen, going ashore, saw the warm-eyed, healthy Deltan maidens, to whom their calls were obviously events; in many families the tradition tells of the sailor who met Grand'mère one day long ago and was back to ask her father if he could marry her. Others deserted their ships at New Orleans or near their future homes. The stories describe a youth's concealment in a hut among the grasses, while his captain floundered about in search of him. Once one left ship here he need not fear capture; a manhunt in the marsh was not a venture in which even a lifelong resident could expect success. The Delta has always protected its people.

Soon the newcomer was acquiring that mixture of daring and nervous attention required for the capture of an alligator. He was trapping turtles on sand hills, and he was swearing at the armored garfish when they depopulated lagoons. And he and his neighbors were turning to a crop that slowly became the closest approach to a staple that the early river people would know: rice. The growth calls for a flat moist ground, covered frequently with water; the Delta provided these essentials as could few places. The crop required no outlay of capital and no great labor force. As a result, those who passed below New Orleans found miles of rustling stalks, tipped with the light golden grain. Wherever the land was lowest, the Deltan and his family scattered the seed. When high waters came, they had thorough irrigation; if they feared that this would not be enough, they made small cuts in the natural river banks, and by gates they controlled the flow. To the back they dug canals to drain off what they did not need. Nature did the rest.

It was a crude method of cultivation, and it remained crude, a system differing little from that used in Egypt or the Orient. The rice was threshed by tossing it in handfuls into the air; the hull was removed by pounding with a pestle in a mortar. As years went by and agriculture changed in lower Louisiana, others smiled at the techniques of these "petits fermiers," little farmers of the lower river. Why, if they organized it, and used new ways, they could produce so much more, and be so much better off. The "petits fermiers" had an answer: If the plantation people knew better, let them try it. This was the Delta way. It gave them all that they wanted—more, in fact, than most others would have consumed. Rice provided the main starch item of their diet. Neither corn nor wheat grew well here; rice was preferred to potatoes. It was combined with fish and game, it went into soups and gumbos, and it was eaten for itself alone. A Delta meal might be bountiful and many coursed. If it lacked high bowls of rice, it was incomplete.*

Papa and the boys maintained a vigil against the grasses. A

* This taste persists. An Anglo-Saxon traveler visited a French Delta family. In the kitchen she spied ten or fifteen sacks of the product, and commented that when the family sold those it would have extra income for a time. They were astounded: "But Miz' Louise, we ain' gon' *sell* that rice, no. Tha's just for a few month'." The Deltan will put his rice into practically everything except his coffee or his dessert. Rice pudding—his expression makes it clear that he regards that as a barbarism.

certain, wild one would creep in at the first chance. Gaining a foothold, it would overrun a whole field in a season or two; then it would have to be cleared at enormous effort, or the field given up. Thereby hangs the tale of a Delta jibe.

One spring the elderly Monsieur Deslondes planted his field, flooded it and rubbed his hands as he saw a fine green line. This would be a good year! Soon other lines of tiny spears thrust their way up. Quick, to work there! With their hands, he and his sons tore out every bit of the unwanted stuff. Then Monsieur Deslondes sat back. The season looked better than ever. But those grains were taking a long time to appear, weren't they? The pale yellow edges were showing themselves elsewhere on the river. Finally Monsieur Deslondes called a friend, and they made an agitated inspection. Oui, it was true. They had pulled up all of the rice, and left the wild growth. The neighbors honored him by giving the useless thing a new name of its own—Rice Deslondes.

So, quietly, lived the Deltans during France's regime. They knew little of affairs beyond their own borders, but events on the Continent were to bring reverberations even to the last Mississippi reaches. France lost the Seven Years' War to England, and Louisiana was an award, not to the winner but to France's ally, Spain—a kind of consolation prize. Spain, uncertain that she wanted a dubious colony that had failed to pay its way, hesitated but finally took it. Up from the Balize, past the rice fields, along the cabins of the alligator hunters moved a caravan of conquerors in the year 1769. Into the Delta would now come new forces—and a new crop.

CHAPTER 2

That Novelty, Sugar

THE Spanish intendant of Louisiana, over an aromatic dessert at a high-piled banquet table, signaled to the waiters. The dark eyes of the Castilian twinkled as the servants came in with platters bearing sparkling white cubes, one or two of which they placed near the cup of each guest. Some fingered the objects; a few nibbled tentatively. A buzz of comment rose, and the intendant stood up.

This . . . er, material, Señores, was Louisiana sugar, manufactured only a short distance away. The intendant was pleased at the murmurs, the lifted eyebrows. He must be having his joke; everybody knew that it was impossible, thoroughly impossible, to make sugar here! Some who were present, French and Spanish, could have so testified from years of losses. The intendant raised his hand. Sugar *had* been produced in Louisiana. The Señor Antonio Mendez, the King's chief magistrate, who lived near the river below the city—he was responsible. Perhaps, Señores, some might wish to take home a sample of this . . . this novelty. They would be hearing more of it in the future, he thought. And the intendant could not restrain his quiet laugh at the wry looks.

The year was 1792. The scene has seldom been pictured in the Louisiana history books. Mendez is almost an unknown name; his first success where others failed has been all but forgotten. As he lost the glory, Mendez also missed the practical return. Had he been able to carry on and capitalize his early achievement, he would have emerged as one of the new sugar lords of Louisiana. He was then only forty-two. He was to live to be almost eighty, and to see others take dazzling places that might have been his.

For many years Louisiana plantation operators had been casting about for a dependable staple. Silkworm culture, blithely recommended by the court, had not worked. Some had thought of candlemaking, using the wax of the myrtle tree. Men tried one crop, then another, often to find that the rigid trade policies of the government shut them from the market. For a time indigo, the unpleasant-smelling plant that produced the commercial dye, seemed the answer. But in the early 1790's ruin confronted the growers; destructive worms appeared almost overnight, and fields were being devoured before their owners' eyes. What was to be done now?

Louisianians had watched the waving of stiff sugar-cane stalks for several generations. The "big grass" had done well in Santo Domingo; the Jesuits brought samples from their plantations there, and the bright banners rose in the air. But it would not crystallize. Men stood before their kettles, experimented, set up new equipment, junked it for yet newer, and failed each time. In one case an exporter sent forth a supply of his product; before the ship was well on its way, it had liquefied and was leaking from the barrels. The best that could be evolved was a substance like jam—not quite what a man wanted for his coffee. It was the climate, some said—a factor that has been blamed, correctly or otherwise, for many Louisiana mistakes. Sugar making was a highly difficult process, requiring specific skills and a "strike" at exactly the proper moment of concentration. None in Louisiana had mastered it.

For some years interest lagged, but Louisianians still raised cane for syrup and for a rumlike drink called tafia. Hundreds took to the latter as their favorite beverage; one worrisome official wrote in 1764, with what seems an untypical excess of Puritanism, that "immoderate use of tafia has stupefied the whole population." Even the manufacture of this delightfully stupefying drink was not a major enterprise. Fewer and fewer Louisianians bothered with the pursuit of the elusive sugar.

In 1791 a Spaniard named Solis, a former Santo Domingan with experience in the subject, was operating a distillery ten miles below New Orleans in the Delta. In that year Magistrate Mendez purchased Solis' holdings, including his cane acreage. He hired an assistant, Morin, who had spent many years in sugar work in Cuba. Their men stirred the bubbling black kettles, sweated in the hot, cloying atmosphere of the steaming workhouses. Magistrate Mendez moved among them, sampling, pursing his lips. Again and again he was on the point of success, and missed it. More inspections, more testings, more mixings—then suddenly, he stared hard at the fragrant mixture. Crystals formed. He had done it!

The result was the banquet at which Delta sugar made its first appearance. But having gone so far, Mendez halted. He did not produce in quantity, and he did not extend the process. Two years passed and Etienne de Boré, who had a plantation above New Orleans, took over where Mendez left off. Dropping the diseased indigo, he called upon Mendez, purchased cane, hired Mendez' helper Morin, and produced the first full commercial crop.

The events set in motion by those experiments about the sweet-filled kettles culminated in one of the great changes of Southern agriculture. Louisiana was to become the sugar state. Slavery was to advance more than ever as the basis of labor over wide areas too moist for cotton. And the thick grass of the cane stalk, and not the alligator, was to become the symbol of the Delta.

For years before this the plantations had been extending into the upper Delta. Large land grants were made under the French, and slowly the infiltration increased. Spanish families of privilege moved among the French; and when it was demonstrated at last that sugar could be crystallized, the locality saw a sudden spurt of prosperity. The old owners installed equipment, new ones joined them; both set about the pleasant task of acquiring wealth. Judge Alexander Walker has pictured the Delta plant of the next few years: a small circular mill of cypress plank, mules to provide motive power, "a very simple, though awkward and uncertain, mechanism to press the juice from the cane." Collected in successive kettles, the liquid was boiled in the open air under large fires; then the kettles were emptied into troughs and put out to cool. From them came fortunes. In 1806 the governor of Louisiana declared that "the facility with which sugar planters amass wealth is almost incredible."

A small France, lightly touched by Spain, was thriving below the city. It was not the France of the Revolution or of Napoleon, the disquieting France of which the Louisianians read in their journals from home, but a manorial regime with forced labor to provide, sometimes, a greater ease than would have been possible in the old country. The file of protective levees now advanced downward from New Orleans on both sides of the river, and behind them extended a thick strip of waving cane banners. One plantation elbowed the other, separated by cypress fences and deep ditches bearing the family name: Canal Villeré, Canal Rodriguez and others. Each property extended as far to the back as the owner thought safe; and like the "petits fermiers" below them, the plantation men extended canals to the rear to carry off the excess waters. A man watched his canals as closely as he did the cane itself. If he kept them clear, he could expect good days; if he neglected them, his crop and his basement would be flooded one morning.

The manner was expansive, but not yet the Greek-templed, elaborately pillared expansiveness of the traditional South. The Delta mansions were Creole * in design, French and Spanish, modified by available Louisiana materials and by climate, with influences from the West Indies. The buildings were generally of wood, for brick was difficult to obtain in large quantities; often, too, in this moist air, the soft bricks crumbled easily. The house was one- or two-storied, almost always white, almost always raised from three to ten feet above the ground, often on thick piers with basements beneath the main level. There was a good reason for the elevation—protection against water—but it also gave coolness and a view over the surrounding flatness. Everything was designed for a maximum of satisfaction with a minimum of perspiration.

To wander about some of these remaining houses is to study spaciousness in union with simplicity. What came afterward did not fit the scene half so well. A wide, deep gallery at the front was open at both ends; on it, except when the mosquitoes were out, the family spent most of its time. Light columns of wood preceded the ornamented magnificence of later days. A steep roof, cypress-shingled, provided an attic with dormer windows. Within sparkled splendor, the family possessions brought from France, or acquired from artisans who knew that certain clients

* The word Creole, as used generally in Louisiana, applies to white descendants of early French and Spanish settlers. In connotes also a high native quality —Creole furnishings, Creole vegetables, Creole manner.

would demand the best they had to offer. As the wealthy Creoles dispatched their sons to Paris for an education, so they sent there for other things to distinguish themselves from the barbarian.

The house faced the river at a distance of a few hundred yards. Before the family on the porch a panorama of vessels moved as on a stage, up and down with wind and current. When the water was high, the sailing ships seemed to ride above the house itself, in the air between the levees. At the Mississippi's edge extended the family wharf, and to it led the gardens and lines of trees. Cypresses, pecan trees, and fringes of orange and lemon provided the setting, growing so thickly that the building was lost a short distance off. The gardens, the responsibility of Madame, were thick with hedges of roses, yellow and scarlet. Sundials rose among parterred flowers, but the formal touch was offset by the tropical lushness of banana trees and the splashing oleanders. The plantings, however arranged, soon lost their complete symmetry in this land of perpetual bloom. The lofty, far-spreading live oaks were mounted by creepers and ferns, contesting for domination with the gray-green moss; and near by stood the magnolias, leatherlike glazed leaves and fragrant cream-white flowers the size of a child's head. At the back, less conspicuous, stretched the slave quarters; at this period they were huts whose wooden frames were filled with Mississippi mud, mixed with moss as a binder. And all along the river's course marched the cane, the source of it all.

Directly and indirectly, the scene was tied to New Orleans. The family had its friends and relatives, usually its town house in the capital. The father maintained business connections, property, and sometimes a government office there. Between the plantation and the capital the family moved by boat, not risking the roads or their good horses. If Madame decided that the season was especially gay, she and her daughters could elect to extend their stay indefinitely. They received their new dresses from Paris as quickly as any residents of La Nouvelle Orléans; they heard the gossip from abroad and the whispered words among the interesting émigrés who came to this corner of France over which the guillotine's blade did not flash. The way of living offered the attractions of both the urban and the country scene, with a background of swamp and lake to provide rich supplies for the table, rewarding hunting for the men, and light excursions by boat for the women.

This was the day of the de la Rondes, the de Marignys, the DeClouets, the Ducros, the Philippons. Of them all the dominant name for years remained that of Pierre Denis de la Ronde—distingué, impeccable, and proud, of a family whose assurance rose above its caprices. Like others about them, the de la Rondes came directly from Canada but spoke of a heritage far back in the mother country. The original Pierre was the son of a Captain of Marine, a Chevalier of the Order of St. Louis and an officer under Bienville. His son prospered with the Spanish, serving in several military exploits. By the time the Americans acquired Louisiana in 1803, he was a sugar master. In 1805 he gave lower Louisiana something to talk about—his new home which he called, simply, Versailles. One admirer wrote, "What Versailles was to France in unparagoned magnificence, the Versailles on the bank of the Mississippi was to Louisiana." To friends it was "The Palace."

Located about eight miles below the city by modern road, the Louisiana Versailles maintained a salon supreme, at which the visiting great were entertained, informed and displayed. Two-storied, sixteen-roomed, it anticipated the later era in size and formal elegance. Double-leveled galleries extended about all of the house; upon them opened long lines of French windows. To his emerging Versailles, Pierre Denis de la Ronde called artists, French and Spanish, for hand decorations on the walls. The crystal chandeliers, flashing, many-hued in their reflections, were of a design similar to those of the Petit Trianon; marble mantels, intricate cornices and friezes—these, too, came from across the ocean.

Years earlier, on his twenty-first birthday, when he had already been knighted by Spain, the second Pierre had planted a double line of oaks from the house to the river. His diary told how he approached the task with care, spacing the trees so that there would be considerable yardage between each, permitting them to grow high and wide. With every season he could feel a greater satisfaction; eventually the powerful oaks became what some have called the finest row of its kind in America. Seventy-five of them still remain, their enormous, gnarled branches interlacing to form an arched passageway, an unbroken parade of commanding patriarchs, trailing garments of moss down a dim vista to the Mississippi.

Among his oaks de la Ronde sat with his wife and children. He sired one son and nine daughters. The romantic Creoles called the girls the Nine Muses, the boy Apollo. He was Pierre Denis de la Ronde III; the girls, Eulalie, Elizabeth Céleste Héloise, Joséphine Pépita, Marie Manette, Adélaïde, Adèle, Marie Félicie, Isabelle Emilie, and Magdalena Azélie. Eventually the house was hailed as Parnasse, or Parnassus, home of the divinities. All nine girls married, and I think this not the least remarkable fact about the remarkable family. Apollo had one son, and that son had none; there is no longer a descendant to bear the name.

But Monsieur de la Ronde had meanwhile embarked on a project that kept his memory alive for generations—a scheme that might have made New Orleans a shanty town. Watching sugar millions pile upward, he conceived a large thought. His new scheme involved his Versailles itself; he would make it the metropolis of Louisiana. Calling together his fellows, he outlined a grandiose enterprise: towering wharves for ships of all nations, shops, stores, and in the center, his estate. Some were intrigued. Versailles-on-the-Levee! De la Ronde looked farther ahead; he would give the world also a new Paris, a twin city of matching grandeur, Paris-on-Lake-Borgne. It would be a back door to his Versailles; he would connect the two with a superb roadway, Chemin de Paris, the Paris Road. He built part of this link; but several events, including a war, intervened, and it all collapsed.

The home held on for decades. When it was up for sale, a Parisian banker, remembering the place, sent here to purchase the furnishings, which made a trip back across the sea. The building saw worse days. A dairyman rented it and stabled cows in its high-ceilinged grandeur. One winter night, heating the place for the animals, someone upset a lamp, and most of Versailles disappeared in smoke. The exterior walls held until a storm destroyed most of them. The route of "Paris Road" remains, but the name has degenerated to "Parish Road." Most who use it believe that it signifies merely the civil parish or county. Sic transit. . . .

About fifteen miles below New Orleans, a small stream reached toward the lake from a point near the river. Though few realized it, the main course of the Mississippi had once extended through this vicinity; the land still projects itself sharply eastward. The old water passage had become a mere distributary of the river; then it was closed off to prevent floods. The fertile earth saw few permanent settlers under the French. It now remained for the Spanish to settle it and provide Louisiana with a colony within a colony.

Spain soon learned that one of the main things which Louisiana lacked was people. She welcomed Frenchmen, Acadians, Italians, Germans and others; but outside of the officials and merchants, only a few Spaniards came. The government made several attempts to remedy the deficiency. From the Canary Islands it brought over hardy peasant people, placing them in groups at scattered points. The government went to some pains to assist them; for four years they were to be provided with cattle, rations and other supplies from the King's stores. Below New Orleans the highly placed Pierre Philippe de Marigny de Mandeville received a large concession of land on condition that he give supervision to several hundred of the Islanders. Outside the Delta the Isleños fared badly. This Louisiana was so different from what they had known, the people about them so confusing. Their holdings were flooded; crops failed; they dropped into listless discontent. The settlements dissolved. Only in the Delta did they maintain themselves.

Along their excellent watercourse the Isleños built rows of small huts, with mud and wood walls, palmetto roofs, and floors of earth. Cheerfully hot in winter, such places were cool and restful in the warm months. They fished right in front of their doors and to the side they raised thriving green things. Governor Bernardo de Galvez had a patron's interest in his countrymen; he erected a home nearby and visited them regularly, smiling at their dances, joking with elderly grandmothers who were not sure this was a proper place for good Isleños. In time the grateful colonists gave their district and the surrounding acres a name to honor him: St. Bernard parish. The title remains.

To the French the area was known as La Terre aux Boeufs, Land of the Oxen. One explanation is that the first arrivals found it the haunt of vast herds of buffalo. Another declares that the Canary Islanders brought over their oxen, which they drove yoked at the horns in the fashion of the old country. In any case it soon became apparent that a superb breed of oxen was here being developed. Other Louisianians came to obtain the animals for use in their farming, or to leave them there for training. It is said that the Isleños turned out oxen "as docile as spaniels."

Set away from the rest of Louisiana, the Isleños were not dissatisfied with their status. Their nearest neighbors were French; they would remain Spanish in language and in custom. They were not interested in visits with others; they did not marry outside their own lines. The men hunted; the women looked after the crops when their husbands were away. A swarthy, handsome people, they lived under the Delta sun and their natural complexions darkened slightly with the years. This and their glistening black hair made their strong, regular teeth seem the whiter. They remained hardy workers. And they still spoke of themselves as Isleños, for another reason. Most of them were shifting slowly toward the eastern fringe of their stream, their Bayou Terre aux Boeufs, where a ridge of earth stretched above the marsh and water. It was, to them, La Isla.

Shortly after the United States acquired Louisiana, Governor Claiborne visited the Isleños and found them "an uninformed, inoffensive, humble people, whose primary cares are the support of their families and a rigid adherence to the principles of the Catholic religion." They seemed "equally removed from riches as from want"; but, showing himself something of a prophet, the governor noted the nearby presence of the large planters and expressed fear that the lands would "ultimately be engrossed by a few individuals." He added, "They are well fitted to the culture of Sugar, and Altho the Cane cannot fail to enrich those who grow it, I must be permitted to regret the degree of debility which it will entail on a considerable portion of this territory." The plantations would encroach, and the Isleños would retreat, but it would be a slow process.

Year after year, the Isleños supplied New Orleans with a large part of its fresh vegetables. Regularly they made slow trips to the old French Market, their oxen drawing their heavy-laden wooden carts. The editor of the Weekly Picayune in 1838 told his readers of their unchanging ways. During the afternoon a family filled its cart with its produce and also hay for the animals' feeding and the owners' own comfort. Over everything went a blanket held up by cane stalks, to keep the sun off the vegetables and the family alike. Man, wife, and children slipped into the back, and the oxen started without guidance. Once the animals had traveled the course to the city, they never forgot it; and the training which the Isleños gave them assured that there would be no mishaps. The driverless teams continued on their way; at intervals the carts were joined by others, each with its sleeping family within. For hours the creaking caravan continued with never-changing gait. Other vehicles moved out of its path. Reaching the river roadway, the file shifted and plodded forward without hesitation or delay.

About dark, still without orders, the animal procession stopped at a halfway house, a tavern. Here the oxen were fed and also the families. The meals were always on credit; they would pay on the way home, when their pockets were full. Back to the carts again, and to sleep, went the Isleños, and the march was resumed. Shortly before midnight the oxen halted; they had traveled through all of the lower city and reached the Market, each yoke moving to its regular stall. The family could now stretch and display its wares. For nine hours or so they remained at the Market, then crept back into their empty carts, sleepy again and ready for a peaceful trip home.

Going and coming, the Isleños skirted the long files of sugar cane and the lofty homes of the sugar lords; and their snores were their only comment.

CHAPTER 3

Cannons Among the Chateaux

CLAIBORNE, the first American governor of Louisiana, was a haggard man in the year 1814. His lack of understanding of the Creoles seemed not confined to their language. The term "Américain" was not one to cause pleasure here. The United States had purchased Louisiana, but not the good will of the Louisianians. Between the Yankee republic and the colony that had always looked to Europe, differences went deep. The new Americans were still a minority, an element whose actions and assumptions grated on French nerves. What cared they for our civilization, Monsieur, for the arts of life? Crude money-grubbers, they had come only to take what they could. And in their Congress they had treated us as stepchildren, casting slurs, wondering if we were "ready" for full statehood . . . The Americans in turn showed only wonder and occasional disapproval. Why, Cal, this was a foreign country, like. People sittin' around in shops and sippin' strong drink all day and talking who knew what tongues!

The two sides quarreled, fought duels, refused to associate in business or in anything else, and certainly not in their social affairs. There were exceptions, of course, but this was the prevailing attitude. In places a pro-Spanish feeling appeared to thrive. Neither Spain nor Britain had fully assented to Napoleon's sale of the vital territory to the United States. Both of those governments at various times called the transaction a fraud. Why, Napoleon had no right to make the sale; he had violated the agreement by which Spain had passed it to him only a short time before then. Louisiana, they insisted, was anything but part of the upstart Yankee nation. Any impartial observer, visiting Louisiana at this time, might have agreed with that statement.

This year of 1814 opened without ill omens in the Delta. The planters made trips to New Orleans, sat about the coffee houses, and talked with their friends. This war of the Americans with the English, it was not going so well, was it? Eh, it all seemed so far away. Pierre, did I tell you of that fine lot of wild geese we caught last week, in the marsh back of the Villeré place?

Yet the months were ripe with danger for Louisiana and for all the rest of the United States. The hostilities against England had turned into a series of sickening defeats. Washington was burned by the enemy. Recruiting lagged; here and there mutiny broke out, and malcontents cried for peace at any price that was necessary or expedient. Worse, Britain had been fighting thus far with only one hand. Now she had bested Napoleon in Europe, and could concentrate on the smaller enemy. In New England objectors prepared for a convention to urge an end to the war, threatening secession if it went on. The new country was close to disaster.

And unknown to most, Britain even then was preparing the mightiest single blow that she or any other power ever aimed at the New World. Her greatest armada was approaching one of the least defended parts of America—the Delta of the Mississippi. Separate English land forces turned to the southeast, moving into Pensacola and fraternizing with the "neutral" Spanish there. From the British an appeal was dispatched to Louisianians to "assist in liberating" their soil from a "faithless, imbecile government." "The American usurpation must be abolished, and the lawful owners put in possession." Louisianians received jubilant letters from Havana and Pensacola; Spain, with England's help, would soon have Louisiana again.

To the defense of the southern shores went Major General Andrew Jackson; and the hopes of many well-wishers had fallen at the news. This lanky Indian fighter, politician, and backwoods brawler, untrained in warfare as true military men knew it! But Andy Jackson showed what he could do. He invaded "neutral" Spanish Florida, ousted the British, put up defenses at Mobile, and moved toward New Orleans. Claiborne poured harassed messages in his direction. The governor was finding a "much greater Spirit of Disaffection" than even he had expected; even among "faithfull Lousianians" he saw a "Despondency which palsies all my preparations." At that moment the armada, sailing up from Jamaica, was a week or so from the Louisiana coast.

The sanguine heart of Old Hickory Jackson sagged when he looked around South Louisiana during the first days of December. His own forces were a few thousand, scattered, many inexperienced, often of dubious dependability. Many lacked basic arms. Washington could spare little; the nation itself was staggering toward bankruptcy. Surveying the place, Jackson frowned. This puzzling terrain! No map gave an accurate picture. Even the Louisianians had trouble explaining it, with this bay leading to that lake and that bayou to a canal. And so many ways to get to the city; at least six or seven suggested themselves at once. He gave orders to block every possible entrance. Then other troubles confronted him. By an act of apparent bad taste he offended the Creole leader, Bernard de Marigny. Surrounded by Americans, Claiborne and others, Jackson alienated part of the other group.

But Jackson did not mull over the difficulties. He pitched into activity, relentless, almost sleepless. Weakened by dysentery, at times barely able to sit upright, he continued nevertheless. He was a shrewder man than some thought, and skilled in ways of appealing to others. His first messages stirred the Louisiana heart, touching on the love of the native soil, rejecting the thought that the people would embrace the appeals of the enemy—and also warning that death would follow treason.

Louisianians listened, nudged each other, and leaped behind Le Général Gjacksong. There was something about this man that quickened their hopes; and also, let it not be forgotten, Louisiana saw the shadow of invasion. Out came forgotten equipment, and money for defense funds. Old men became home guards. From the Delta, from the plantations, from the small farms and from the marshes, moved the volunteers. A company of Choctaw Indians presented itself; free men of color were formed into a unit. In marched pirates of the Gulf, Lafitte and his men, who had rejected enemy bribes to cast their lot with Louisiana and the United States.

Now formed one of the nation's strangest armies: helpers in city taverns, Frenchmen from palmetto shacks near the river mouth, courtly dragoons, bankers and smugglers, doctors and oyster-diggers. With them marched Jackson's Tennesseeans and Kaintucks, men skinny like the general himself, with tobacco-spotted shirts and caps of coonskin. A veteran of the Grande

Armée of Napoleon stood next to a sunburned Indian fighter who scratched himself as he gaped at the sights of this New Orleans place. Not least should be counted the contribution of "Grand'mère Dévince"—the elderly Madame Dévince Bienvenue, of St. Martinville. She had seven sons—Théodule, Terville, Térence, Timoléon, Timecourt, Casimir, and Dévince. Bidding each goodbye, she wrote the Gouverneur that she had no more sons but offered herself for any service. She did not wait for a reply, but hurried by boat to New Orleans, and demanded a place as a nurse.

Within eight days of Jackson's arrival, the British fleet rode unexpectedly into sight of the Louisiana Delta. Here came England's splendor and the confidence of her death-dealing might—a force of twenty thousand men on fifty vessels, two great squadrons, some of the most celebrated of her regiments. The men and their commanders represented the picked perfection of their day: the conquerors of Napoleon; the 93rd Highlanders, men chosen for size and endurance—none less than six feet, kilts swinging above sinewy legs; the North British Fusileers, the Duchess of York's Light Dragoons; Vice-Admiral Sir Alexander Cochrane, Sir Thomas Hardy—in whose arms Nelson died at Trafalgar—and Sir Edward Pakenham, brother-in-law of the Duke of Wellington. Among them stood ready a force that had only recently put the torch to Washington. This amateur American rabble would be easy targets!

The expedition arrived in holiday spirits. In favored place sat wives of the officers, some having closed splendid country homes for "estates along the Mississippi." The ladies arranged dances, musicales, a small play or two to enliven the long trip. Authorities had prepared full lists of officers for the Province of Louisiana—tax agents, clerks, government editors. A high official of Bermuda resigned to become "collector of customs," and brought with him five pink-cheeked daughters of marriageable age.

The armada scored at once. Following the route of Iberville, passing Ship and Cat Islands, it paused briefly, then approached Lake Borgne. A meager American force of five gunboats fought hard, but was taken. The British now had an arm of the Gulf that might give entry at any one of several points. Jackson redistributed his men, called upon some to march without sleeping until they reached the city. From the corners rang the notes of "Yankee Doodle" and also "La Marseillaise." Yet could a place so situated, torn so recently by conglomerate loyalties, be held against the enemy?

Ill fortune struck again. Every line of passage was protected, it seemed, but one. This the enemy took. The British collected most of their army on little Pea Island, and there they had their first taste of the Delta. All treeless marsh, with alligators in the small stream that crossed it, the island gave no protection of any kind. Immediately there fell a heavy rain "such as an inhabitant of England cannot dream of," one officer wrote. The men had no tents, no coverings. At nightfall severe frosts "congealed our wet clothes upon our bodies." The British brought with them a supply of Jamaica Negroes, thought to be accustomed to a climate such as Louisiana's. Many of them died on the spot.

Deserters conferred with the British. They gave an alluring picture: a few thousand soldiers in all, rich supplies of cotton and sugar in the city ready for conquest. Reconnoitering, British officers reached a point on shore, Bayou Bienvenu, leading to the plantation of the Villeré family along the river. At the entry stood a huddle of palmetto huts, quarters of Spanish fishermen. Poor, ignorant, they were allowed by the Villerés to use the plantation canals. The British arranged an inexpensive deal; officers donned native attire and went with them to the river, a scant eight miles below the city. Here one slipped to the bank for a long drink of Mississippi water—an exploit of which he could boast. The place was near English Turn, to which other Britons had penetrated within reach of an empire those long years ago.

From Pea Island, small boats put out for the shore. Silence was the order; this magnificent surprise must not be spoiled. The reedy coast loomed; a pelican or two wheeled ahead. At the fisherman's village an American guard of several men had meanwhile been stationed. One or two escaped to the marsh but lost their way and could not give the alarm. One of the captured men, the Creole Joseph Rodolphe Ducros, was questioned. A common story is that he lied skilfully, exaggerating Jackson's strength. Jackson's biographer, Marquis James, holds that he probably made a common mistake of amateur soldiers, unconsciously overestimating the forces. He declared that Jackson had 12,000 to 15,000 men at New Orleans, and some 4000 at English Turn. Ironically, the British believed this and other similar reports in preference to the truth told by their spies. Now they decided that they must not be too hasty; they must stop short of New Orleans until their full strength waited on land.

In secrecy the British moved up the bayous until their boats touched bottom. Advancing, they found themselves in slush to their knees; they fell headlong and dragged themselves forward. Eventually the land grew firmer and they passed enclosed fields rough with the stubble of cane. They were on plantation property. Oaks and rows of orange trees appeared, and beyond them the long white home of the Villerés, gleaming in the morning sun. On the gallery sat young Major Gabriel Villeré, who was in general charge of defenses in the area. At the first glimpse of an advancing red-coated column, he ran to the back of the house. Another file trapped him in his own home.

The British now had New Orleans at their mercy. As yet Jackson had received no hint as to what had occurred. Had they pushed on at once, the city might have fallen. But they remembered Ducros' words; they encamped here, and lost their chance. Confined under guard, young Villeré was meanwhile in agony. This, mon Dieu, would give excuse to some who would say the Creoles had been faithless. The soldiers saw a flash of color. Villeré leaped through the window, spurted across the yard, and hurdled a cypress picket fence at a leap. "Catch him or kill him!" the officers cried. But Gabriel Villeré knew this soft land. They did not catch him.

He stole through the moss-hung trees and over ditches to the adjoining plantation of Colonel de la Ronde. He and the colonel rowed across the river, obtained horses from a friend, and the three spurred them on to New Orleans. Jackson leaped up at the news: "By the Eternal, they shall not sleep on our soil!" Another man, so caught, would have prepared a hasty defense. Jackson ordered an attack.

All available men had to be concentrated in the Delta. Plauché's Creole battalion was brought in from Bayou St. John, running most of the ten miles. Up rushed free men of color, pirates, and others; in all about two thousand converged on St.

Bernard parish. The struggle was to take place upon the estates of the de la Rondes, Bienvenues, Jumonvilles and others. These rich properties, with chateaux that were monuments to a way more continental than American, were now to be the theater of a frontiersman's war, in defense against a threat from Europe itself.

Past rows of white houses, past groves of graybearded oaks, moved the mixed forces on this night of December 23. One double line of trees drew Jackson's eye. He might have admired their beauty, but he quickly appraised their military value. They were the majestic oaks of Versailles, the high-named mansion of de la Ronde. About them Jackson's soldiers took silent places. Only a few hundred yards away the enemy rested. The men, enjoying a welcome letup from their privations of the past days, sat or lay about bright fires. In the high-ceilinged rooms of the Villeré home the officers lounged. A fog drifted from the river, and behind it slipped the American schooner *Carolina*.

Suddenly came booming death from the river. One volley, another and another, and the camp was in wild uproar. The men pitched helplessly about until ordered to hide behind the levee. In the night the officers turned their forces toward the schooner. Jackson's land forces maintained quiet, their presence still a secret. Then at a signal they leaped from the other direction. A British officer later described it as "a tenfold panic." "No mob," he added, "could have been in a more utter state of disorganization." Fighting was hand-to-hand in darkness; the Americans used tomahawks, hunting-knives, feet, and fists. Sometimes each side found itself killing its own men.

The fog slid in more thickly. Jackson had scored, and heavily. As the British brought up reinforcements, he withdrew his men across several plantations in the direction of New Orleans. The imminent threat was lessened; but worse was to come. He and his men dug in at the Rodriguez canal, a small abandoned waterway, reed-covered, extending all of the way from river levee back to dark cypress swamp. Every available spade was commandeered to deepen the opening and build an embankment behind it. Into the mud parapets went whatever supplies could be found, logs, stray wooden pickets, a number of cotton bales. (The old tale that the country was saved by lines of bales is a pleasant exaggeration.) Such was Christmas Day in the Delta. Jackson settled in the Augustin Macarty mansion; from the upper windows, using a telescope, he would have a box seat when he was not among the men at the front.

The British concentrated reinforcements. From the lake, with incredible effort, heavy cannon were dragged over the half-liquid ground. The *Carolina* was blown up, but a sister ship escaped. The morning of December twenty-eighth saw the enemy in full land attack. Jackson ranged the battlefield, slapping his men on the shoulders, dodging bullets. One of his aides halted him. The legislature was about to give up to the enemy! puffed Abner Duncan. The Creole Colonel Déclouet said so. Jackson, with the British approaching, cried out that he doubted it. Duncan hesitated; the governor, he said, wanted orders what to do. Jackson yelled that he still didn't believe it, but that the governor should investigate and "if they persist—blow them up!" Then he turned to his main task.

With the intervening plantation buildings as protection, the British came forward at the river and along the rear swamp. The Americans blasted away several of the great buildings; on the British column marched, in superb file. The Americans had their heavy guns ready; the number was limited, but they were handled by the expert former crew of the *Carolina* and by the not less expert former pirates of the Gulf. In marksmanship, even against the celebrated British military, both groups were scoring. The battle guns of the enemy were being ripped and silenced by deadly fire. The Americans possessed the advantage of a finely entrenched position, dominating all of the restricted field. The Indian fighters and backwoodsmen also picked their targets well, using their lifelong experience at the frontiers. They could load, fire, reload, and fire again with a dismaying quickness; and the long bore of the hunter proved far superior to the English short rifle. The enemy went down like toy soldiers in white and red. But the British column at the swamp, meeting Americans standing in water to their knees, was beginning to succeed. Then, the terrible havoc of the other lines brought an order for general withdrawal. The Americans had won this encounter.

In a few minutes Jackson had the problem of the home front before him again. Bernard de Marigny, member of the senate, raced down from New Orleans. Governor Claiborne, it developed, had not "blown up the legislators," but had closed the halls. The members were aghast; de Marigny grew vigorous in his insistence that the body was entirely loyal. There had been a terrible mistake, Monsieur le Général. The legislature was allowed to meet again, and the matter ended, for a time.

The British determined to use their last piece of artillery if necessary to blast away the motley opposition. More weary days were spent in bringing up additional batteries. The British soldiers rested, or tried to rest. Many were dying of diseases or, as some said, of the Louisiana marsh and swamp. Sometimes they had to stand in mud to their waists. The mosquitoes gave them no relief—nor did the Americans. The frontiersmen formed parties that sought out British sentries and shot at them as they might have done at a flock of ducks. They dispatched small bands of troops to make the enemy think it was a full onslaught, setting up an alarm, then withdrawing in a moment. Many of these tactics, then deemed ungentlemanly, later became standard practice.

The Americans transferred some of their forces to the west bank of the Delta. By terrible labor the British did the same thing. Extending the Villeré plantation canal to the river through painful hand-digging, they pulled barges over the levee for the task. January eighth was to be the last of these Battles of New Orleans. With every skill at their command, the British drew up for a coordinated offensive that must not fail. Throughout the previous night they worked without letup. The drive must come before dawn, before the American marksmen got to work on their targets. But everything went wrong. The boats to take the British soldiers across the river proved too few; only half the troops could be accommodated. Then to get the men aboard the barks from the slippery banks took unexpected hours. The unknown Mississippi worked against them; the current drew the vessels three miles below the Americans.

Pakenham, commanding the main British land forces, waited in a rage for a signal that the hostilities had begun as scheduled on the west bank. It did not come. Should he wait longer? He dared not. On started the British in precise files. The early morning fogs began to lift, and they were open to American fire. The backwoodsmen had their directions: Wait until they are in close range; pick your targets; *then don't throw away a single bullet.* They could not afford to lose ammunition. The rifles cracked; single men, pairs, dozens, sank down. The brave red lines opened, staggered, then closed again. Behind the American line moved Jackson, always Jackson: "Give it to them, boys. Let's finish the business today!" All that he knew, all that he had learned in border fighting, he was pouring into this struggle.

Again the British were caught by their own blunders. It had been arranged that the 44th Regiment was to carry fascines for crossing Rodriguez canal, and ladders for mounting the fortifications. Now it was discovered that the supplies were missing. Back went three hundred men for them. Confusion grew worse. The American riflemen were working in alternate ranks, one wave of murderous fire succeeding the other with a speed seldom beheld in battle up to that time.

The British broke, leaping into wet ditches, seeking cover in the grasses. For officers who had never seen their soldiers fall back it was a galling spectacle. The superiors came far forward to spur their men, calling out commands, cheering a laggard section, reminding others of their heritage. Some knew that they were doomed, and they left whispered messages: Tell my wife. Remind my family . . . Pakenham, the general of whom the empire had expected a long glory, was a hero. His horse went down, his right arm was broken. He grabbed the mount of his aide in a desperate attempt to rally his army. In a moment he pitched forward, grapeshot in thigh and groin. The soldiers looked about in indecision, as one officer after the other fell prone before them. And there was Wilkinson. He led his men through the canal, atop the mud fortifications themselves, and winced as a volley cut into him. He fell over, into the arms of a Kentucky major. The Kaintucks told him he was too brave to die. He thanked them and asked a favor: "Get word to my commander. I fell on your parapet . . . died like a soldier and a true Englishman."

On the west bank of the river the story was different. Despite their advantages the Americans faltered and retreated. The city might yet have been taken by the British from that direction. But in view of the debacle on the east shore, surviving officers gave the order to British troops to withdraw. The Battles of New Orleans were all but over. Back through the marsh and soggy bayou edges went the enemy. On the vessels of the armada waited the wives, who had come only a few weeks earlier in their light finery for the conquest. To some of the women the litters carried torn bodies; for others, there was only word that he could not be found. In a cask they returned the body of Pakenham to the woman who might have become First Lady of the Province of Louisiana. She and most of the others put away their laces for the black of widow's despair.

Meanwhile part of the British fleet had moved up the river. Jackson had realized the hopelessness of defending the Balize at the Gulf. But twenty-five miles above the Head of Passes two forts waited along a wide bend. The French had first set up defenses there in 1746; the Spanish had strengthened them. This was Detour des Plaquemines, Persimmon Bend, so named because of the rich yellow growths that early visitors saw there.* Now the British units opened fire. For nine days they blasted away with their guns, without success, and then withdrew.

The sugar fields and the gardens of the Delta, with their broken orange trees and crushed hedges of heavy flowers, became the burial grounds of the British. Some of the mansions were gone. That of Chalmette was packed with explosives; one of the family set a match to the rocket. Proud plantation owners later displayed walls pierced by cannonballs. One declined to remove the pair in his walls; he had them gilded. The Villerés pointed to a pecan tree under which, in keeping with the sanitary custom of the day, the viscera of General Pakenham were buried before the body was taken to his ship. For years the natives said that the pecans bore streaks of red. Pakenham died under the oaks of the Colomb house not far away, but through an error the scene of his death has become associated with the great de la Ronde oaks. Almost any Deltan will tell you—"Those are the Pakenham Oak'."

Most of the fields over which the men fought still grow no cane. Since then the only planting has been the bodies of more soldiers.

* The name Plaquemines, from the Indian, clung to the area, and in time the whole lower Delta became Plaquemines parish (or county).

They form a national cemetery. The sites of several of the American batteries have disappeared into the river; but where the *Carolina* poured her broadside into the enemy, dry land rises. The Mississippi has given as well as taken.

There remained a matter for dispute. Had the legislature or any large part of it planned to give up the city to the British? Of the loyalty of the great body of Louisianians, there could have been no question. The legislature had numerous Creole members who fought with distinction, who headed citizens' movements to back Jackson to the limit. But an element of the group, as members of a political body, differed strongly with the American Governor Claiborne and with Jackson as well. Part of it was a matter of personalities, part of it a reaction to Jackson's forthright use of powers under military law. The reason for the temporary closing of the legislative halls remains a mystery which has not been entirely solved.

At the time when things had looked their grimmest, Jackson had superintended the raising of rear defense lines, one of them only two miles below the city. Colonel Déclouet, a former state senator, a Creole commanding a regiment of militia, was in the city. He called on his friend, Magloire Guichard, speaker of the House, holder of large properties in St. Bernard. (He was a French refugee from Santo Domingo, where he had once before lost considerable property under stress of war.) During the evening Monsieur Guichard spoke at some length; what he said became afterward a subject of bitter argument. According to Colonel Déclouet, Guichard observed that it was a terrible kind of struggle that Jackson was conducting, a "Russian war"; Jackson would burn and destroy everything; Jackson might be worse than the British; the legislature should be ready to take measures, if needed, to preserve the country. Further, Déclouet gathered from him that other legislators might be inclined to make terms with the British in case the battle line cracked, so that New Orleans would not become "another Moscow" on Jackson's orders.

It was no secret that some were alarmed over the nature of Jackson's plans if the British were to score further. The president of the Louisiana senate put the matter directly to the officer in charge of the city, and received silence for an answer. Jackson later said he would have "fired it and fought the enemy amidst the surrounding flames," then moved up the river and fought again. No evidence was offered of a definite scheme to deliver New Orleans. But it appears that there might have been some men of property who weighed the chances, somehow, of saving their possessions if worst came to worst and the cause seemed lost. Here was the same problem which faced the men of Paris and the men of Stalingrad during the next century; in each of these cases, a different answer was given. The Louisiana legislature later conducted an elaborate inquiry in which Guichard could remember saying practically none of the things which Déclouet quoted. The legislators exonerated him. Years afterward, Bernard de Marigny, in a sprightly discussion of the matter, agreed that Guichard was "worried by pressing anxieties because his plantation and slaves were in the hands of the British," but maintained that even so concerned, he had not uttered such thoughts. Monsieur Guichard, averred de Marigny, might have had a nightmare during the long winter evening, and talked in his sleep. Beyond a nightmare, he would concede nothing.

The declaration is often made that the Battles of New Orleans were useless. The final land encounter took place fifteen days after the signing of the Treaty of Ghent, which declared the holdings of both nations to revert to their status before hostilities. Yet some have noted that the treaty was only a preliminary to peace, and have wondered if England would have given up Louisiana to the United States in the event she had won the engagements. Regarding this nation as an interloper at the river mouth, Britain had never been reconciled to the legality of its claim. The treaty dealings were long drawn out; at several stages the American ministers felt that the Britons were prolonging them in anticipation of developments on the battlefront. The British repeatedly proposed that each country keep what it held at the time the treaty was signed; and almost to the end, they demanded "restoration" of all territory which did not "belong" to either party. Such phraseology might have permitted a question as to whether Louisiana really "belonged" to the United States.

The battles accomplished a number of results. The unexpected successes brought a wave of new national feeling after the dark doubts of the war. They ended the incipient rebellion against the national government in New England. In the fields of the Delta were sown the seeds of a broader American unity.

CHAPTER 4

Imperial Highway

For years Captains Bradish and Johnson, both Americans, had been passing up and down the Mississippi, gazing at the Delta greenery and the Delta people in cabin or plantation. Alert fellows, they remembered what they saw; what they proceeded to do as a consequence, is in some ways the story of the place for the next half century. The Anglo-Saxons filtered in, looked about, and if they did not conquer, at least they climbed up to sit beside the French rulers and squirmed about in so lively a fashion that the Frenchmen were forced to move over to make room for them.

The Messrs. Bradish and Johnson had entered the Spanish marine service during its last days in Louisiana. As pilots, they were employed under a tight monopoly operated by Señor Juan Ronquillo. They did not roister as did most of their swarthy colleagues; they saved their earnings, and they got along well. Like their associates, they memorized the route from the Balize up the winding passage to New Orleans: that sharp turn, the long clear reach, the point where the waters eddied dangerously. One day one called the attention of the other to a fair stretch of soil on the west bank about thirty-five miles from New Orleans. No, come to think of it, he had never seen it under water, either. The best ground for many miles, it was then occupied by squatters, fishermen, rice farmers, and others. You know, if a man had a little money. . . . The captains pooled resources and before long they had a small plantation in operation. The French snickered at these funny Yonkees; some canny official had disposed of a bog. The captains told them they were wrong. It was going to be something big yet, by God. Wait and see.

When word spread that Louisiana was about to become American, the captains sensed chances in the making. One Spaniard after another prepared to give way to an American. The captains called on Señor Ronquillo and bought him out. Now the piloting system was a two-man monopoly. They hired others as Ronquillo had hired them, and the number quickly increased. The first years of the American regime saw an amazing procession of new vessels moving up the Mississippi. The plantation of the captains also grew. They were pioneering in virgin soil, and they were working at the proper crop—sugar.

After a few years, complaints developed against the method of pilotage; the legislature ordered reforms. (These brought only worse conditions, but that is beside the point here.) The captains retired rich. A new landmark for travelers rose, the first mansion of any size on the way up the river, a heavy brick structure looming two and a half stories high above the flatlands. No harking to Europe for supplies; it was all home-built, home-decorated. The slaves baked bricks of Louisiana clay; they dragged the lumber from near-by cypress forests; the carved wood, interior and exterior, was their work. Walls were two and a half feet thick, and they still stand. The captains built their Magnolia for posterity.

As they managed together so easily, the captains saw no reason why their ladies should not be equally congenial. Magnolia had two mistresses. Few heard of this, French or American, shrimp fisherman or master, without making predictions. The captains were tempting fate! Yet it worked well, at least for a time. Mrs. Johnson had a son, and the partnership was further cemented; to applause on both sides, he was christened Bradish Johnson.

Existence was restful down at Magnolia, among the oaks and the flower-covered trees which gave the place its name; and it was also somewhat unconventional. Leading into the Mississippi was a side stream, Grand Bayou, connecting with the Gulf. Along it appeared men at whom Mesdames Bradish and Johnson might have looked with wonder in another locality. They slipped about quickly, their eyes darting in all directions, and they came at odd hours. The women did not have to ask; they sensed that these were smugglers or pirates. Mrs. Johnson several times told of finding the celebrated corsair Lafitte at Magnolia; she recalled that he was "very, very handsome and very, very polite." The smugglers, evading the Mississippi mouths, used this point for transshipment, and Magnolia and other plantations along the river obtained their slaves in this way. To have turned one's back on such opportunities would have been poor business; operations of this kind were regarded as neither reprehensible nor unusual in their day.

But the captains gradually found other problems than pirates. The prophecies were coming true. The estimable ladies were having tiffs, then differing with fury; then, worse, with ice in their eyes. The house could not be divided in half; reluctantly the captains sat down to settle the matter while the women tapped their feet. Bradish bought Johnson's interest, and Johnson purchased Woodland, a property some miles to the north. As to little Bradish Johnson, his name a symbol of the partnership, it was too late to remedy that. He remained Bradish. Inheriting riches, he added to them, investing in more cane and other properties. He acquired éclat, and finally he reached a stage in which he need remain only half the year at Woodland, spending the rest of the time at his Fifth Avenue residence in New York. During one of his stays in Louisiana he entertained Dom Pedro, emperor of Brazil, not far from that happy point at which his father and his namesake had spied a slightly elevated stretch of land.

A former Delta planter has a clear memory of Bradish Johnson in these latter years. When he went to the Delta he wore a tall silk hat, Prince Albert coat, and striped trousers. None ever saw him in different attire; and his manner almost never changed. "It was frozen dignity," my friend smiles.

These were the two themes of the days that followed: Americans and sugar. With each year or so a new plantation appeared. Sometimes the owner was a French Louisianian, but generally the Creoles clung to their possessions near the city in St. Bernard, while the new arrivals took the unoccupied land. Turning to the land-ownership maps, one finds that the French accent marks and spellings grow fewer with each mile or so to the Gulf; the Villerés give way to the Morgans, the Jumonvilles to the Packwoods. And now and then, as the years passed, amalgamations of the two strains took place, the daughter of a Creole looking with favor upon an American—a thought at which her grandmother would have blanched.

Regardless of the national background of the owner, sugar was paying more than ever. The example of experimentation that had been set here found followers. The Delta saw a succession of planters who fostered further pioneering. J. J. Coiron, a native of Martinique, imported a new cane—the purple or striped Java variety—which was more resistant to frost; and out of his plantings evolved the parent stock from which almost all Louisiana cane can be traced for the rest of the century. Others tinkered with the machinery, evolved refinements and improvements. Sugar making was becoming an industrial process, requiring hundreds of hands for a fairly large-scale operation.

Meanwhile in Paris in the 1830's a young Louisianian was working tirelessly over a set of test-tubes. Norbert Rillieux was a brilliant but unknown figure; almost any native of his home state might have surmised that he would remain unknown. To those about him in the laboratories he was merely another student, a retiring boy who had little to say. In Louisiana he was marked off—a quadroon.

For generations there had been white blood in his family. A newcomer to Louisiana could have taken him for a member of the ruling race. But somewhere, years ago, one of the women had been dark. Legally Norbert Rillieux was free, yet there were many things for which he might not hope. His white father had perceived an unusual engineering skill in the boy, and made it possible for him to carry on advanced studies. At twenty-four Norbert Rillieux published technical studies which won quick praise among scientists in France. Within a short time he was directing a course at the Ecole Centrale. He seemed happy in Paris, for there he found friendships as well as rewards. Presently it was suggested that he go back to Louisiana; perhaps surprisingly, under the circumstances, he accepted an offer there. A planter, Theodore Packwood of Myrtle Grove plantation in the Delta, knew of his interests in the field of sugar engineering. Month after month Rillieux worked down the river and in New Orleans under Packwood's sponsorship.

During a half century, research workers had been trying to perfect an evaporating process for sugar. As the Louisiana Planter and Sugar Manufacturer has pointed out, Rillieux used a sharp originality, cutting to the center of the problem, then striking in a direction that few had previously attempted. His apparatus for evaporation by multiple effect, for which he received patents in 1843, "laid the foundation for all modern industrial evaporation. . . . He went into the matter so long in advance of the investigations made by our modern scientists such as John Tyndall, Lord Kelvin, and others, that his success was a far more wonderful thing than can be appreciated by those of this generation." With his machinery, the profit to the planter was estimated at seventy percent greater than before, while the fuel cost was reduced fifty percent. A practical revolution in sugar culture followed. For decades most of the large plantations used his invention. Many failed to understand it; others tried to make duplicates and failed. A disparaging rival took down one of the elaborate machines, then found himself unable to put it together again. Rillieux was called upon to reconstruct it.

The invention spread to Europe and Asia, to beet and other sugar factories throughout the world. When at some time in the future Rillieux is accorded his full recognition, it may be judged that few of his contemporaries in Louisiana matched his accomplishments. But he apparently realized that his opportunities in the state of his birth were limited. He went again to Paris some years before the Civil War and there continued his researches; and he never returned to Louisiana.

Now came the height of the plantation day, when the families of first settlers found their small holdings jostled by those of the new men. Steamboats brought surveyors and their instruments, and the natives sat silently on their galleries and watched the strange goings-on. The newcomers were taking risks where others would never have done so. And spurred by the wealth that they saw in the distance, they were making changes in the scene. Each owner who moved toward the river mouths became automatically an advocate of levee extension. The American planters demanded that the state take an interest in the raising of the river banks; and local laws were now requiring settlers to look after the mounds at the front.

The machines of sugar production had other uses. Steam pumps, wonderful sights to the earlier settlers, rose toward the marsh, to suck out the water and throw it to the back. Drainage meant that the fields could be extended farther to the back than men had ever thought possible. Levees spread on four sides, so that the sugar acres became rectangular islands of dry soil in the surrounding wetness. Ditches crossed and recrossed; the land was cut into cubist designs. Water gates punctuated the canals and ditches, to hold out the seepings from the back or front, marsh or river, and to allow them to enter when they were wanted.

The economist DeBow prophesied the extension of the plantations almost into the Gulf itself. For fifty miles below New Orleans, he wrote in 1847, the section might already be "compared to a beautiful town with only one street—the great Mississippi." He went on to declare that "the labor of man and his enterprise are creating for our city an avenue to the sea, studded at every pace with all the results of a high and attractive civilization." Warming to his subject, he made a prediction: "A prospect, wanting scarce in any element of beauty, shall open ere long, from the very mouth of the mighty Father of Waters, upon the traveler as he approaches its great city, even as it opens upon him now at many an hour's distance." In the center of each estate was the white mansion with its tall pillars, its lines of trees and flowers, and always the pavilions and statuary. A sure criterion of the planter's prosperity, or the ambitions of his lady, was the number of marble Jupiters or Kneeling Maidens that were outlined against the leaves or the moss. Behind the temple-fronted house rose the sugar factory, thrusting its brick chimney into the air, the marker by which the river pilot could guide himself up the river. Some used the term "Imperial Highway" for the grandeur that unfolded itself.

The proper way to see it all, said the owners, was to travel by one of the local steamboats. This was an education in leisurely ways. The course zigzagged from bank to bank to take in almost every establishment en route. When the water was high and the current strong, the pilot went through what appeared to be fantastic maneuvers, frequently heading a half mile or so upstream beyond the desired point, in order not to miss it. At each stop the captain was expected to have ready a free copy of a New Orleans newspaper for the owner. None knew exactly why; it was "just the way." The owner in turn must invite the captain inside for a drink or for a meal at the proper hour. Other customs were in the same hospitable tradition. When dinner time arrived, almost any stranger who came forward was to be invited to the table. A special practice in some stretches seems to have been that of ringing a bell outside just before food was served. The wayfarer would know that this was his signal to present himself!

Regularly the planters observed their lesser neighbors at their rice growing, and speculated over the possibility of turning much of their own broad acreages to the crop. Their commercial journals urged them to do it, and the idea was often discussed. Robert A. Wilkinson of the Delta was talking in 1849 of a large scheme to use the water which he drained with such effort from the sugar fields, to flood the lower lands at the bank for rice. Some planters raised the commodity, but largely it remained a business of the yeomen or of the man who combined farming with fishing and hunting. Sugar was a demanding crop; and as soon as sugar's needs called, everything else had to be dropped.

Whenever a bad year came for sugar, when the price fell alarmingly, the possibility of rice was put forward again. In the 1850's, for instance, many of the planters tried rice. But sugar picked up again, and the same men forgot the other crop. When sugar paid, she paid well! Let others worry with that rice.

For nearly fifty years following the Louisiana Purchase, it would not have been possible to discuss the Delta's planting affairs without considering Maunsell White, an example par excellence of the non-Frenchman who made himself at home along this Imperial Highway. An Irishman, he had gone first to Kentucky. There he heard of Louisiana and was not long in deciding that the fast-opening region presented even better prospects. To some Louisianians he might have been branded a Kaintuck, meaning a coon-skinned barbarian of that day. But for this cheery Celt—a good eater, a good worker, a bon vivant—the name obviously did not fit. His spirit appealed to the Creoles from the start.

Arriving in 1801, in his early twenties, he found New Orleans little more than a village, with a straggling settlement below it in the St. Bernard district, and a few scattered others in Plaquemines toward the Gulf. He applied himself to something with which he was familiar—trading—and his eye turned toward that almost empty, almost beckoning Delta. He also directed his attention in time upon the Versailles of Colonel de la Ronde, and especially upon that handsome circle of the nine de la Ronde Muses. Completely at home, he soon wooed and married Céleste, second of the Muses. (The first Muse went to Gabriel Villeré, the same Villeré of the Battles of New Orleans.)

When Andrew Jackson arrived in the city, White came forward with his own volunteers, a peppery company of Irish-born, ready to show that no Frenchman could hate the British as the Irish did. During the Battles a wounded English officer was taken to Maunsell White's home. His recovery was slow, and a friendship grew between Irish captor and British prisoner. When the officer left, months later, the Whites and the de la Rondes lined up to bid him a regretful adieu. By this time the guest found found himself penniless, and White provided means for him to return home and re-establish himself. For twenty-five years the two men corresponded. Then White learned through others that his friend had fallen into money troubles, and that his large family was approaching distress. He got into touch with a trusted merchant in England who arranged a settlement of all obligations. It is not difficult to see why the Louisianians, French or American, liked this man.

He was prospering beyond most of his colleagues. His own firm became one of the best known in the Valley; contemporary sources valued his property at more than two million dollars. He moved farther into the Delta, forty miles below the city on the west bank, to his Deer Range plantation. Within eight years of the Battles, his young wife had died, and their child did not live long afterward. For a time he grieved; then in the consolation of the de la Rondes he found himself drawn to Héloïse, the third Muse, and he married her.

And now he was enjoying his Deer Range to the fullest. DeBow described it as "the elegant seat of Colonel White" and added, "On the river it presents an imposing front, which loses nothing by the closest inspection, amid shades and walks and rural improvements." Here the colonel lived "with an honest and republican simplicity, but with no want not abundantly satisfied"—clearly a happy combination. Another visitor found a front fence of boarding three miles long, with a thick hedge of sour orange trees, "many of them loaded with fruit glittering through the handsomest foliage in the world."

Yet all was not entirely favorable. It was of a Plaquemines parish plantation that Mark Twain made a much-quoted remark: "The cane is cultivated after a modern and intricate scientific fashion, too elaborate and complex for me to attempt to describe; but it lost forty thousand dollars last year. I forget the other details." The planter could forfeit everything as easily as he made it, in two seasons or in one. A heavy freeze, or a bad levee break, or an especially low market—and the owner quietly closed his ledger book, to walk slowly away from his sugar house. A woman cried as she stood on the broad white gallery that looked to the Mississippi. And they went back to New Orleans or New York or Kentucky and advised their friends never to break their hearts with such a crop.

Maunsell White underwent a series of setbacks. Shortly before 1850 he had to withdraw from control of his firm. For the satisfaction of creditors he offered over eight hundred thousand dollars of properties. Then, for the first time in many years Colonel White was seen no longer on the steamboats, and in the lobbies of the planters' hotels. But he was not yet broken; a note that appeared three years later informed his friends that at sixty-nine he had "resumed commercial business." A letter declared: "I am now working silently, and I think surely, to the accomplishment of my views, viz: the payment of all the debts due to the late firm, and the collection of the debts due to them." Within a decade he died.

Irrelevantly, Maunsell White is remembered today mainly because he liked pepper sauce. Years earlier, he had become an oyster fancier. At Deer Range oysters were a part of almost every meal, including breakfast. In New Orleans he discovered a place of particular delight, the old Gem Restaurant on Royal Street. Anyone who wished to find Maunsell White, it was said, should go to the Gem, locate the highest pile of shells, and there he would be behind it. His servants grew expert in the preparation of a certain highly spiced sauce. Nobody, even at the Gem, could match that; and so the Colonel took to carrying a bottle of the mixture with him, in his coat pocket or in the hands of his servant. Everybody heard of "the Maunsell White sauce." The recipe or an approximation of it was recognized all over Louisiana. "Pass me the Maunsell White," said one man to another. The planter had become an aromatic ketchup; and so he remains.

To the side, holding to their small plots, the original Deltans fished and trawled, and watched the arrivals and the departures of the Bradishes, the Johnsons, the Whites, and the rest. They paused sometimes to inspect the laughing visitors as they came down the Imperial Highway and stepped from the proud and puffing steamboats to the platform wharves at which the Negroes waited. Perhaps they wondered what such a life could be like, without animals to trap and skin, turtles to chase when they climbed out of the water, or frogs under the house. Eh bien, get along, Antoine. Those shrimp won' wait for you all day.

CHAPTER 5

The Gay Picaroons

ONE sunny morning in June of 1811 a pleasant-faced, earnest merchant of Schoharie in central New York summoned his five children, kissed them and then his wife goodbye, and set off for a business trip to New York City. There Benjamin Miles passed an uneventful few days in trade. He met warehousemen, he arranged credits, and after dark a week later he left Corlear's Hook for his lodgings in Cortlandt Street. He had two thousand or more dollars in his wallet; it was a hot night and on his way Mr. Miles felt thirsty, as even earnest men sometimes do. He picked a small drinking place on Water Street and proceeded to enjoy some beakers of cooling porter.

About him sat a cheerful male company. Mr. Miles heard someone remark that he had seen a "black-looking schooner" near by the other day and suspected it was a French privateer. Mr. Miles lifted his head and gave his listeners the benefit of his thoughts. Yes, those scoundrels were out there waiting to prey on the commerce of good citizens and businessmen. Before God, he wished someone would put him in power for a little while! He would order the American Navy to capture every one of them and hang them at the yardarms. He uttered the grim word "picaroons" and, he said later, he might have made use of "some other rash expressions." Time went by; Mr. Miles took his last cheering mouthful. On his trip home he passed three dark men, talking together; and then, he surmised, one or more of them hit him on the head.

Benjamin Miles woke up in the bottom of a sailboat in the East River, with the three men about him. He felt for his pocketbook; it was gone. He complained about the money, but his main thought was for his life. He was certain that they planned to drop him in the water. They told him that they knew nothing of any money; and he was not going to be killed, they assured him. They bound his hands, covered his eyes, and before long he was hoisted up, placed in the forecastle of a vessel, and was on his way to sea.

Twenty-four hours later, Mr. Miles was lifted on deck, to learn that he was in the hands of the very "picaroons" at whom he had sworn. Some of the crew had heard him; now he was to be their guest for a cruise, to show him that they were only clever, agreeable fellows after all. The vessel was the six-gunned *La Vengeance;* and Mr. Miles was, in truth, to be shown a number of things. The trip led all of the way along the Atlantic coast, into the Gulf, and up the Mississippi River. Mr. Miles had to work, but was not mistreated. The scoundrels took it as something of a joke, Mr. Miles was forced to conclude.

Now he learned about the business of buccaneering in the Gulf. He watched the sighting of various ships about the Mississippi mouths, the preparations of men and guns. In each case he was removed below deck just before the moment of seizure, but he missed nothing else. He saw vessels taken as prizes, cargoes dispatched up the river or adjacent Delta waters. It was all handled with the ease and dispatch of any of Mr. Miles' transactions in Schoharie. The supplies were awaited by merchants in the city, and no one seemed upset at any part of it.

Finally on August 15th or 16th the *Vengeance* was in the Mississippi near English Turn. Mr. Miles was transferred to a small boat and taken to New Orleans. At two o'clock in the morning he was deposited on the levee, without a penny, and ordered to get out of the city without delay and to keep his Yankee mouth well sealed. Aware of the port's reputation among God-fearing people, Mr. Miles did as he was told. Working his way laboriously overland, he arrived by mid-November in New York, to find that after much search, officials had given him up for lost. At Schoharie his friends had even settled his estate, dividing his assets in several directions. Whether he liked it or not, Mr. Miles had discovered more than he had ever suspected about this strange modern world of the nineteenth century. He knew also by this time that there was such a thing as pride among rascals. Don't call a picaroon a picaroon, especially if he can hear you.

The Gulf had long been a lake of corsairs. When Spain claimed it, the French had been among the first to sail it for purposes of robbery on the waterways. One reason why the Spanish had been concerned over the French settlements was their fear that this would be a fine place for pillaging their commerce. Even the founder Iberville did a bit of singeing of the Castilian's whiskers; for a time he seemed to envision a privateers' empire over the southern waves. Other Frenchmen regularly swept down on the galleons. The lure of the Spanish Main was impelling, and youths of many countries and many backgrounds joined the shadowy navies of sea-rovers. The captains had letters of marque, giving them the privilege of pouncing upon ships of this or that enemy nation. But the margin between privateer and pirate, as has often been noted, was a thin one. A man and his crew had to live; when a master heard his followers cry for money and mutter mutinously, his eyes began to blur as he tried to tell the flag of one nation from that of another. The leaders and their outlook became truly global; they would plunder anything, without discrimination.

Men learned early that the Delta offered unrivaled natural facilities for informal dealing. It was all too easy to creep along the endless flats and shallows, to hide when necessary among the grasses bordering the indented passages. A separate, smaller breed were the local smugglers, who did not range the waters but would take what others brought them. A rough partnership grew up between the two elements. The Deltans could negotiate the rest of the way to the city or arrange to meet New Orleans friends with whom they had understandings. Sometimes the officials knew little of this. Again they sensed that it would be hard to curb, and that in any case the contrabandiers served a community need, and let it go. Restrictive trade rules of the home governments made a certain amount of smuggling not only advisable but even imperative. Also, government agents in these lonely stretches were human and liked a fair bit of luxury as well as the next fellow. It paid a smuggler to be reasonable and share something with them. During the eighteenth century the trade waxed and waned, but it was seldom absent for long.

Ships disappeared in the Gulf, and at some port a year later trinkets turned up with the initials of a missing passenger, or a bolt of costly silk that had been part of the cargo. That was all that would be known. From time to time those at the Balize would sight a speck on the horizon. Rescued, the survivors whispered their stories: men hung by the thumbs at the masts on the shimmering sea, moaning as the death for which they prayed came only by slow degrees; a guffawing circle that watched a wretch, clothes ablaze, run shrieking to the edge to plunge into the waves. Generally, however, there was only the soft beat of warm, lapping waters with their hint of the tropics.

The nineteenth century opened new, rosier opportunities. French privateers expanded their quarters at Martinique, at Guadeloupe and other islands to the east. Into the Delta poured new piles of goods. England captured the Caribbean strongholds; the pirates moved to the Gulf, to center their undertakings about the ragged shores of Louisiana. Other factors entered. The United States was barring the slave trade from her boundaries, which now included those of the Delta. Louisianians were horrified. Slaves were wanted more than ever; from no place was the demand for black flesh more insistent than from the fast-developing sections below New Orleans.

To an extent that some have underestimated, much of the privateering was commerce in human beings. Ships were intercepted near the coasts, African or American, and men and women were shifted from one captor to the other. Hijacking would be the modern word. These men showed as little compunction, when pursued, at tossing overboard screaming captives in chains than at throwing out bales of inanimate contraband. One sank almost as quickly as the other. About the Mississippi mouths crept individuals of all types and elements: cutthroats who had turned to the sea as an easy path to lucrative larceny; adventure-hunting youths who enjoyed danger; snarling exiles wanted by the police of scores of places. In New Orleans and in the Delta the picaroons had quiet but important "connections"—merchants, financiers, and plantation owners. Among the mercantile men of the city there developed organizations with large treasuries, which equipped captains and their ships much as later industrial operators hired gangsters for their purposes. Such arrangements were not limited to South Louisiana. The investors often lived in New York or New

England. In a burst of pride or of injudiciousness, such individuals sometimes named their privateer ships after wives and sweethearts, to their embarrassment when matters reached public print.

New Orleans emerged as the spawning place of countless undertakings of dubious character. It became also the point to which prizes were dispatched after capture. More or less officially recognized practices were established. A captor communicated with an owner and let him know that for a certain consideration he would return the ship. The owner received his property undamaged. The privateer obtained less than he would on the open market, but both sides were spared a great deal of trouble.

Breton Island to the east of the river, and the Chandeleur chain along the St. Bernard coast, became favorite stopping places for corsairs with prizes or with booty for disposal. A ship bearing contraband goods approached as close as the shoaling waters permitted. Word had meanwhile arrived at their friends' quarters, and vessels of smaller draft were dispatched to make the transfer. A few more miles of curving passage through the Delta, and the cargoes were at hand for sale.

Some operators also dabbled in filibustering in the interest of new Latin American governments or elements in rebellion against Spain. Louisianians gave money, equipment, and occasionally their lives in these efforts. Land expeditions were organized, sea battles fought, Spanish ports blockaded. Many who left the Delta on such occasions were zealots afire with a yearning for liberty; others were mercenaries, taking pay from one side to betray it to the enemy. And between them were soldiers of uncertain fortune, who would cut the heart out of any designated chest for a fair consideration.

The era of privateering which lasted until the 1820's and with waning intensity for some time afterward, was one of duplicities, of crossings and doublecrossings. The most publicized of the actors were the pirates Jean and Pierre Lafitte; but others operated on their own, preceded and outlasted the Lafittes. Shortly after the Battles of New Orleans, the Lafittes were gone. Others remained on, though history has generally not been fair to them, denying them their full recognition. To attempt any full account of their fantastically interconnected manipulations would be futile. Instead, I have selected several representative episodes, case histories of the time. It was, I submit, a lusty period.

A man of gall was William Mitchell. He came to recognition in the Delta only after an apprenticeship to the southward. An Englishman, he involved himself in a number of exploits in the vicinity of Nicaragua in 1816. Descending on the island of San Andrés, he captured it for the rebels and proceeded to divest the royalists of all movable possessions. Then, as the Louisiana Gazette described the incident, he shot and then hung up the bodies of the governor and his force of six soldiers. Let that teach tyrants a lesson! About the same time he went to the aid of beleaguered republicans and rescued them with their hoarded belongings. Stopping to repair his vessel, he put his passengers ashore, and sailed away with all of their property. None could call Mitchell a one-sided man. Shifting to the Mississippi, he suffered bad fortune when he was arrested at the Balize. He must not have been worried; he had influential friends. Escaping conviction, he went on to other things.

A group of Louisiana merchants made him commander of a "mosquito fleet" of open boats and tiny schooners operating in and about the Delta. Stanley Faye in the Louisiana Historical Quarterly comments that a single remittance to the silent partners, after deductions for officers and men, totaled nearly two hundred thousand dollars. Lakes Pontchartrain and Borgne and the Chandeleur Island chain were Mitchell's favorite hunting grounds. Several times the unpleasant federal customs collector arrested him; once he was shot. Mitchell called this simple harassment. He would get revenge. The collector earned his livelihood from cargo duties, did he? Mitchell would fix that. There would be no cargoes!

He almost succeeded for a time in bringing about just that situation. He sailed up the river near Fort St. Philip at Plaquemines Bend, held up a ship and escaped by a side passage. Then he moved on the Balize and took the collector's revenue cutter with her six guns. For a time he was the scourge of vessels seeking entrance to the river. Then, when search came close, he fled to other scenes.

Several years later, in 1819, news arrived that a small marauder —just a rowboat, some said—was loose in the Gulf. "Sounds like that Mitchell," declared New Orleans. It was. The pilots at the river mouth remembered the last time, and appealed to Fort St. Philip for help. Reinforcements were sent to them, but Mitchell slipped in anyway. Eluding all manhunts, he raided and terrified ships of all countries; and then, with his unfailingly good judgment, he glided away. Lest it seem that the enterprising Mitchell failed to receive a just reward, Mr. Faye notes that he captured a man-sized vessel to replace his rowboat.

The next decade brought the Delta the case of the *Bolivar,* a vessel with good connections. Its owner was Thomas Reybaud, former Mexican consul at New Orleans, who acquired the *Bolivar* at auction after she was condemned by a prize court. Perhaps he thought that a vessel once connected with privateering should not lose its identity; in any case the *Bolivar* was reconditioned at Mobile and started forth. She was in luck; or perhaps informed Mobilians were her friends. A short distance out, she made a fine capture, a schooner that had just left the same port for Tampico. The officers of the *Bolivar* told the proper persons at Tampico that they would be glad to release the schooner for a moderate sum. The proper persons declined, and the *Bolivar* rode the waves with the prize along. Then, ready for anything, and taking along the captured vessel, the *Bolivar* headed for the Mississippi river mouths.

At Southwest Pass fortune was again with the *Bolivar.* A second vessel moved within range, the *Isabella,* with a cargo worth forty thousand dollars. The *Bolivar's* captain told the other ship to give up. The *Isabella's* master replied that these were obviously waters within the territorial limit, and that he intended to do anything but that. From the *Bolivar,* as her guns stood out clearly against the Gulf sky, came an ominous message: Heave to, or be sunk where you are. The *Isabella's* officer replied by giving his opinion of the *Bolivar* and her ilk.

The *Bolivar* moved into position and fired. Perhaps the crew had suffered by lack of practice, but the *Isabella* was able to pull away into the river. The heavier *Bolivar* started after her. The *Isabella* gained; the *Bolivar* lowered a man-of-war boat with a dozen sailors aboard, firing at intervals, to speed up the chase. Over the bar in the river mouth went the *Isabella.* (To hell with a pilot at a time like this!) After her spurted the man-of-war boat; after that, lumbering, the *Bolivar.* The small boat advanced on the *Isabella* in the approaching dusk; the victim seemed about to fall into enemy hands when the Mississippi came to her rescue. The *Bolivar* stuck in the river mud, and called back her men.

The master of the other ship, the *Isabella,* was out of danger, but he had his dander up. He was going to do something about this. He slipped up the river and found his way to a federal revenue cutter. Shortly afterward the cutter came upon the *Bolivar,* still in the mud. The adventure was over; the *Bolivar,* the small boat, and the crew were hauled up to New Orleans. Just off the river mouth, the government men found the *Bolivar's* first prize from Mobile, and confiscated it.

Piracy was charged to the men of the *Bolivar.* (But not, let it be noted, to the owner. It was always so.) Many Louisianians were stunned at the action. Here was an unwarranted governmental interference, a barefaced attack on the principles of individual enterprise in privateering. On earlier occasions when pirates had awaited trial, their followers had threatened to storm the jails and burn the city. New Orleans was slowly quieting, and the crew of the *Bolivar* went unrescued. Yet they came off rather lightly, with sentences of one to three years. It was not a result to deter others, and it did not.

The years passed, but traffic in contraband, with related enterprises, did not pass with them. Increased federal forces were making it all more difficult; Louisianians assured each other that piracy was over. Last year's affair was the end, certainement, don't you think? Then another foray was staged, and the general opinion changed again. Through the 1830's and into the '40's this situation continued. In 1842, for instance, sudden excitement ran through lower Louisiana when a dramatic message came from the Balize.

Out in the Gulf the ship *Charles* had been discovered by river pilots, floating helplessly. Not a person was aboard; trunks had been torn open; everything of value, except a lumber cargo, was gone. On the decks one of the pilots almost slipped in blood, still wet, and there was more at the deck edge and over the vessel's sides. Men looked at each other and did not have to say what was in their minds.

The pilots scoured the surrounding waters, without result. In New Orleans anxiety spread. The *Charles* had left only a few days earlier, bound for Bordeaux, and aboard were relatives and friends of many Louisianians. The newspapers reported a "disastrous panic" in commercial circles; few merchants would send out ships until this threat was removed. Mass meetings brought demands: Catch them, catch them! Volunteers came forward and a steamer, the *Neptune,* was chartered under the command of General Persifer F. Smith, of military celebrity.

The *Neptune* hurried about the Gulf waters. The adventurers could not have gone far; most Louisianians were sure they were lurking near here. All vessels were stopped; the shrimpers and oyster people pointed out possible hiding spots, while certain small smugglers carefully made it clear that they knew nothing. Information spread that on an island in the Chandeleur group, directly in the path of earlier pirate routes, suspicious men had just set up a camp. The *Neptune* hastened there in the dark.

The general and his men crept up in a boat. As it struck bottom, they leaped out and ran forward. Before a tent stood a man, gun in hand. "Who goes there?" he shouted. "Surrender!" they told him. The sentinel handed over his gun; simultaneously a man ran out with a knife and slashed at two of the volunteers. One of them fired into the assailant's stomach. Reinforcements from the *Neptune* rushed to the tent. More bloodshed seemed imminent, until the leaders enjoined them all to be quiet. The injured man lay dying. It became suddenly clear that an error had been committed.

The island party numbered only four, three adults of the Faubourg Marigny and a weeping nine-year-old boy. A doctor had suggested a rest in salt air for one of the men. On their way they had been stopped by others scouting for pirates, had identified themselves and received warnings to watch against the marauders. When the volunteers appeared in the night, the man inside had taken them for the sea bandits and come forth with the knife to save his brother. And now the moans of the victim were the only sounds above the beat of the Gulf waters as the volunteers looked in horror at what they had done.

The trip back was a longfaced one, in contrast with the pomp, the high hopes, the smiles and tears of the embarkation. The general disbanded his men. Shortly afterward the roll of the expedition disappeared, according to the newspaper The Herald; "and it was always very difficult to discover who were the members of it, though when it started they were all well-known citizens." The general and several others who had received considerable attention at the beginning were called by authorities on capiases charging murder, but the matter was ultimately dropped.

Yet where were the people of the ship *Charles* and the pirates? Men with former buccaneer connections found neighbors' fingers pointed at them. Individuals who whispered suspiciously about the incident were rushed before officials for long questioning. Then the papers of Charleston carried a small and not entirely enlightening note. Into that port had come "the late captain of the *Charles*" with his crew—but without the passengers. The officers and men arrived on a schooner from Southwest Louisiana. The tale that they told was this: The *Charles* had sailed into the Gulf but had sprung a leak about fifty miles out. She had started toward the Balize, but the water had mounted rapidly in the hold. Another vessel, bound for Le Havre, moved into sight, and the crew and passengers transferred, with all of their belongings. As for the blood, the captain and mate had cut their hands and someone had killed a few chickens on deck.

Then, a little later as the account went on, the rescue ship had fallen in with the schooner from Louisiana on her way to the Atlantic coast. The crew and officers had no wish to go to France with the passengers and they had made a second shift. The schooner herself was long delayed. Struck by lightning shortly afterward, she lost weeks before she could reach Charleston. Eventually, arriving in France, the passengers on the other ship appear to have given a roughly similar story.

And so the incident was explained. But was it? Some circumstances were highly unclear to men familiar with such matters. The *Charles* had not sunk; many in New Orleans insisted that its cargo—timber and staves—would have prevented that, and that the captain should have known it even if the panicky passengers did not. Also, since they were so near the river mouth, why had no greater effort been made to reach the pilots? And why was no note or message of any kind left to inform others and prevent the terrible concern of the families in Louisiana?

The contemporary attorney, Henry C. Castellanos, observed that the vessel could have been claimed as a prize after its abandonment, by the first persons who came upon it. Had certain of the crew members planned everything with this in view, expecting to return to the vessel as quickly as possible and take it to another port for admiralty sale? Such things had happened before, and were still happening at that time. If this had been the purpose, they were frustrated by the element of time and the accident to the schooner that followed.

Because of the circumstances an investigation was held in Charleston, and a judge found no evidence to warrant suspicion. But New Orleans was not satisfied. Regarding the captain, one editor wrote: "A fearful weight of accountability attaches to his infamous conduct. If we have a counsel to offer him, it is to avoid Louisiana in all his future peregrinations." As to the truth, it was and is any man's guess.

CHAPTER 6

Loss and Survival

THE Delta, which had saved New Orleans in 1815, lost it and the valley in 1862. On that earlier occasion Louisiana had been sharply apprehensive. Now it seemed almost serenely confident. "Nothing afloat could pass the forts," wrote George W. Cable, retelling the days of optimism. "Nothing that walked could get through our swamps." Yet as before, the Delta entranceway to the continent was almost doomed. In 1815 the invader gave away his chances; in 1862, facing the men from the North, the Confederates made the mistakes.

Once again an expedition was launched in secrecy, its men numbering almost the same as the twenty thousand of the earlier armada. When the news arrived, Louisiana guessed correctly that the Federals would not repeat the British strategy of trying to slip in through the lakes; and when it thought of the river route, it felt safe. In 1815 the small Fort St. Philip at Plaquemines Bend had resisted the enemy nine full days and nights, hadn't it? Since then the government had enlarged it and erected an additional, greater defense on the opposite bank, Fort Jackson, commanding the sweep of the Mississippi. Now both were in Confederate hands, further strengthened, ready for any callers.

As important as the forts was a device that went with them—a raft of logs and abandoned schooners, chained together from one river bank to the other. A short time earlier, high water had poured down with an unusually heavy volume of driftwood, piling up for a half mile along the stream. The line then broke; but it had been hurriedly repaired, and most Louisianians were certain that the Yankees could never hope to surmount this barrier.

Admiral David Farragut arrived with fifty vessels, large and small, at Ship Island in the Gulf, the same landing place that so many before him had chosen. Thence he advanced to the river mouth; and there, as some expected, his first ships were caught in the mud. Dispensing with the regular pilots, whom he suspected of Confederate sympathies, he used his own forces, took weeks to make thorough soundings and finally moved into the Mississippi.

Sun-darkened trappers and blue-clad oyster-tongers gazed at vessels—wooden gunboats and mortar schooners—such as they had never seen or imagined, sending high waves toward shore, forcing small floods over the low-lying fields here and there. How this will affeck the oyster market, you think, Gus? Mon Dieu, tha's true, you got your boy in the army north in Georgia!

The Battles of New Orleans had taken place among the plantations; the struggle of 1862 was to rage about the cabins and rice fields below. Never had these thin edges of earth known sounds like these. Every rebound of the heavy cannon made the rockless soil quaver. "It was like a big paw hitting at us, all the time," one ancient man said. Mud chimneys collapsed; houses swayed. Some took their boats to the Gulf borders and lived on the islands for a time. Others felt another, a worse fear. Inside those forts were their men, volunteers or pressed into service. Women refused to leave their flimsy homes but sat huddled at their windows, fists over ears, waiting to see how it would end.

Hiding the masts of his vessels with willow boughs as camouflage, Farragut ordered an almost continuous bombardment. For five days thousands of heavy shells and cannonballs buried themselves in the marshes, in the moats, occasionally striking the forts. The Confederates fired back, but both sides did surprisingly little direct damage. In carriages and small boats, plantation people and their guests watched the brilliant fireworks. Look at those Yonkees; it was droll, wasn't it? And all for nothing, too!

Nearby residents also crept up to see. On the west bank two children, Josephine and Robert Smith, hurried to the levee. They gazed entranced until the brother noticed that the battle was directly upon them. A Union man called: Get out of the way! They crawled behind a heavy oak. For an hour they stayed there, faces half buried in the earth as fire flashed about them.

The fighting grew heavier than ever. Robert whispered, and Josephine nodded. Hand in hand, they dashed across the level ground. A few feet more; a swamp was ahead. Robert felt his sister's hand tighten, then go limp in his. He turned. A wild bullet had hit her; she was dead before he could kneel beside her.

The battle raged on. Farragut now decided that the forts could not be taken by direct attack. He turned to the obstruction in the river. His forces tried to blast it but failed. A gunboat slipped up in a foggy Delta night, and the men cut the cable. The Confederates spied them, too late. The water washed heavily through the gap. The first obstacle had fallen; but greater ones lay ahead.

The Federals pressed forward, to attempt passage of the forts, and to meet the blasts of waiting Confederate vessels. Death cracked on all sides. Combat was at close quarters, cannons pounding, smoke swirling. Farragut said afterward that it was almost guerrilla fighting: "We had nothing to aim at but the flash of their guns; it was very difficult to distinguish friends from foes." His flagship caught fire; several times the Federals seemed doomed. But they pushed on and won. Along the Delta they sped by levees lined with men and women, past rows of slaves who were frightened and slaves who were joyous. Up at New Orleans the bells clanged, and for the first time the city realized that it had lost.

Battles would follow in other parts of Louisiana, to the north and to the west. The Delta would be held by the Union until the war reached its weary end. When Vicksburg fell during the following year, the vital river was in Federal hands. The West would be cut off from the South; down the stream would move heavy Union tonnage from the rest of the country. The Confederates had been struck a blow from which they could not recover.

Of the Louisiana names that rose during these years, those heard most often were of Pierre Gustave Toutant Beauregard, who fired the shot that began the war; and Judah Philip Benjamin, who has been called an American Disraeli, and the brains of the Confederacy. Both were of the Delta, the first by birth, the second by choice. To both, the fates promised much that they did not fulfill: each said later that he remembered his years in this water-bordered earth as the happiest in his eventful life.

Pierre was the son of a Beauregard and a De Reggio, related to the Ducros, the De Vezins, the Villerés. Any of the older Creoles, hearing any one of those names, would have nodded quickly: He was well-born, that one. His was that simpler, older French regime; I have a faded sketch of the home, Contreras, a large, one-storied place, rather less than pretentious. Yet it was against a background of Latin gentility that Pierre spent his youth. He rode his pony about the fields, he heard his Père give quick directions at cane grinding time. He paddled or was paddled in small boats along the bayous to the lakes, and he watched while sweating workers dragged in their shellfish. At an earlier age than most, the dark-eyed, solemn boy was handling firearms, and well. He heard of the great Jackson, and he wandered over the fields of Jackson's command.

Soon he was showing that he had a good French temper. Hamilton Basso in his biography tells how, returning from a bad hunting day, when Pierre was about ten, he was taunted by a cousin, aged twenty. In a moment his olive skin paled; he dropped rabbit and gun, grabbed a heavy branch, and made after the other. The cousin fled to an outhouse; Pierre threatened to burn it down. The elders intervened, but Pierre did not forget. He seldom forgot.

After early study under two former officers of Napoleon, he went to West Point, from which he was graduated with high honors. A professional soldier, winning credit in the Mexican War, he returned to Louisiana, to enjoy visits to the family home; hours of hunting—snipe, mallards, wild geese—and boat rides in the bland blue evenings. Here he reread his books that told of the great Napoleon, and rehearsed his lessons in military strategy. Here, too, he met or remet the beautiful, brunette Marie Laure Villeré, and soon she was Marie Laure Villeré Beauregard. Receiving Army assignments that brought him home, he stayed for a time with the Villerés.

One of his projects was the rebuilding of Forts Jackson and St. Philip in the river's bend; it is of record that he predicted failure for any future effort to hold the Mississippi unless vastly greater expenditures were made. Marie Laure died; peace, or the assignments of peace bored him, a soldier born and trained. He passed a listless, restless period. Then he married again, Caroline Deslonde, another Creole. He became commandant of West Point, but resigned in less than a week; for this was 1860, and the war was very close. Before long the incisive Beauregard, eyes flashing, in his element at last, was at Charleston, to give the signal for that famous volley at Fort Sumter. The conflict was on. He became a hero; all over the South, men shouted his name in happy non-Gallic mispronunciation. For a time there was talk of Beauregard for Confederate president, with the support of the Army.

Almost immediately, Beauregard fell into disagreement with Jefferson Davis, the first of dozens of furious differences that were to last on in controversy beyond their deaths. President Davis held for a careful defense; Beauregard demanded a slashing attack. The two men came to detest each other. Blamed for losses, Beauregard defended himself; Davis relieved him of command of the Western Army. His dimmed star seemed to be rising again, but the war was over; and Beauregard returned not to glory but to a Louisiana that had lost. Davis preceded him in death. Invited to a place at the funeral, Beauregard declined. He would not, he said, be a hypocrite.

Today the Beauregards are gone from the Delta. There stands a tall, stately building which once belonged to the general's son, but it is of another period. The abandoned family home that Pierre had known remained until a few years ago. Then people who needed wood began to pull away at the galleries and the walls; one day it fell into a broken heap. Only occasionally can an elderly native be found who remembers anything of him. One led me this year across Bayou Terre aux Boeufs to a small cemetery that was partly lost in its twisted, thickening foliage. He pointed to a gravestone, that of the delicate Marie Laure, first wife of the general:

"Ici repose M.A. Laure Villeré, épouse du Major G. T. Beauregard, officier de l'armée des Etats-Unis, née le 22 Mai 1823, décédeé le 21 Mars 1850. Esprit descendu du ciel, tu y es remonté; dors en paix, fille, épouse et mère cherie." ("Spirit from heaven, there you have returned. Sleep in peace, daughter, wife and dear mother.") Marie Laure is alone. Beauregard was buried in New Orleans, where he lived out his final days.

Judah Philip Benjamin was not a Creole, not a Louisianian by birth, and never did he inspire the adulation that was Beauregard's. Yet Benjamin may be remembered longer by the Deltans. He left not a tomb, but a monument and a brilliant one—a house. Of poor Jewish parentage, he was born on the English-owned West Indian island of St. Thomas. Judah entered Yale College at fourteen; two years later he was in New Orleans as a notarial clerk. Studying law at night, he tutored in return for lessons in French and Spanish. He learned quickly and was well liked. At twenty-one he became a member of the bar; two months later, to the surprise of many, he married a Creole girl of high place, the handsome Natalie St. Martin. Not long before this her father had retained Judah to teach English to Natalie; now he had a son-in-law in his French Quarter home.

In other directions Judah made equally quick conquest. Within a few years he won reclaim, more than surprisingly, as one of the best attorneys in the crowded field of Louisiana—remarkably skilful in argument and a master of technicalities. Inevitably he went into politics; first a Whig, he later shifted to the Democrats. Sometimes he seemed to yield to pressure from below, but he remained essentially an advocate of the status quo, and a sharply conservative one, in the Louisiana legislature, in the Senate at Washington. From being a representative of sugar planters he became one himself, acquiring an interest with Theodore Packwood in the many-acred estate of Bellechasse in the upper Delta.

The small Creole home that stood there for years was not quite adequate for the flush 1840's. It was single-storied with galleries at only two ends. The new place would have great, double-leveled porches, almost fifteen feet across, a parade of massive, rectangular pillars and everything else in proportion: curving stairways of mahogany, massive carved decorations, silver-plated door knobs, extensive rose gardens between the house and the levee, and an enormous bell into which Benjamin was said to have dropped five hundred silver dollars during the melting, to "sweeten the tone."

The charming Natalie and their child remained with Judah for some time, but it grew increasingly clear that she found life in Louisiana, and perhaps life with the plump and hardworking Judah, a trifle dull. She went to Paris, never to come back to Louisiana. Judah brought his mother and sisters to Bellechasse; he went to Europe to visit Natalie every year or so, as Dr. Robert Douthat Meade has noted in his biography. And they seemed to get along pleasantly when they were together. But Natalie continued a wife at a distance.

Benjamin became an enthusiast in scientific sugar culture. He read about sugar, he met such men as the genius Rillieux, and with the practical help of his partner-manager Packwood, he made Bellechasse a success. Dr. Pierce Butler in his earlier study quotes the partner's wife: " 'There goes Theodore with Mr. Benjamin! I never see them riding about the field together without trembling. . . . Mr. Benjamin can talk him into buying any newfangled pot or pan he's pleased with for the moment, and then Theodore has the worry of making the thing work.' " Among the curious trinkets was a "domestic ice machine" which would, or perhaps would not, put forth pretty sticks of ice when the crank was turned. But their sugar won prizes.

In 1852 the river broke near by; backwaters slipped in until all of the cane was ruined. Other financial problems rose, and Benjamin sold his interest, leaving Bellechasse as part of his past. When the war came, he was named Confederate Attorney General, then Secretary of War, then Secretary of State. As perhaps the closest associate of Jefferson Davis, he quarreled with his fellow Louisianian Beauregard. Men disagreed about him even more bitterly than they did over the Creole; through it all Benjamin carried on, "smiling as usual," in the words of a wartime observer.

Eventually and without a smile, Benjamin urged a realistic plan which alone, he thought, might have saved the crumbling Southern regime—a proposal to free the slaves, as a means of obtaining European aid. It came too late. In the collapse, Benjamin fled to the Florida coast and after a number of perilous adventures, reached England. Then ensued perhaps the most incredible phase of an incredible career. At fifty-five, ruined, he began close to the bottom of the British legal profession, to become one of its important figures. Though his American accent grated often on his listeners' ears, he emerged as Queen's Counsel and a wealthy man again. No other individual has had quite his experience as a leader of the law in the two countries. And now at last he could be at home from time to time with his wife Natalie.

For years the elaborate, twenty-roomed Bellechasse remained in preservation, and crowds attended the parties beneath its ornamented ceilings and walked in the curving gardens about the silver-toned bell. It was notable, from an architectural point of view, not only for its great size but also for the complete third story extending high above the galleries. The stranger who had made himself so much a part of Louisiana and the Delta had given them one of their show places. Then the house fell into disrepair. The silver-plated doorknobs disappeared; the white enamel that covered the interior woodwork cracked and broke away. A tenant family occupied the former drawing room, and a nurseryman planted tuberoses on the rotting floors. The river cut closer, through the wrecked gardens; in the silences, the lapping of the waters was very close. A memorial association moved the house and saved it; today, in Benjamin's name, it still towers over the river bank.

In the meantime the Delta knew the confusion and the violence of the Reconstruction and the years that followed, the period that saw an attempted social-economic revolution and its eventual failure. In South Louisiana as elsewhere, many of the lesser whites came to the forefront, fighting for a new place in the sun. Their allies included some of those from above, who had been Unionists, and the mass of the Negroes, striving also for a position that the older way had denied them. The decades were acrid with the fury of deep-searing resentments. Not for some time had New Orleans and its surrounding parishes been known for gentle politics.* The Civil War and Reconstruction witnessed a series of shifts of power in Louisiana: first to a city laboring element, not necessarily friendly to the Negro; then to

* See Chapter 16 for some of the earlier irregularities involving the Delta.

some of the native whites, the Negroes, and their Northern allies; and eventually back to the planters. Hatred met hatred, and corrupt methods spawned more corrupt ones.

To many of the former Delta slaves, freedom meant primarily the right to move from a region to which they had previously been tied. During the war and afterward, they wandered to New Orleans, to the Federal armies and elsewhere. Often they were told that they would receive land, and they looked for it and asked for it. But few obtained it. For a time Federal military authorities supervised the operation of sugar holdings in Plaquemines and St. Bernard. Growers agreed to pay wages of ten dollars a month for able-bodied males, and soldiers took charge of "discipline." Later this ended, and the planters sought other adjustments to the problem of a free labor force.

Disruptions ensued, dissatisfaction on both sides, with occasional strikes for higher pay. Crops failed, and operators swore that the plantations could no longer exist. Yet despite everything, these great holdings, symbols of the older regime, remained generally intact. The Delta parishes had a number of Negro officials; riots broke out, and there were killings from ambush, clashes between Reconstructionists and groups of men who moved down from New Orleans. But older plantation owners held on with tenacity; the economic base was shaken, but it did not collapse. New owners moved into the Delta, and usually they were Anglo-Saxons, individuals from other parts of the South, or Yankees who might or might not be in sympathy with the national government. These newcomers, like others before them, saw in the sturdy green stalks the true wealth of the state; and to the winning of that wealth they applied new methods and new ingenuities. The post-war officials were ousted; the sugar men generally stayed.

For most of the other Deltans, the fishermen, the oyster diggers, the men of the frontier, much of the political turmoil seemed rather remote. They followed their cool water paths between the curtains of reeds and grasses, they dredged the sandy shores, and they traded with the city people when the occasion arose. To many, the matter had ended when that man Farragut had pushed up the river. The plantation owners offered some of them jobs in the fields or in the sugar houses. Frequently, having been their own masters for so long, they failed to fit themselves to such routine; and the sugar men had to look elsewhere. The growers spoke often of substitute labor, and often they tried it. Chinese coolies—they seemed to serve the California railroads well; European peasants, such as the Easterners and Midwesterners were importing with success—perhaps they would be the answer. Long editorials appeared in the New Orleans newspapers; "immigration leagues" and similar organizations were formed. When a supply of Chinese railroad laborers passed through the city to the West, scores of curious men and women went to the station to watch and comment.

Finally the Chinese were brought here. Usually they remained a few weeks in the furious sun, they fought with the overseers, and they slipped away in the evening or quit in a body, to go up to New Orleans or to join the fishing industries of the Delta. J. T. Trowbridge has described the landing in New Orleans of one hundred Germans, who had been hired in New York for sugar work. Within twenty-four hours about a third of them had asked higher wages and "deserted when they did not receive them," with the result that "planters, who had hoped to exchange black for white labor, were very much disgusted." We shall, in accounts of years that followed, see other attempts of this kind. Generally the planters found that they must continue dependent upon the Negro as a worker; and, despite threats and adverse predictions, the great estates continued in operation.

Into the Delta there moved a figure extraordinary; politician and plantation-man-to-be. Henry Clay Warmoth, Reconstruction governor of Louisiana, was a character unto himself. As Beauregard and Benjamin represent the Confederacy, Warmoth personifies a phase of the period after the war. A man of engaging manner, handsome, big-framed, the possessor of an ambition to match, he was at one time the most hated person in the state. With the years feeling altered and he entered alliances with some of those who had condemned him most. In an interesting combination of terms, a recent newspaper commentator called him "one of Louisiana's most distinguished carpetbaggers." Yet Warmoth could point to a Southern ancestry.

In the pattern of the self-made American, he was born in a log cabin in Illinois, set type in a printing office, and studied law in his spare hours. A district attorney at twenty, he left office to fight on the Union side. He developed early a talent for contention. On a furlough after being wounded, he was accused of exaggerating losses, and dishonorably discharged; he sought out Lincoln himself, and was reinstated. Eventually a military judge in New Orleans, he became an influential figure in the state's new Republican politics. In the several transfers of political power, Henry Clay Warmoth emerged at twenty-six as the youngest governor in the state's history.

The new official charmed, infuriated and puzzled many men and women. He was, at the least, an adaptable man. The terse accusation was made by one enemy that the governor rejected a bribe of fifty thousand dollars, because it was too small. The governor said it was all a lie. But he himself declared that during his first year in office he received more than a hundred thousand dollars. Since the governor's salary was eight thousand, some have observed that this accomplishment must have represented considerable scraping and saving.

Warmoth was not above a certain appealing frankness. When others protested to him of corruptions in his administration, he replied: "Why, damn it, everything is demoralizing down here. Corruption is the fashion." A delegation called a pending bond measure a steal, and the governor retorted that he agreed. He had walked into the senate that day, he said, and discovered "nearly every prominent broker of the city lobbying that bill through!" And he liked to tell of the disillusioned Democrat who investigated various shady Republican schemes, only to find that involved in almost every one were certain respectable supporters of his own party.

Like others, Warmoth looked down the Imperial Highway of the Delta. The boy who was born in the log cabin now found himself a plantation master. The establishment was the spreading Magnolia, first set up by the pilots Bradish and Johnson, the plantation at which the pirates had called in earlier years; and certain Louisianians saw in Warmoth's connection with it a matter for mirth. The prevailing spirit soon possessed Warmoth; he formed a refining company for seven near-by plantations, and, wanting room for his own expansion, he purchased a line of neighboring properties. He now had more than five thousand acres. He and his associates built a sixty-mile railroad, the first on the west bank of the Delta. Opponents said that it was put up at the suggestion of Mrs. Warmoth, because the trip by carriage was wearing, and a bore by steamboat! There were, of course, other reasons and good ones. The line crossed a succession of large plantations and proved a profitable investment.

The Deltans offer the tale of a desk that came with Magnolia. One of the Warmoths was told that it had a hidden compartment. For a half hour or so she tugged at it. The Negro servants tiptoed to the door and watched. At last, with a sharp breath, she drew out the concealed drawer. Inside was a file of letters and a velvet case. The attendants edged in; it must hold a fortune left by the pirates, sure! The mistress worked over the catch. The case snapped open and at the servants sprang a horrendous sight—a complete set of grinning gold teeth. It was the closest to picaroons' booty ever found at Magnolia.

"There was nothing in Louisiana," Warmoth wrote, "more alluring and charming than life on a sugar plantation." Magnolia, with its much-increased production, became a place to which visiting scientists, businessmen, and celebrities were escorted. The government, recognizing the highly modern innovations introduced by Warmoth, established a sugar experiment station on the acres. Warming to the prestige now accorded him, the former governor made a trip to Europe with an agent of the United States Department of Agriculture to study sugar industries in France and Germany. Many planters, including prime enemies of other days, turned to him. He was asked to conduct several tariff fights; he addressed meetings, he led parties to Washington. After a number of years, Warmoth enjoyed a city home in the fashionable residential district of New Orleans, occupied a pew in the Episcopal church, and listed, among his closest friends, a former Confederate officer!

Yet despite the streams of awed guests at Magnolia, he was finding the credit entries growing smaller on his ledgers. There was fame and position in sugar, but also increasing debt. One year the management spent three and a half cents a pound to produce the commodity, and from it earned two and a half. Some adjustment seemed necessary. Henry Clay Warmoth called for the accounts and sold to somebody else.

PART II

MELTING POT

CHAPTER 7

The French All Around

A YANKEE husband watched his Delta wife in the kitchen. She was trying to follow his suggestion that she prepare something he remembered from boyhood, a New England boiled dinner. She cut the vegetables, she washed them, she put them in the pot; and then she added tomatoes, bayleaf, thyme, onions, and five or six other items without which she was sure no dish was complete. The husband, grinning, told her: "Bébé, no matter what you put on that stove, it's going to come out French—your own kind of French."

The Delta began French, and despite contributions and mixings from many other sources, in most matters it has stayed that way—its own kind of French. Through all of the nineteenth century, the number of "foreigners" increased, but France held itself intact along these river banks.

Between the plantations and below them, the original Deltans were busily engaged in making their scene a far-removed, moderately drenched, slightly foggier version of Normandy, Brittany, Gascony, Provence, and the other places from which they had come. They re-established what they remembered, with differences and concessions to their land and waters.

The new arrival quickly learned his first lesson. There had long been a saying here that no matter what you wanted, if you kept your eyes on the Mississippi it would come to you, whether it were a baby carriage or a mate in a skiff, a casket or a crate of apples. Any spring could be counted upon to wash down the makings of a house for a man who needed one—boards, stumps, sometimes a whole tree with green leaves. The river was a casual provider. A levee break above brought table tops, broken windowsills, half of a roof, and chairs. "Me, I hate to see that sight," a Delta woman once told me. "I think of the terrible day our own house was wash' out." But her husband had no time for pity. He was out snaring the wreckage.

What a man reached first was his. Simply to see it as it bobbed along—that was not enough. When a choice item appeared, a heavy trunk of cypress in some cases, eight or ten might spy it at the same time along both sides of the stream. Each would run to the water edge, give a shove to his skiff, and from then on it was the back muscles that counted. The man who got there first would put his hand on the wood, drive in his spike and tow the prize home. Then he would go to work in his yard just behind the river bank. For miles about him stood houses erected in conformity with the river's varying burdens—boards unmatched, the front of one material, the rest of another or several others. And if the family did not mind, who were you to ask questions?*

With the river also came food. Upstream, at New Orleans and elsewhere, people were always dropping or tossing away edible stuff. Workmen were careless at the wharves. Foremen gave orders to cast out cargoes for which there was no demand or which showed a trace of spoilage. As years passed, the importation of bananas from the tropics reached sizable proportions at New Orleans, and large supplies of the fruit were discarded. Much of it looked barely ripe, but by the time it reached the customers in other parts of the country, it might have rotted. Soon this produce would be moving past the Deltans.

A family that kept the Mississippi under close scrutiny was one that profited. A father told his young son, "Take the levee, and call me when you see something, you hear?" In heavy spring, when the stream poured strongly past, an endless file of Deltans were to be seen squatting at the river bank. Talking of a wise man, the neighbors said, "He don' let the river slip anything pas' him!" Here was the ultimate compliment.

When a ship anchored for repairs or overhauling, the nearest residents rowed out to make friends, and barter took place. The native had his rice, his ducks, and his fish. The ship's people had

* E. P. O'Donnell used this practice as the basis of his richly amusing novel, *The Great Big Doorstep*. His Delta family retrieved a magnificent set of steps from the river, then decided to get a house to match.

cigarettes, tinned goods and foreign fruits. Now and then a Delta man paddled near the path of an approaching vessel and asked for gifts. One who possessed no other words of English learned the names of a commodity or two, and the effect of the word "please." Amused officers or crew members tossed out small presents and the Deltan smiled his appreciation. When the ship produced nothing, he shook his fists. All that trip for nothing; and now it was the turn of the crew to grin.

A few have told me how shrewd husbands donned their wives' sunbonnets, tied their dresses about them and made high-pitched appeals. The scheme generally worked. One sardonic Frenchman, as soon as he received a gift under such circumstances, would stand up in his boat, lift the dress high in the air to display his full male costume beneath, and yell, "Ya-ah!"

Along certain stretches of the shore a stranger, unless he were well guided, could drown in trying to get from house to house. Various points were too low for habitation, marked by bogs and pools just behind the natural bank. At night the yellow-red lights of the line of houses reflected in several directions. A mud road along the river, half-lost in the thick grasses, could be followed; but for months at a time this became a creamy mass, and a man unfortunate enough to lack a boat might be marooned in his house. Even then, he need not worry about food. Ducks floated in his yard; he could cast a fishing line out of his window, and if he waded to the back, he would soon be in reach of a turtle or two. (And within wrestling distance of an alligator, whose hide he could eventually sell.)

The smaller Delta house was reduced to essentials, but like that of the plantation man it was adapted to its setting. The first few settlers who built close to the ground and then watched the water rise over their floors learned the value of cypress stumps to elevate them. A sweltering summer or two, and the owner added a wide gallery like that of the manorial establishments. For the roof, the Deltan cut cypress shingles or used the not less serviceable palmetto leaves. When he wanted a chimney, he mixed river mud and Spanish moss and fashioned a tight and roaring fireplace. The family kept warm, and Maman also cooked here. For many years brick remained a rarity. The plantation people gradually imported it; for one of the other Deltans to do that was to invite the derision of his neighbors. So he thought he was going up in the world, did he?

The home was a small box: two or three rooms in a row, thick batten blinds, an attic for the storing of animal traps, pelts, and rice. Over a bush near the gallery hung the drying nets; against the wall stood the poles, some for pushing a way through the shallow waters, others for fishing. With them were worn rectangular arrangements in wood, fish cars, in which the catch would be dropped as the receptacles floated in the water, to keep them alive until needed. From the ceiling inside hung smoked fish and animal skins that had not yet fully dried; and with driftwood for the fire and a neat grass switch to beat off the mosquitoes, the Deltans felt well equipped.

To his boat the Delta father gave attention such as he bestowed on nothing else, cleaning, scouring, caulking. One of his first lessons from his Père, which he passed on to his sons, was that the boat must be maintained against water, sun, and wind. Much of it was a matter of necessity; this was his major asset, his capital in a daily struggle for a livelihood. The rest was pride and an attachment such as he might feel for an animate being. "She know how to handle herself. You ought to see her fight when a storm come." And the affectionate blow upon the prow was proud and proprietary.

The Deltans farthest to the north had the best places, driest, least exposed to the winds. Later arrivals took the next, and with each advance of settlement existence grew more and more amphibious. Most men and women clung until the last possible moment to the way of their grandfathers, the farm life. Even in the river's final stretches, some attempted crops while the rest shook their heads. Along the inner sides of the bends, where small half circles of rich soil still showed themselves, only a kind of desperation made a living possible. On these narrow skirts of ground they could hear the waves to the back, and the softer, but hardly less ominous, suction of the river just below the bank at the front. To remain here as a grower was to break health or heart. I have met some of these determined farmers. One lost a wife because the two of them insisted upon staying through a single turbulent night. Another buried two children during a struggle that lasted for years. When they talk of these days, their faces darken and their eyes are lusterless.

Others tell of group movements brought about by the changing forces near the Gulf: "That was the year all the families had to move away . . ." "Use' to be a lot of farming here. . . . Now they got nothing." Farm colonies altered in a season to settlements of hunter-fishermen; and though the women cast backward glances, they knew that they had said goodbye to their years as farmers. Now they would be people of the marsh and the lakes. Their skins would brown with the greater exposure, their frames would grow more wiry, the palms and soles of their feet would toughen. And they would hold more than ever to themselves.

Everywhere the Deltans, from birth to death, were surrounded by the chatterings and the wing beats of birds, in the trees along the river, in the gloom of the swamps, over shore and marsh, or riding the Mississippi on logs and broken furniture. Many remained the year round: the friendly mockers, those mimics whom the imaginative French called "voix d'amour"—"voice of love"; the whistling cardinals, the ever-active sparrows, the glossy boat-tailed grackles, their rear feathers in the shape of a keel, and the impudent red-winged blackbirds, hated by the rice growers.

To the south and the east and west were others of the waters and water edges: shore birds, waders, habitués of ponds and lakes and the lonely island fringes. The gulls swooped by in sociable flight, graceful white wings flapping as they competed noisily for scraps from the fishing boats. The Delta children smiled at the laughing gulls, commonest of all, the dark-headed creatures whose cry was like that of a deranged woman. Among them glided the smaller terns, gentler, well-called "les hirondelles de mer"—"swallows of the sea." About the mud flats at the Mississippi mouth congregated the silent brown pelicans, lifting themselves in solemn group flights, plunging suddenly under the water after fish. In the air above waited the sinister black frigate, or man-of-war, birds with their enormous wings, forked tails, and down-hooked bills. These were Delta pirates no less than those in the ships. Watching the gulls, terns, and others, these predators descended as soon as the smaller ones caught mouthfuls of food and forced them to disgorge.

Twice a year, in the fall and with spring's approach, the residents saw a new winged populace in teeming migrations. Back and forth over it flew most of the wandering creatures of the central continent. As cooler weather approached, the heavens filled with the rustling flights of hordes on their long trips toward Central and South America. Here many paused for a rest before taking a last sight of land. Food was plentiful. In the marsh and at the river entrances the waterfowl congregated by the hundreds of thousands, eating the roots, seeds, and young shoots—Delta duck potato or wild onion, banana water lily, widgeon grass, three-square grass, cattail sprouts, and others.

Sometimes the roar of the birds could be heard for a mile or more away. One type moved excitedly across a flat, digging at the shreds of green that rose above the mud. Behind them came an advancing army of another kind, to take what was left, and then a third, to pick up seeds and specks passed over by the rest. Storing up strength, the birds were ready for the hard lap ahead. Then, as warmer days approached and the Delta green grew richer, the skies to the south were darkened by sweeping lines of flight. Men on luggers gazed up to see dozens of almost exhausted creatures clinging to the sails and ropes for a respite before continuing on to shore. There they dropped, hungry and spent, but soon were feeding clamorously again.

The Deltans watched the clouds for game birds, for the early arrival of the blue-winged teal, for pintails, for the incomparably swift canvasbacks, and for their favorites, the heavy-bodied, succulent greenhead mallard or "canard français," "French duck." The first blue-wings sent excited youths racing to tell Papa the news. They were prepared for the season; they had been practicing and re-practicing their duck calls and they had the decoys lined up in the kitchen. For a time the oldest boys and the father would drop everything else. They were supplying the family, but they also knew the old-time thrill of the hunt. Yet they did not waste ammunition, these people of the deepest Mississippi. A boy learned caution and skill. He tracked the birds quickly to their feeding grounds, he studied their habits of flight, their tricks of hanging for a moment or two in the wind, their slow climbs upward; and he returned well rewarded.

The rest of Louisiana knew of this concentration of game in

the Delta. During the 1880's and '90's, with improving communication, the old market at New Orleans did a thriving business, taking almost as many ducks, geese, or other game as the Deltans could provide. Some had their first direct contact with the city in supplying this demand. As one recalled from his youth, "We went out to take whatever number we wanted—two hundred, three hundred in a day." Gutting the birds quickly, leaving the feathers on, they kept an appointment with the captain of a freight boat or a man along the railroad track. With cool weather the birds would remain fresh; expert cooks maintain that game should age at least twenty-four hours before it is eaten. Sometimes the Delta produced too much; newspaper reports as late as 1913 tell of overstocking of the market, with ducks going at three pairs to the dollar. Not long after that date, stringent new laws were enacted, leaving room for only a furtive flow to the city. To violate the laws for their own uses would not be hard, but no more would the Deltans hunt so extensively for the market.

The family enjoyed game through the season, usually fricasséed in fragrant style, and throughout most of the year. Geese and duck were picked, breasts neatly halved and inserted between blankets of salt in a barrel. Each family had such a barrel. Nearby was a second and not less important barrel, for wine. From their orange trees the river people evolved their favorite drink, a heady concoction of water, sugar, and juice in fermentation. When they had the two barrels ready, after a hard winter of work, they were ready to relax. The plantation man went to an Eastern watering place; his plainer neighbor had his own facilities at home. At any place for miles along the river, the caller would find him stretched on his gallery or in his yard under a hackberry tree, listening to his food digest and talking to his friends.

Over glasses of wine, the conversation could be soothing. Again, the hearty spirits of the men asserted themselves, and the host fell into violent disagreement with his guests. Hands flew about and also words: "Nom d'un chien! Pig! Snake!" A gift of gusty invective was not among the lesser talents of these people. Words sharpened, cries grew until Maman would step outside, wave her sunbonnet and outshout the men. Think of the innocent children! (The innocent children, packed on the gallery, watched fascinated by this not entirely novel, but still wonderful clash.) The premises were cleared. Papa grumbled that Maman had not given him half a chance at that Ledet villain. Maman said something, and Papa chuckled; and the laughter that echoed over the soft borders of earth had a tropical note.

Only seldom did Maman assert herself. In most things her husband was the ruling figure. Papa, he knew. It was the way it had always been. She stood by to lend a hand, to help pull in a log, to dress the skins, to bring in the rice. Through the year she wiped at the moisture that dripped from her walls; she fought ants, lizards, and the rest of the creeping life of this over-fertile place. When she had no soap, she found that river-bottom mud made a good substitute. She scraped and cut corners and she did not complain.

The children usually worked for Papa. He set them about their duties in the morning: one to scrub the boat, another to set a box in the water and watch for big river shrimp; this one to look for wood, one of the boys to go to the swamp for frogs, or to drop nets for the squirming red crawfish, ever present in the springtime; another, in proper season, to work at the thick bushes on which the blackberries waited in the sun, or at the trees with their burdens of rich brown figs. Only when Papa had no assignment would the child be Maman's for the day. In the evening Papa met each member to inspect the return. A poor batch, and they would have a hard time explaining the reason.

The life about the house was different from that of the usual farm, even if the family had a green garden. The few cattle lived in and about the marsh, taking care of themselves, partly amphibious like other forms of life in the Delta. The chickens and hogs, too, foraged largely for themselves, living off fiddler crabs, fish and shrimp scraps that they found about the house, and other items. (Flesh of all types took strange flavors under the circumstances; I have had fried chicken and pork that tasted more like fish than like anything else.) Wallowing happily about in the liquid mud, the hogs had a real and persistent enemy—the alligator. Many times the trail of a sow led to the water edge, and the trampled grass told of a brief struggle. The 'gator had lain in wait, and in two or three quick moves it caught the prize in its jaws and sank beneath the water. A few bubbles, and that was all.

Meanwhile with every year or so, Maman was producing an addition to the family. The early Louisiana French believed that the Mississippi had a property which induced fecundity. If this were so, the Deep Delta waters must have possessed a particular concentration of the substance. Yet it seems hardly necessary to blame Father Mississippi. These were French people; this was the equivalent of a rural territory, and what was there to discourage a family? Seldom did a doctor see Maman during all of the time between marriage and the birth of her thirteenth or fourteenth child. She could say with pride that not once had she missed the preparation of a meal. Even on the day of delivery she had the vessel brought from the stove so that she could measure the seasoning herself. Papa would not like it, a gumbo that was wrong.

Sometimes, in this man's world, she found herself suddenly a widow. In the city her cousin would have put on a long veil and black dress for the rest of her life and fallen into periodic fits of weeping. The Maman of the Delta had no time for mourning à la mode. She tonged oysters, she paddled the boat, she followed a trap line in the marsh. Sunbonnet on head, in homemade trousers, she took up where Papa left off. For another fifteen years, until she had the last girl married, she would work with the seasons. Only then would she agree to buy a something dark and sit on her gallery and think sad things about Papa!

The river bank, whether it had only a natural elevation or a lesser extension of the levee from upstream, was becoming a variety of things in one. As their houses faced it, so the Deltans lived with it. It was the driest, most dependable path of travel, the means of access to other dwellings, the place of meeting and the route of promenade. Here the news was canvassed, digested, and passed along: The Bourgeois family had three bébés, all at the one time. But yes, it was true! Who would have thought ol' Bourgeois had it in him, that skinny lil' fellow. . . . They said the government was sending a lot of new soldiers to the forts. Mon Dieu, not more war! . . . Was it true one of the Songy boys shot his brother by mistake, for a deer in the swamp?

One who had nothing else to do "took the levee." Many a

fifteen-year-old, parading with her friends, was chosen by a silent watcher or two, to be fought over at the next dance, and married before the time of the following one. And others sat on the top, watching the ships as they passed or waiting for friends to come along. Sooner or later, everybody that a man knew would walk along the levee.

Since the Delta people had only to look from their front window to see what was going on, they kept a steady, unending vigil upon the world which passed before them. A husband could not hope to deceive a wife with a quick visit to the store for whisky. Everybody knew. Some on clandestine errands tried to creep quickly over the levee, follow it along the river edge (in low water this was possible), then slip over to the other side at the proper point. They might succeed once; not more often. Ah, but non, he was up to no good, that one. A suspicious housewife, catching a glimpse of such a movement, was known to dart to the levee top, the better to see where another went. Curiosity wore no camouflage.

The world was working its way into the lower Delta. Trade is trade, water or no water. Peddlers came on steamboats, on foot or by cart. They carried their supplies in hand-trunks or holders about their necks, Pandora's boxes to open wide with inexhaustible supplies. Usually they were French, sometimes Jewish, from Southern Europe. In all cases the Deltans called them "Arabs." They offered colored cloths, buttons, dishes, and dresses. Did the boy need glasses? How about shoes for the little girl? Every little girl ought to have one pair of shoes; who knew what would happen? The caller was glad to barter for rice, for pelts, for alligator skins, or for anything else.

Soon, too, came the "chalons," floating department stores in miniature. The owner, arriving on an infrequent trip, tooted his whistle and for miles the housewives ran over their lists. This was commerce with a luster; as one woman sighed in recollection, "It made paying out your money a nice pleasure." In the nineties, several vessels brought a particular wonder. A family sat together in front of a black box and then, there they all were, on paper. Some families dated events by the years such tintypes were taken.

Ultimately the travelers found that this was a place of quick return. "Drummers" let it be known that they would arrive on a certain week end, ready to pay a good price. Out of the marsh would come the trappers, their pirogues low in the water with the weight of the skins. The drummer had a drink or two ready, a bargain was reached, and everybody was satisfied. The traveling men hired assistants and before long they opened small stores along the river. The people walked or paddled the distance and set up accounts. Between seasons, the merchant staked them. Later he made advances to permit purchase of new boats. One phase of modern life was penetrating the Delta, be it for better or for worse.

In a room off the store, the families gathered for occasional dances in the French tradition. Fiddles and accordions came out and couples, old as well as young, moved through gay rounds, while orange wine was passed about. An old man rose to sing a ballad that went on and on, a story of unrequited love and suffering; or a more impish one, of husbands and wives and best friends. Then bowlfuls of succulent food were passed about, always with rice, and everybody got into his boat to go home.

About 1825 one of the fabled families of the Delta arrived—the Burat brothers, seven of them. Why they selected this vicinity is a question; but they were men of prodigious energy and equally prodigious accomplishments. Each married a Delta girl, and their many children married, until for miles, nearly every resident was a Burat by birth or by marriage. The section took the name, which was eventually softened to Buras. And today in the town of Buras, all or practically all is Buras.

In this lower section, one of the traditional controls of French life advanced only gradually. For years much of this combination of land and water remained outside the reach of the church. The priest who planned to cover the territory rolled up his trouser legs, carried extra clothes and vestments in a bundle tied to a stick over his shoulder, and made his way partly by boat, partly by horse, partly on foot. Returning, he would usually discover that he had missed half the families. On his next trip he found that high water prevented him from reaching his destination. At another time most of the people were in the far marshes for the trapping. When he did get to the families, he saw that they had come to live without the church. Lethargy had settled, especially among the men. Religion? They had to make their livings. This was not true in every case, of course; but barriers had grown up that were greater than distance. One settlement, receiving a mission, decided that it did not want it continued. The trapping season had been bad; the church, they were sure, had "brought bad luck."

Here and there flourished the custom of "sauter ballet"—leaping the broomstick. A couple wishing to be married took part in a ceremony. A broom was lifted a foot or so off the ground; man and woman jumped together across it and thereafter were considered wed. In other instances, natives took two or more wives at the same time. The late Captain Horace Hale Harvey told of one dweller in the backlands who possessed a trio. "Why, you have a harem," the captain told him. "What that is?" Gus inquired. "That's having more than one wife in a house." "Is that all?" Gus asked. "Eh, that ain' nothing!" Later, a priest held services near by. To them went Gus and his harem. As was the custom in calling after long periods, the priest announced that he would hold wedding services. The captain nudged Gus: "Go on."

Gus stared in indecision at the three forms before him.

"Make a choice."

"But I wan' 'em all!"

"Then close your eyes and pick."

Gus chose the middle one, but whether he was thereafter a reformed man is not included in the story.

By contrast, other Deltans remained strong church people. An account is given of a marriage planned far down the river for seven one evening. The priest learned that afternoon that the boat, his only means of the reaching the place, was out of commission. He and the pilot worked over it until dusk and for hours afterward. They arrived at their destination at three in the morning. The wedding cake waited; so did the couple, holding hands at the dock.

Determined ones frequently went forth to find the priest. The two families and most of the relatives formed a wedding party and boarded the largest available vessel. Someone brought a fiddle, another his best orange wine, and the company danced and sang on the way. Along the banks watchers waved and called out jokes; other boats kept well out of the way. The Deltans explain that you knew it was a wedding party by the aroma a mile off.

On other occasions a group of women with babies devised ways to get them christened—"have the water poured," in Delta parlance. If the family never set foot in a church again, Bébé must be "poured." A lugger would set out with as many as a dozen babies, and also fathers, mothers, godfathers, and godmothers. The journey might take a full day each way. The rectory would provide sleeping quarters between trips. Then again, a boatload of children seven, eight, and nine years old would arrive for the ceremony. "It was our first chance to get here," the parents explained.

In 1834 church authorities had sent a priest to Pointe à la Hache, a cluster of farms and homes on the east bank fifty miles from New Orleans. The first of a succession of buildings rose on what often seemed an ill-omened site. The highest ground in the area was an ancient Indian burial mound with a shell base; atop it was placed the first permanent cross in this part of the Delta. Several priests died here, of yellow fever and other illnesses. During the 1850's the violent "Know Nothing" movement, in part an anti-clerical activity, spread over America, to find a surprising strength in Catholic Louisiana. Down at Pointe à la Hache, to the accompaniment of a number of confused charges, Father Nicolas Savelli was stabbed to death by a mob. Traditions of the present-day devout describe ill fates that stalked participants in the killing, on ships at sea, in the North, and on foreign soil.

Conditions altered with the years. In 1863 the newly ordained Father Mathurin Harnais arrived from France to take a new post at the thriving center of Buras, on the opposite shore a little below La Hache. As Father Robert Wilken, O.F.M., has noted, this was only a few miles above the point at which another priest had blessed ashes and said a Mass in 1699 when the French came to colonize Louisiana. As on that occasion it was Holy Week; some thought it a good sign. By the next spring a newly painted building was ready. From France the priest had brought a painting, Christ walking on stormy waves, and the edifice was dedicated to Notre Dame du Bon Port, Our Lady of Good Harbor—

a name with meaning in a place of encompassing waters. From all directions arrived the people, many in luggers with white and red triangular sails bulging in the breeze. Many wore no shoes, but carried them to show that they owned them. Quietly they took their places; through the opened windows, over the fragrant orange trees, echoed the notes of sacred songs in French. That morning young Father Harnais must have remembered his home across the sea.

Yet all was not a quiet hymn for the priest and his successors. Often they felt that they were striving against the land itself. No circles of homes spread out from the place of worship, as in other parts of the world. Those single files of dwellings, up and down the river and toward the back, meant that the parishioners had to come long distances, against obstacles and handicaps. The initial spurts of enthusiasm died like squalls from the Gulf. The priests found that many of the people had forgotten the simplest parts of the services. Yet always they wished earnestly for two things: their children must "have the water poured," and all must be "passed through the church" at death. Not to be buried by the Father—it was a terrible thing, yes.

When a sufferer closed his eyes, a neighbor was quickly called. He must go to the river bank and fire three shots into the air. The Father, the Son, the Holy Ghost—it was a benediction, and also a way of notifying all friends. Several of the sons went back to the swamp to cut boards for the coffin. The women stopped the clocks, turned mirrors to the wall, and got ready for the wake. That night hot stews of duck and seafood waited on the stove, with pots of coffee, and on the table rose piles of rice and home-made bread. Throughout the evening came callers; the orange wine barrel was open, and everybody stayed until dawn when a long water procession began, up the river to Buras or Pointe à la Hache.

Sometimes death came with greater drama, from the river itself. A Deltan misjudged the changeable river. His pirogue was found later against the bank. For many miles, friends watched the stream. When the body did not appear, the family brought candles, fixed them on wooden bases and set them forth on the water. This should "tell where it was." For an hour and more a crowd would follow the bobbing points of flame in the night's blackness, until they blinked out. Word was sent up to the church—"A Mass, please, Father, to find the body."

And the boys of the family set to work with a paint box on the gallery posts. From a neighbor or from the store, the proper black would be obtained and the supports would gleam darkly in mourning. If the columns went without black, there would be talk for miles along the river.

CHAPTER 8

Dalmatia on the Mississippi

ACROSS from Italy, against the blue of the Adriatic, lay Dalmatia, a place of warm winds, beach, and jagged mountains. Its people had enjoyed little of the soft peace that their scene might have indicated. For they were Slavs, and their home was one of the crossroads between Occident and Orient, the Balkans for which Turk and Roman, German and Italian and others had fought during long eras. Between hostilities, the Dalmatians knew want and oppression, often a drudgery that brought only slow starvation.

It was a southern land, of olive and orange and tall flowering shrubs. The population of its islands and coasts were partly of the farm, partly of the sea, living in the shadow of churches and palaces dating from the Roman emperors. Nature provided a number of admirable harbors, and from them in the nineteenth century, as in earlier ones, men went out in sailing vessels.

As early as 1825 or 1830, seamen and ship captains of Dalmatia were finding their way up the Mississippi. The crews went ashore in prospering New Orleans and thought of their lovely, poverty-pinched country, and some did not return to their ships. A few became merchants and traders, but most of them transferred to vessels of Louisiana. Moving down the river, they marveled at the superb residences surrounded by their green banners of cane. But this scene, they knew, was not for them. Farther south they went ashore and watched the French. It seemed like home, this place and climate, these men whose living was along the waters.

The first arrivals took ridges that no one else claimed and set up small cabins. A few countrymen joined them and they held apart, a quiet people, little inclined to chat, almost morose. When they did talk, their thick, guttural tones perplexed the French.

Beside their neighbors they seemed hulking men, with broad faces, high cheekbones and, always, the wide handle-bar mustaches that made their neighbors grin.

One would take a barrel on his thick shoulders and lift it over the levee with the same ease that others would show in rolling it. With a single lunge they poled their vessels astonishing lengths through a canal. Frenchmen nudged one another as the big fellows passed. Before long they were further amazed at the attraction that work of all sorts seemed to have for these people. You look at them at dawn, and you look at them at night—late, late —and Nom de Dieu, you know they haven' stop at all between! I see it with both these two eye', I tell you. The Dalmatians kept this up, whether their fingers turned blue with cold or sweat darkened their garments from throat to ankle. Only occasionally did they take a glass of wine at the store; and then, before they had time for their last swallow, they were off, not caring if it were the heaviest of rains, or the most scorching hour of the early afternoon. The French, who thought they knew how to live as this climate dictated, were perplexed. What sort of behavior was that!

When one Slav met another, his greeting was *"Kako ste?"*— "How are you?" The answer was *"Dobro"*—"Good." The amused French called them "Kako ste's"; eventually the word became "Tocko," and it has never been lost. The Dalmatians themselves have taken it over and use it of each other, generally in friendliness or in light joke. (The well-advised stranger will exercise care in applying it.)

The Tockos fished, they tried shrimping, they hunted. Then they turned to oysters—and some of the commercial history of lower Louisiana was changed. Man had met job. The Delta is the New World's greatest potential center for this shellfish. The oyster will develop neither in fresh water nor in the sea; it requires certain combinations of the two elements. The steady outpouring of the Mississippi makes possible a succession of mixtures, spawning grounds of peculiar suitability. The Gulf winds force the river water into the grass-fringed bays and inlets east and west of the river mouths, where it mixes with the brine. The silty Mississippi flow is packed with minute food particles; the saline waves provide additional elements, and the mildness of the Gulf permits the oyster to multiply through long productive seasons.

The earlier Deltans had found the oysters readily accessible in low, thick, natural reefs along the shores and about the river passes, cool bits of fleshy nourishment in their rocklike protections. For years the gathering of the shellfish had continued in haphazard fashion. Men waited for low tides, or felt about at the water edges, and there they were for the easy taking. Depleting one area, the diggers moved to another. They gave a few of the cool months to the enterprise, then turned to more inviting seasonal occupations. If the oyster' were hard to find one year—eh bien, the nex' would be more better.

The oyster, she was a funny thing, said the French. A small break in the river bank—others looked sad, but the oyster gatherer smiled. The new yellow tide, reaching across the broken banks to the low places along the shore, would feed the oysters until they were fat and juicy. But then sometimes a storm came, and look, the little things were dead or dying, smothered in mud and sand. More than that, in one bay the oysters would be swelling with health; in the next, unaccountably, they were anemic, "jus' a bladder of water." Gradually, for miles, what had once been the best of reefs were producing poor, almost worthless growths.

Now the Tockos advanced upon the oyster beds with determination. They ripped at the stony clusters until they had torn them apart. Their palms and their wrists poured blood; when it got in their way they doused their hands in the salt water, shook them and went back to work. They experimented, they tried new locations and, most important, they devoted all of the year to the operation, turning it into a kind of continuous farming in the water. They developed tools to fit their purposes—tongs that were a pair of hinged rakes eight feet long, operated with both hands like awkward scissors to draw up the oyster clumps. And they built a special lugger, low-hung, wide-beamed, with a deep hold for large hauls.

Regularly the Tockos went up the Delta to New Orleans with their oysters. Using ingenuity and muscle, they followed the backwaters as far as they could. The sailboats strained and creaked over their curving paths, through waters that rippled with silver in a good wind, through others the color of wine, motionless and spotted with lilies, or across deep bays in which the boats rocked and tossed. At certain points they came upon shallows and had to stop a few hours until they deepened. When the wind was dead, they cordelled or pulled themselves with ropes along shore. Every delay worried them; every hour that the oyster was out of water counted heavily. On clear days the Tocko could hear small clicks; the shellfish were still alive in their piles. A warm, foggy period, and he muttered imprecations. "Fog same like smoke; then you work like hell. Inside pile, they living; outside, die fast."

Emerging from the rear passages into the Mississippi, the small vessels of the oystermen could not make headway against the current. They hailed towboats moving up the river. To the towman these were small fry, but they helped reduce the cost of his trip. For a total payment of twenty-five dollars he would take them. If he asked too much the Tockos shook their heads and waited for the next. Arrived at the city wharves, they went promptly to the dealers. Good oysters, yes. They could sample them. The dealers usually did not bother. The Tockos had a reputation for reliability.

At intervals they met with bad news. Too many others had come at the same time; the wharves were packed with oysters. A Tocko then called a boy, gave him a bottle of wine, and let him shovel all of his produce into the river. Perhaps the fish would enjoy them. Generally, however, the oysterman received a good return; and soon he was back in the Delta, investing it in expanded holdings.

For years they lived lonely, grueling lives, these men without their women. They moved out to the places where the oysters were most plentiful, along the back bays and lakes, in lines of settlement along canals that they dug. Their places were camps, cabins on birdlike wooden legs, five or six feet in the air at windswept edges, over which the water piled high during storms—specks in the immensity of grass and sky. The men rose just as a glow of pink was beginning to show in the east. A crimson radiance soon lay over the shells, the roofs of their cabins, the flowers among the waving meadows. But the Dalmatians had no eye for the loveliness about them. They had "job to do." They worked in open boats through fog and rain, wading in water up to their waists for hours, sitting in the wet vessels for the rest of the day. The incandescent sun beat down upon them, the waves of heat crawled like living things, and the sea birds gathered in raucous flights.

The Tockos were away all of the day; when they returned they were often too tired even to talk. They had little to keep them awake. Their huts, primitive even to their humbler fellow Deltans, held only beds, ropes, clothes hanging from the rafters, and tins of food. Night after night the Tockos guided themselves back to their homes in the distances. To be in these marshes after dusk is to sense a vast serenity such as I, for one, have known nowhere else. The moonlight strikes the edges of the grasses, like the blades of spears. The stars glimmer against the fathomless black; all about us is a living darkness, many-tenanted, creatures stirring, chirping, bellowing, calling softly. In our watery tunnel between hummocks of heavy growth, the paddles lift and fall. A sudden turn, and before us, ghostlike in the moon rays, stands an oysterman's cabin, its walls a dull brown smudge, the shells about it gleaming in the cold light. From within, a lamp is lit to greet us after our hours in the marsh.

Sometimes death awaited the return of the Tockos from their labors. Every few years the waters rose suddenly to trap the occupants of the cabin, and others died in blasts that tossed their camps aside in broken pieces. Those who lived repaired the wreckage as best they could and went on as before. It was not long before the French were assuring each other: "Those Tocko', they work so hard to earn their money that when they get it, they don' know how to enjoy it."

Their honesty matched their frugality. The camps remained open at all times, without latch or lock. When a man found himself out of tobacco or rope, he did not want to make a special trip to the front—the river edge. He went to the place of another Tocko and took what he needed. His friend, returning, understood; the borrower would be back with a repayment. Eventually, enterprising members of the group established themselves as small wholesalers, handling supplies at a saving for their people. A benevolent medical and burial organization was formed, which became one of the oldest in Louisiana. Through it all, though they toiled without letup, they remained men of moods, brooding on their troubles, killing themselves in times of sudden disappointment. A French Deltan sighed and waited for the tide to change. The Tocko took a gun and rowed to the end of the shell ridge, where they found him later.

Yet they knew a few pleasures: those visits to New Orleans, calls on relatives there and on some of the friendly girls about the waterfront. To their camps they brought back red peasant wine, cheap and strong. They diluted it with water as was the custom in the old country, and drank it in the morning before they left and at night when they returned. The mixture must be a proper one—"too strong, no good taste. Too little vine, taste like not'ing."

And on special occasions, in their badly heated huts, as the flames of their candles shook with the winter winds, they took out the accordion and the gusle, the long, single-stringed instrument of their people, and played and sang. Perhaps it was "Maritza Moya," a love story of a Slavic Mary waiting on an Adriatic beach. More often it was an epic, a composition from the hearts of their fellow countrymen, a part of their ancient, tragic history. In interminable stanzas it described guerrilla warfare against the Turks, battles in which warriors were slain one by one but never gave up until the last man collapsed with a shouted message of resistance. Another had the picaresque touch, its heroes Robin Hoods who met bejeweled Turks, walking globes of fat and malice, and sent them away naked, bellies bouncing as they scurried. Or the words were grim, telling of conquerors who liberated Slav babies by tossing them in the air and catching them on upthrust bayonets. These were the themes that brought tears to the Tocko in his Delta isolation, that saddened and then eased the pain that they evoked.

The Dalmatians prospered; collections of camps thickened back in the bays, and a number of the settlers moved to the river bank. Along the Mississippi appeared Olga, Empire, Ostrica, Oysterville, and others. To the Legendres, the Robichaux, and the Bourgeois, were added the Zibiliches, the Jurisiches, and the Popiches. The French told their friends: "If it don' got an 'itch,' it ain' Tocko." Many from the Balkans joined them, Serbians, Montenegrins, a few Greeks, Albanians, and others. But the Dalmatians remained in the majority of the foreigners. Into Buras moved more Tockos, for this was a central point from which scores of camps fanned out.

Ultimately, some felt themselves sufficiently established to send home money for a bride. Seven or eight years had passed; the girl that one remembered—was she still single? If not, his family would know of another proper, obedient maiden, who worked hard. Infrequently a Tocko, feeling that this was one time to spend his money, made a trip back to the old country, and was received like a small millionaire. His cousins importuned him for loans, and the rulers tried to impress him into military service. He returned to Louisiana with his new wife, to stay.

If the sturdy, large-boned Slavic mother found the ways hard to understand in this far-off home, she did not protest. She was more stoic even than her husband, and she lived only for him and their children. To the French women she was polite but she did not tell much, as she did not ask much. Neither the goings-on along the levee nor the wares of the boat-merchant drew her attention. Of these hard-hewn housewives some remarked, "You could grate cheese on the ridges of their palms." When she was needed, the Dalmatian wife dug for oysters with her husband. She helped build up the shells at the base of their hut-on-stilts, so that she and the young ones had a few feet of firm ground. She acquired several cans of paint, and among the bird-bordered pools of the marsh the homes shone neatly. Doors were splashed with bright yellows or light blues and greens; about the walls colored friezes depicted flowers, ships at sail, and peasant girls. And the children grew up to Slavic songs and instruction in the native tongue.

But as the boys and girls reached seven or eight years old, a sharp change was made. The children must have an education; to that all agreed. Facilities were meager in the Delta; the mother and children stepped aboard one of the luggers to be taken to New Orleans. There they remained for months of each year; the father could join them only from time to time, for a day or an evening.

A steady procession of Slavic youths came to the Delta, brought over by relatives or friends. They made "bargains"; a relative in Louisiana would pay for the passport and transportation, and in return the apprentice agreed to work for him, say, for four or five years. He would receive food, clothing and expenses, and he would earn a few dollars a month, at a slightly higher rate each year. It was not until the newcomer was not so new that he began to wonder. Others, at lighter tasks, were earning far more. Cousin, this was not right. Under tightening immigration laws, Cousin stood as sponsor, guaranteeing that the new arrival would not become a pauper. Would the young man want to go back to the Adriatic? (In some cases, it is said, the Slav was a stowaway, or had violated some other rule to reach this better land, and that made him more or less amenable to Cousin.) But competitors, spying a hefty, energetic boy, sought him out. How much did he say he earned? They were willing to give double. Cousin would charge that his friends were "stealing" from him when his back was turned; in the end he usually met the offer.

By degrees the Dalmatians were changing in the Delta atmosphere. Tocko girls married only Tocko men; Tocko boys now and then took French brides, and their children grew up French in most things, but with the high cheekbones and something of their father's stolidness. The older Slavs, though they never entirely lost their accent, took on a bit of the speech of their Gallic associates.

The Tocko was making his own contributions, including his food tastes. His dishes made the French shake their heads in wonder, then sample, then adapt with extra seasoning. The French told each other: "When you say Tocko, you mean oil." Into practically every dish he poured his olive oil. Some drank it with salt added. (Doctors found that the first Dalmatians warded off intestinal disorders with this lubricant.) He stirred a cup or so into his oyster soup. He introduced his neighbors to the oyster salad. To the cooked oysters and their water he added grated onion, black pepper, "yusta bit vinegar" and a heavy dosage of the oil. Thoroughly mixed, served cold, the preparation has a flavor that neither the French nor the American oyster dish can duplicate. After the Tockos arrived, olive oil became one of the main imports to the Delta. From the old country, from Cuba and other places, heavily laden schooners brought the commodity. When large American duties were adopted, it was smuggled in. Vessels with "hot" olive oil slipped into the lakes and bays, and the saving was not a small item.

Gargantuan men of gargantuan appetites, the Tockos were inviting their fellow Deltans to their homes. A Frenchman, his eyes wide, told me of one occasion. At the door he stumbled against two barrels of red wine. A heavy goblet was shoved into his hand; he was led to a table. In a wide dishpan were twenty or thirty heads of lettuce, over which oil, warm vinegar, and other mixtures had been poured. Each guest took a whole head. Next to the lettuce was a large pig, freshly cooked. Each man cut off as large a hunk as he wished; to the astonishment of the visitor who had seen the size of the first portions, most went back for second and third helpings, and made additional trips to the salad. Everybody enjoyed himself; but at the height of the evening, the Frenchman noticed that one of the lustier participants now sat in gloomy thought. The guest asked him what was wrong. The answer was plantive: "I yust realize—if I hadn't come here, I would have another reef finished!"

But on one day of the year every Tocko indulged without stint or regrets. This was St. John's Day, June twenty-fourth, an occasion which his people made one of the great festivals of the Delta, next to Christmas and Easter. The observance went far back into the early folkways, its origin lost in the pagan period. In the old country the elders led their sheep to the Adriatic for immersion; all bathed; men leaped over bonfires; the priests held Mass for thousands who knelt at the water's edge. In the Delta the old custom was modified; the day was celebrated by visits from camp to camp and bathing on the shores of the lakes, by joke-telling, eating, and dancing. Tockos, French, and others traveled by boat to the back sections for the wine, beer, and the rest. Out came the accordion and the gusle; a climax was invariably a chant of home, the ranges and the hearths of Dalmatia. When it was over, a silence would fall and some of the older people, weeping, would say that they must manage somehow, before God, to get back to the Adriatic ere they died. Then an elderly Tocko called out, "Boys, let's march!" Brisk, semi-martial music rang out, ranks formed, and shells along the beaches scattered with the thumping of the ground. The gulls and the terns swept down for the bits of food, and the memory of far-off Dalmatia was strong again.

Though they remained at peace with outsiders, the Tockos wrangled among themselves. Highly individualist, they differed especially in their oyster marketing. Feuds were common. In one instance, after years of operation, a quarrel arose within a profitable organization and the holdings had to be split seven ways. They were divided into more or less equal parts, designated by letter, and slips of paper were dropped into a hat. The members drew, nodded their heads sharply, and most of them never spoke to each other again. The French have laughed at such disputes, and said, "If those Tocko' ever really got together, they'd be king' down here."

Kings or no kings, the Tockos had converted oyster production into what is probably the most efficient of the Delta gathering enterprises. The French remained in the business, but it expanded all about them, and the expansion was Dalmatian. Between the Frenchman and the Tocko, little friction developed; the French shrugged and concentrated on their trapping and their various other callings. When a Dalmatian oysterman needed extra help, the French did not object to digging and tonging, though they complained that he was a hard driver. But occasionally a Tocko would find oysters missing from his reef and accuse certain of the earlier Deltans of stealing. The reefs until now had been more or less public property; and among some it was not regarded as a mortal sin to draw out a few shellfish. A man moved his pirogue into low water, slipped over the side, and felt for the oysters with his feet and his rump. When he dumped his catch at home, he rubbed his trouser-seat and said, "I *worked* for them;" and the family knew what he meant. Gradually, however, the poaching decreased. The Tockos were willing to kill for their oysters.

On each side of the river the Dalmatians had evolved a different type of operation. To the east rise most of the natural reefs. Here the molluscs multiply at a quick rate; as a matter of fact, they grow too fast. The Dalmatians have found that the oysters overcrowd and starve each other until they become "coons"—stringy, lacking in favor. So the farmers thin out older reefs and encourage new ones in which conditions are better. These beds provide the "cooking oysters."

On the west bank of the river, however, Tocko persistence has brought the Louisiana mollusc to its high point. The waters are saltier; drainage seems to concentrate the brine to produce an oyster of richer flavor. Yet too much salt interferes with ready reproduction. And so the Tockos have created a cross-river culture. From the natural reefs on the east side they take the well-grown molluscs and transfer them to selected bedding grounds of the west bank for final, improved taste. The result is an oyster for the raw, halfshell trade, combining the advantages of both locales.

Unwieldy to handle, likely to die at any stage, the oyster requires unending attention. The fisherman collects his shells, loads them on a large lugger, approaches a shallow bedding ground east of the river, moves the shells to a small oyster skiff and then scatters them in wide outward sweeps. The young "spat," floating about in the water, find the shells, "set," and grow there. Development takes about two years. Going to the scene from time to time, the oysterman tongs up the shellfish. He finds heterogeneous masses, the molluscs beginning to cluster thickly. Squatting in his boat, he uses his hatchet for culling, removing the dead from the living, clearing away additional, undesirable incrustations, taking care not to crack the shells of the maturing oysters. Now he separates them into two piles, ready and unready. The latter are dropped back in the water for further improvement. The others are shifted across the river, to imbibe the brine that is there.

Months pass; the oysterman samples the product in the saltier beds. When he decides that they are right, he tongs them up, reculls them and shifts them once more, to a last, temporary bedding spot near his camp. Freight boats arrive; the oysters are brought up, placed in sacks, and started toward New Orleans. They arrive at the French Market or one of the many wholesale places that line old Rampart Street, a few squares from the river front; and the purchaser begins to worry over his profit.

The grower also has a number of things to disturb him. When the river is high in the spring, sudden infusions of fresh water bring injury or death to his crop. When the water is very low it is equally bad. "The oyster, he can take change, but not when they come too fast." The oysterman must keep guard also for boring clams, boring sponges, and the conch or drill, which digs a tiny circular hole and enjoys the mollusc, like any connoisseur, in its own shell. Worse than any of these are the drumfish. The owner wakes frequently from startled dreams that a school of these hungry predators are tearing away at the beds, eating him into ruin. It is not a baseless nightmare. Within a few hours, a man has been known to lose a property that took a year to build. The sixty-pound poachers move in heavy formation, equipped by nature to chew through an oyster shell in a minute or two. In calm weather they can be heard over the water, their powerful jaws crunching through the beds. When a grower learns that the drums are over his reefs, he drops everything else and yells to his friends to join him against the common foe.

Thousands of acres of Delta shallows are fenced about by galvanized wire, laboriously installed along stakes in the water. They have been found the only effective protection against the drums. The Tocko watches the brine; if it grows stronger than usual, he may have to cope with these saltwater enemies. And when the Delta wife, Tocko or French, wants to convey the thought that her husband has a hearty appetite, she assures you: "That man—he eat' oyster' like a drumfish!"

As the Tockos prospered, some moved "inside" to the river bank, and sent their relatives or employees to the camps. Eventually they discovered that even their vigorous constitutions were unequal to the burdens placed upon them. Long work in the rain and cold had left them rheumatic, subject to ailments of the bones and of the chest. Various better-to-do Dalmatians have gone to New Orleans to become oyster wholesalers; others have opened restaurants there and acquired a local fame for skills matching those of the Creole cooks. In recent decades the French Market has had a definite Slavic or, as the natives call it, "Austrian," influence. A leading "French coffee stand," at which countless thousands of natives and visitors have drunk the rich beverage, was established by a Tocko.

With the years, certain of the sons did not wish to return to the Delta when they finished school; it was "country," the way of the old people. They went into business or professions. Even the elders are giving up what had once been their most prized distinction—their brci or walrus mustaches. They had been marks of masculinity, of honor. He who did not grow one back home would find the small boys hooting at him on the street; he might hear his smooth face referred to as a Turk's backside, not a complimentary remark to a good Slav. The brci had made the first Tockos convenient bogeymen for the French mothers: "You behave, all of you, or I'll call a Tocko with a great big mustache to get you." Today when a Deltan wants to disparage a Dalmatian neighbor, he snorts, "Him! I know him when he wore a mustache!"

CHAPTER 9

The Mixture Thickens

INTO the river one morning in the 1870's steamed a heavy vessel under a foreign flag. On a green Delta levee several men watched with intent eyes, for the ship bore a cargo that could mean a good season or a ruinous one for them. At the rails crowded scores of men and women, gazing through the lifting shreds of mist. A hand was raised on shore, and instantly dozens returned the greeting with shouts. The Italians had arrived.

The unsettled years after the Civil War found the plantation owners casting about for fresh supplies of labor. The Negroes generally were no longer the docile force of the earlier day. The Italians, amiable and available on easy terms, might be a solution. The men strode forward in their velveteen trousers and vests, speaking in quiet, excited tones. Behind them hurried the silent women, stout, earringed, wearing richly colored dresses and yellow handkerchiefs. Heading them was the smiling agent. The plantation people had agreed to pay him so much a head; he was collecting also from the newcomers, and he was interested in seeing the venture succeed.

At first the Italians were wanted for only the peak period, the months of cane cutting and grinding. Some planters, as Dr. Hewitt L. Ballowe recalls, contracted to pay the costs from Italy and home again for the brief employment—perhaps the longest-ranged transportation ventures in Southern agriculture. An Italian and his wife, it was claimed, could be shipped back and forth by steerage at a rate little more than that for a box of lemons. Eventually, however, they stayed in Louisiana. The wages were seventy-five or eighty cents a day, with cabin provided, and this seemed almost a fortune to the Italians. They remembered days of want, when families crept up the mountainsides to start a planting of a few beans, if they could scratch out the space. In the Delta there was so much land and, to them, so few people. They brought with them only their own zeal; they asked little—wine, macaroni, a little seasoning. It was all buono, buono, signor.

The men and boys worked for long hours in the fields, and many of the women found things to do, caring for the animals, assisting in other duties. At times the Italians superseded the Negroes; again they occupied additional quarters of their own. Miss Florence Dymond of Belair plantation describes the domestic scenes. The family macaroni was always a pleasant sight, hanging on the gallery railings to dry—sometimes more than pleasant to the goats that nibbled at it. The family soon acquired its goats; the milk was preferred to the cow's. The other drink was wine, strong and sour and cheap, purchased in quantity at New Orleans. And life seemed good, with work for everybody, the Delta sun almost as warm as that of their Southern Italy and Sicily and, every year, the St. Joseph's Day altars, with fish and cakes and other foods. The non-Italians of the vicinity were called in, to taste the flour-and-fig-paste figures and the rich dishes in which olive oil and green peppers were leading ingredients; as climax, a small masque or pageant was enacted, in which children played the roles of the holy figures.

At the end of the sugar grinding some of the Italians, both married and single men, were going up to the city and making their choice of jobs. In the East and the West the railroads asked for many to lay their lines. In Midwestern cities other chances offered. As before, the Italian put himself in the hands of the padrone, who had an office near the French Market and was a man of several trades. Often the padrone kept a small hotel which catered only to his fellow countrymen. They boarded with him when they went to the city; he looked out for jobs for them. The men shifted about, but the Delta, which they first knew, was a favored place.

Like the Tockos, the single Italian youths decided in time that they wanted brides from home. A man wrote back. A picture was sent to him; or someone in whom he had confidence arranged matters with church, consul, and others. The girl bade goodbye at the wharf to the family whom she would probably never see again, and waited for the long voyage to end. At the dock in New

Orleans stood several men, the groom, his friends and witnesses. The group went at once to the church on Rampart Street, where everything was prepared. After the ceremony the priest gave a reassuring talk in Italian; the smiling friends escorted the couple to the market for a supper, and then the steamer was ready to take them down the river.

In this arangement the man took his chance; the girl took hers. If the marriage failed, the general feeling was that the fault was hers. It was the woman's responsibility to see that a marriage was successful. Talking with intermediaries who arranged such affairs, I heard of only one case of an unhappy result. A worker in Plaquemines parish, remembering a girl of his old village, had been overjoyed to learn that she was still available. He waited expectantly at the wharf, a bouquet of flowers in his hand. He went aboard and then he stopped before the woman who was brought to him. A few minutes later, eyes down, he walked off the vessel; she stayed there, crying into the flowers. He had only a few words for his friends. She was not the way he had remembered her. She had grown—not pretty. He would pay her way home again. The unwanted bride did not leave the vessel until it returned to Sicily.

Most of the others fared well. With his wife, the Italian saved his money. The plantation owner was amazed when he learned of the account that Lucas and Rose had accumulated. The padrone held it for them; they did not trust too many people. Ultimately the master found the purpose of these funds. The Italian was almost always an excellent farmer; he had an affection for growing things. He liked to labor in the fields. But, it developed, he preferred to labor for himself. He had been watching the land changes about him. He heard of good opportunities; after a shrewd inquiry, he made a down payment and went to work.

Now and then an Italian obtained a segment of the same plantation soil to which he had first applied himself. But there would be no cane for him. He raised what he knew well how to raise, diversified vegetable gardens. He had relatives and friends at the market in New Orleans, who would take his produce. At the beginning things would be hard and uncertain; but by this time the family had many hands with which to strive. They would be up before dawn, moving about their thick Delta cabbages, their cucumbers, firm, moist lettuces, and potatoes; and they did not rest until late in the evening. The children might dream of easier days, but if they did so it was not during working hours.

A story is told of a Delta landowner who had two tenants, a Negro family and a newly arrived Italian family. Before long the Negro made complaint. He and his wife and children labored without stint during every hour of the day; but the previous night he had gotten up and what had he found? The Italians were hoeing by their lantern light! It was not fair competition. Before many years had passed, that Italian family had its own farm. A St. Bernard resident of a later period describes a month of wet weather when others of necessity were neglecting their crops. Riding the slushy road one day, he saw his Italian neighbor. He had obtained six short planks, tied one to each of his feet and to the horse's hoofs, and there they were, making progress across the field.

These were years when the Deltans capitalized on their geographic position and the improving transportation to provide mountainous supplies of greenstuff for the New Orleans market, for Chicago, and for other places as well. Taking advantage of the soil and the climate, they nursed their vegetables until they were ready weeks in advance of those from other places. Men at the French Market knew that the Deltans could guarantee very early deliveries, and a happy profit to both sides ensued. The Delta acquired a kind of celebrity among the produce men for its lettuce and cucumbers. A good Delta "cuke" was a formidable object, long, thick, and solid.

Today the Italians have taken over considerable stretches of the Delta, particularly the upper portions in the vicinity of the Market. That institution, still officially "French Market," has become more Italian than anything else. A latter-day legend of Louisiana is the rise of the Vaccaro brothers. One of them worked beneath the New Orleans wharves, picking up bananas dropped from the vessels. Others served as cane cutters or laborers in the Delta. Eventually they established a fruit stand near the Market; then they formed a fruit company of their own. They expanded, they acquired plantations in Latin America, timber lands and other holdings; their firm was capitalized at fifty millions. In recent years one of the Vaccaros acquired old Magnolia plantation, first owned by the river captains Bradish and Johnson, and later by Warmoth, the Reconstruction governor. Magnolia has been a kind of barometer of social change along the river.

The Italians became shippers of Delta produce as well as tradesmen. Let others dredge it up, grow it, seine it, or shoot it; some of the Italians were ready to move it more cheaply than anyone else. The Spicuzzas became the leaders, but others were close behind them. The Italians would deal in almost any commodity. Down the river the luggers carried freight from the city; that disposed of, they took on whatever would fit into their holds—rice, oranges, ducks, turtles, cucumbers, figs. The owner of a wharf with something to dispose of had only to tie a white rag at the landing as a signal—and be ready to bargain hard.

The Italians were among the first to install motors in their supply luggers, early in the present century. Their business thrived more than ever. When an important contract was to be filled, every inch of space below deck, on deck, and in the pilot's cabin held its part of the burden. The vessel sank perilously low; passengers who made the trip shut their eyes when they saw the approach of larger ships, sending high waves toward them. But the Spicuzzas and their colleagues fulfilled their agreement in every case.

Easy friendships grew between the Italians and the French, Spanish, Tockos, and others. The Tockos and Italians frequently intermarried, for their countries were close to each other in the Old World, and they had interests in common. French-Italian unions have not been unusual; and it did not take a wedding to encourage the French to change an Italian name. Signor Miceli (who pronounced his name Mitcheli) emerged as Monsieur Michel, with or without his permission. In this case some of the Micelis gave up. Legally they became Michels. A man doesn't fight his customers, does he?

For years there had been a few Irish in the Delta, at scattered points, but they were uncommon enough to make the Delta child ask Maman what made them look and talk that funny way.

The middle and later years of the nineteenth century brought these "foreign" people in waves, so that even the young gave them no more than a glance. The Irish came as ditch diggers and construction workers, as many of them had come to other parts of the South. Up in New Orleans the Irish population had increased. There the good-humored, muscular men dug drainage canals, cleared swamps and bogs. The slave owner expressed only a frank truth when he declared that he would not risk his Negroes in such dangerous labor, in fever-infested places. They were worth too much to him. When an Irishman died, sir, the only loss was to his relatives. So the Irish held a monopoly of the heavy construction work in South Louisiana; and as the levees extended into the lower sections of the Delta, especially after the Civil War, they became familiar figures with their barrels and shovels.

While natives looked on, the Irish stripped off their shirts, carted earth over the banks, and set up rows of tents among the grasses and cottonwoods near the levee. They were odd sights to the Deltans, these habitations—and the Irish themselves found them no less odd, sometimes waking in the morning to see their shoes floating out of the entrance.

"Ces vieux Eereesh," the natives called them—"Those ol' Irish!" The word "old" did not imply age in this case. Yet trouble developed rarely, for the Irishmen had a geniality and a warmth of disposition that was not foreign to the place. The natives seldom felt that the Irish were imported competition. This labor was not in the down-river pattern of life. When a good season in the marshes offered itself, who would want to have a shovel in his hand?

Frenchmen began to talk with the Irish, sharing drinks at the stores or from the bottles that the contractors provided to improve morale. Them feller' could tell joke', yes! Good feeling was not confined to the men. The Delta girls found themselves objects of interest to red-headed bucks whose wooing was light-hearted but insistent. These powerful fellows attracted the jeunes filles as glamorous figures from another environment, strange as were their blue or green eyes. Before long the priest beamed to find a man from County Kerry at the rectory, with a girl of Buras. As time passed, pink-faced children with pert noses that were unquestionably not of the old Delta played about the family wharves, prattling French with their cousins. An Irishman's son spoke of him as "mon Papa" and often had difficulty in understanding the words that Papa used. Papa would wonder at the fates and write home that everything was well with him, but still a little peculiar.

Other jobs attracted other Irish. A group of stonecutters, here to prepare the granite emplacements at Forts Jackson and St. Philip, formed a settlement near by. With each project some remained permanently. They worked in the stores, they drifted down among the pilots and some turned to the livings that supported their fathers-in-law and their neighbors. Before a trapper's cabin, one of the alien figures would watch as the others showed him how to skin the day's catch; in a line of slim, dark-haired shrimpers, a heavy man with a fair face scrambled about the waters. With a chuckle he came to call his relatives "Kiskadees," taking the term from the common expression of one Frenchman to another: "Qu'est-ce que tu dis?"—"What are you saying?" One cheerful Irishman sold a sign in ornate English letters to a grocer, with the assurance that it meant "God Bless Our Home." Not until months had passed, when an English-speaking stranger inquired, did the merchant learn that it declared "Credit Given Freely."

All that glittered was not Irish, but most of the levee workers were Celts and that was enough for the Delta. They were all "those Irish," whether they derived from England or Wales, Finland or Norway. Today the French inform you that certain residents are "real Irish, yes." But Johannesen isn't an Irish name, you tell them. "Tha's all right; the gran'papa was." The grandson in this case says casually that the family came from Sweden, but at an early date he gave up efforts to persuade the Deltans to draw distinguishing lines. He and his descendants stayed "Irish."

Sugar brought the Italians, construction work the Irish; and seafood drew the Orient to the Delta. Visitors were frequently surprised when they caught sight of a lugger man of yellow-brown complexion, with slightly slanting eyes, calling instructions to another in high-pitched, unfamiliar notes. A series of slow trickles had been opened from the East, from the Philippine Islands, China, the Malay Peninsula, and other scattered places. Their exact origins are matters of speculation. As early as the eighteenth century, the ships of Spain numbered among their crews the wiry men of the Philippines. The Islands were then the possession of His Castilian Majesty, and the natives, always excellent seamen, were forced into service in Mexico and other parts of the New World. When Louisiana became another of the crown's holdings, a certain number of them went to New Orleans and then drifted down the river among the bays and marshes. Men of the East were in the conglomerate mass that formed the pirate fleets of the Gulf and Caribbean in the early 1800's. But for years afterward little mention can be found of them.

Along Lake Borgne, near the Terre aux Boeufs area of the Spaniards, a colony of Filipinos gathered during the last half of the nineteenth century. Some have believed that it was first formed by seaman who deserted ships in New Orleans to escape their brutal Spanish officers. In the port, when a Filipino seaman went to a particular neighborhood near the market and inquired of the proper men, he would be directed there at once. On the lake, the colonists carried on an existence that differed little from that which they might have known at home. Fishermen born and trained, they turned to the catching of Louisiana shrimp, raising ocher-dyed red sails and scouring the shallows for the darting, light-colored shellfish.

The French and Spanish residents saw them from a distance, barefoot figures wearing pajamalike, collared costumes of neutral color that merged into their background. Their odd, triangular-shaped palmetto hats were as fine a protection as has yet been devised against the Louisiana sun. But these men did not fear the sun; they rejoiced in it, worked in it without letup, lay in it between tasks. The locality had a tropical languor, with its light brown sands and gnarled roots of mangrove trees, its grasses and palmetto leaves. Bayou St. Malo was the colony's waterway, skirting a tall Indian shell mound. The outlines of the huts, seen from far off, were in contrast to those of their neighbors. Sharply pointed, paintless, they seemed more fragile than even the lightest of the French and Tocko stilt-camps. One who came upon them in the late hours of the day, with their slanting shapes against the darkening golds and reds of the sky, might have thought himself viewing some drowsing scene on the other side of the earth.

To the French and Spanish children, the people of St. Malo were objects of an emotion between amusement and fright. Dr. Louis Ducros recalls the time in his boyhood that he first beheld one of them. "I stood in the road and gaped and gaped, and in my excitement I told a friend to look at the Chinaman. The man, Marcelino, turned on me and pointed—'Look here, boy, I'm no Chinaman. I talk Spanish like anybody else, and I'm a Christian!' " Under their Spanish rulers, the Filipinos had assumed the speech and the religion; and these factors made them seem not the less bizarre to the natives of the Terre aux Boeufs district.

Judge Albert E. Estopinal remembers hunting trips to the vicinity with his father. The Filipinos welcomed them, took them to good grounds, and fed them dishes of rice and boiled fish, with a flavor such as he had never tasted before or later. Every night, under dark rafters from which hung carcasses of dried fish, the colonists gathered and played card games. Fish-oil lamps lighted part of the room and the winds whistled outside. Others agree that cardplaying seemed to be an obsession with the Filipinos. Excellent players, they almost always defeated their visitors.

For years this was another place without women. It never saw girls from the Philippine Islands. As one of the men of today puts it, "Our women did not travel. Their place was home." As time went by, callers saw female figures in the background, sad-eyed women whom the men had brought from New Orleans. Some were said to be German: others spoke Spanish and had a Latin appearance. A few stayed for long periods; for the rest, this strange life seemed too difficult, and they went back by cart or boat, curiosities to many among whom they passed, in particular to those of their own sex.

The women remained much to themselves at St. Malo. From darkened side rooms they stared in silence at the outsiders; when the visitors were leaving, they sometimes smiled tentatively and murmured a brief goodbye, as if unsure of their status. Toward their men they were dutiful and submissive; if flare-ups occurred, none heard of them. When children were born some had a markedly Asiatic look, while others were more European, wistful, fragile-formed, with olive complexions and large, luminous eyes. Now and then a Deltan would hear that tiny Manuelita or Anna had died after weeks of fever, and that the men had buried her with rites conducted by one of these Christian Orientals.

Though the Deltans accepted their neighbors, few in New Orleans knew even of their existence. Suddenly in March of 1883 a well-spiced rumor spread: There was an Oriental settlement in the city's shadow, and they had never had a woman there until they sent to Asia for a lithe beauty; then the men had fought so violently over her that the elders ordered her cut to pieces and thrown to the alligators! The Times-Democrat foresaw a startling story; its staff included that richly-endowed student of exotica, the Greek-Irish Lafcadio Hearn. Following a series of clues, a party of newspapermen chartered an Italian lugger, and made a roundabout water trip, passing lonely lighthouse keepers and finally edging into the green liquids of St. Malo.

Hearn, in happy excitement, judged it a spot "as dead to the civilized world as the heart of Cambodia"; the nearest available point, he noted, was "Devil's Elbow." He stopped before a "strange wharf, as ruined and rotted and unearthly as the timbers of a spectral ship in the Rime of the Ancient Mariner." Everywhere buzzed mosquitoes, rising with a sound "like the boiling of innumerable caldrons," and great green-headed tappanoes and sandflies; enormous spiders wove their webs from the timbers about the seines and fishing-tackle.

The colonists were individuals of all sizes, tall and short, and of many hues, light, dark, cinnamon-colored, glossily yellow, "like that bronze into which a small portion of gold is worked." At this time one white man lived there, a Frenchman who was "Maestro" to the rest. A hard-faced, hard-mouthed person, he could yet speak with softness on occasion. Learning that some of the later Oriental arrivals were not Christians, he had baptized them in St. Malo's thick currents. A lone Negro stood about, a Portuguese who was "perhaps a Brazilian Maroon." Only one of the Filipinos had enjoyed much of a brush with city civilization.

This was young De los Santos, whose mother had been an Occidental. He had been educated in New Orleans and had worked in a judge's office, but then had abandoned everything else for the life that he had first known.

Now Hearn learned, alas, that there was no truth in the titillating tale of the lady and the alligators. Yet there were things to see and tell. The colony had a system of laws of its own. It was watched by no St. Bernard officials; no tax-collectors visited it. Arguments were placed in arbitration before the oldest man, whose word was final. A recalcitrant was "liable to be imprisoned within a fish-car, and left there until cold and hunger have tamed his rage or the rising tide forces him to terms."

Yet, it was admitted, there had formerly been women here. One was witness to a desperate attempt to murder her husband. In the night the assailant had entered the cabin, but husband, wife, and son had managed to beat him off. Punishment was quick and simple. "The assailant was overcome, tied hand and foot with fish lines and fastened to a stake driven into the swamp. Next morning they found him dead; the mosquitoes and the tappanoes had filled the office of executioner. No excitement was manifested; the Maestro dug a grave deep in the soft gray mud and fixed above it a rude wooden cross, which still shows its silhouette against the sky just above the reeds." The Maestro pointed to a rotting hut that the dead man had occupied: "only mosquitoes live there now." And he told of the incident with a combination of "religious compassion for the unabsolved soul, and marvelous profanity expressed in four different languages."

The settlement at St. Malo waned. The Maestro left; the Filipinos shifted about the Delta in search of new grounds. St. Malo was deserted, and the center of Oriental enterprises in shrimp moved to the opposite side of the river. To the back there grew up Manila Village, named for the island capital of the Filipinos; Dewey, for the admiral who defeated the Spanish, and other settlements that changed with the years. They were reached through canals or bayous from the Mississippi; about each thrived a miniature industry. The section became a place of shrimp-drying; on wide, slightly curving wooden platforms the shellfish were spread in rows to harden. The market remained largely the Orient; the Delta offered such abundance that shrimp produced here could compete after shipment with those found and processed in the East itself. The population of this vicinity was more mixed than that of St. Malo, with white workers of several nationalities, with Chinese, Malays, Portuguese, and others, including the Filipinos, or "Manilamen" as Louisianians came to call them.

Each platform had a boss, Oriental or part-Oriental. Between seasons the structures were deserted. During shrimping months they were thronged by a drifting population, single men and others with their families. The working forces lived on the spot, for they might lose a day or more in getting to the inaccessible places and, too, they had to be on hand at all hours, whenever the shrimp arrived. The catch must be boiled in brine, then raked out over the wooden expanses. The settlements were small towns on pilings, suspended on the fringe of the shore. Against the sun there was little protection; its heat was wanted, needed everywhere for the drying process. It was a flowerless, treeless scene, gray and weatherworn, the yellow grasses in the distance, the shrimp changing hues in the hot atmosphere, some almost crimson from the cooking vats, others lightening, the rest of almost neutral shades from long hours of drying.

Clustered around the platforms were small, French-patterned houses, some of them slums over the water. Here men and women of all shadings brought their children, to live a teeming existence about the Gulf shallows. Over the platforms moved men with rakes and shovels, changing the supplies of shrimp, turning them, and turning them again, always to get the maximum of sunlight. Those who worked here seemed to absorb a listless quality, a dejection that came, perhaps, from their long hours of waiting and their slow, monotonous chores. Year after year, lines of luggers came out of the Gulf with their burdens of shrimp, and the masters of the settlements increased in wealth and stature. A number of them were Filipinos who had begun as deserters from Spanish merchantmen and were not ashamed to tell of their earlier experiences. A few were Chinese. Gradually the latter have seemed to replace the Filipinos. The Chinese are better traders.

Harder than the work at the platform was that of the seine

crews, using fantastically long nets for the purpose. When they came upon schools of shrimp they placed themselves between the catch and the deeper waters and pushed their way inland. Usually they stood up to their chests, and the labor was unending. They operated on shares, the owner of the boat taking the largest part. Days would pass before there would be anything to share, long, disheartening days as they dragged through the low waters, skin blistering, the salt tearing at their hands, only the pelicans and the terns seeming to find the fish. Then suddenly the water sparkled with the flipping shelled things, and they would strive on without letup for hours, while quantities escaped on every side.

In some cases such workers were trapped no less than the shrimp in their nets. A few operators saw a way to gain by employing Oriental relatives and friends. Unable to speak English or to find their way about, these remained on the Gulf borders in a status approaching servitude. If they were inclined toward rebellion, the head man had a further hold. Certain of them had entered the United States illegally, perhaps through the help of their employer. Would they prefer the marshes and a little money, or jail and none—and also deportation? Nor was this arrangement confined to the Orientals. In New Orleans men who had committed offenses of various natures drifted about the waterfront in search of a quiet place out of reach of the authorities. Agents of the shrimp operators promised just what they wanted. I have talked with some of the Anglo-Saxons who worked in the industry, and they have wry memories.

Word was passed around on the arrival of such men. This one had no passport; another was wanted up in Chicago. So they could be held here indefinitely, paid below the scale, and "deductions" made as desired. The only boats were in the hands of the company, and the company saw that none slipped away. Some years ago the federal government acted. Several casual fishermen were guided about the territory. Then the boss was arrested on evidence of these agents. Peonage in the Delta came to an end.

In recent decades shrimping has expanded, to become a vastly more lucrative undertaking for the Deltans, French, Filipinos, and the rest. The state produces more than half of all shrimp taken along the coastal waters of the United States. The shellfish move inland, up the bayous and inlets and along the lakes, and then move back again into the Gulf. Only during the past few years have scientific inquiries disclosed some of the details of the shrimp migrations; and it has been discovered that superb "jumboes" thrive out from the shores. Heavier, more seaworthy luggers have been acquired and motors installed for longer trips into the blue waters.

The old hand-seines have died out, and the luggers drag heavy mechanical trawl-nets, scouring the waters, lifting the nets from time to time to the decks to inspect the contents. The catch goes into the hold, to await a meeting of the lugger with an ice-supply boat that will hurry the produce to the shrimp factories. Girls, in some cases children, stand ready to pick the fish, which are then cooked in brine and canned. And recent improvements in refrigeration, including "quick freezing," are bringing about new markets and further possibilities for enlargement of the trade.

But in its essentials the industry remains the same. Men still set out to find the tiny fish wherever the signs indicate that they may be. They study the water surfaces, they recall their experiences of other years in certain places, they watch for the down-sweeping gulls that may indicate a concentration of the shelled things. As during the earlier years, rich days will be followed by empty ones and men will wait in the bitter glare of the waters. They must guard against sudden, furious storms, against sharks that will rip their trawl-nets apart; and once they have their delicate, perishable shrimp, they will worry lest the heat get them before the buyer. A long day's catch can spoil in a bad few hours. So it always was; so it will be until still greater revolutions in refrigeration are brought about.

CHAPTER 10

"Stop Acting Like a Pilot!"

OF ALL the callings in the Delta, the highest stands that of the pilot. To be a pilot—ah, that is a thing for you. The youth who sits on the levee and studies every vessel that passes—almost certainly he is thinking of the day when he may be out there, riding high above the world, guiding the ships to and from New Orleans. The wrinkled old man who runs from his store toward the river—he wants to call an "Eh, là-bas!" to the Capitaine, whom he has know since he was no higher than a big muskrat. And the smiling girl who is pinning a flower at the neckline of her dress and embellishing her lips—it is all for the passing of the young pilot. You think he cannot see her close enough for such preparation? Then what does he have his telescope for? And if he is a real pilot, he will be using it! To be a pilot, that *is* a thing for you.

He is the Delta's local hero, neighbor-who-made-good, and village spender, all in one. His is a calling of pulse-quickening possibilities—danger, adventure, and the obvious opportunities it affords for monetary and social advancement. When a friend questions the actions of such an individual, another is likely to interrupt, "But he's a pilot!" That explains, and takes care of, a great deal.

For two centuries and a half, piloting has flourished as an occupation with a special color of its own. Concerning the pilots and their methods Louisianians have grown voluble, now enthusiastic, now apoplectic; and with the years the position has undergone violent change. "Where they's pilots, they's alway' something happening," the Deltans tell you. Things began to happen early in the history of the region.

The pilots first established themselves at the Balize, when the engineer Pauger created that small island stronghold at the river mouth in the 1720's. Their work was closely related to the military defense, and the occupation was not a sedentary one. The trip up the Mississippi with the sailing vessels often took weeks. Where the river made a curve—and especially at English Turn—they might spend days waiting for a change in the wind. Between trips the pilots had to accustom themselves to a life of almost complete exile. Rulers might fall, new tyrants rise, the shape of world events alter and alter again while they remained among the shrieking shore birds.

They built stockades and fortifications and saw them washed away. Hurricanes struck with full force on these unprotected corners, and at intervals the governors recorded, without much excitement, that the Balize had been destroyed by the winds. The buildings were replaced by somewhat sturdier ones, and the pilots saw these also demolished. Sometimes man was responsible. One afternoon in 1795, when Louisiana was still a Spanish colony, the pilots and soldiers caught sight of a six-gunned vessel moving upon them. It was French, *La Parisienne,* and a privateer. The crew trained its guns on the Balize, then disembarked to enjoy a week of light carousal at Spain's proud outpost, drinking Spain's wine, and eating her food. Word had been sent up to New Orleans, but it was not until the eighth day that help was seen approaching. The men of *La Parisienne* then made off with all movable equipment and furnishings and set the torch to the rest.

Under France, under Spain, under the early United States, complaints were many against the piloting service. With the Spanish, as already noted, it become a monopoly directed by Señor Juan Ronquillo. Visiting during his regime, the Frenchman Perrin du Lac found problems traceable to nature and officialdom alike. Risks at the river mouth were manifold; the look of things deceived the most experienced of officers. The Gulf shoaled; bays that seemed clear and deep had only a few feet of water. Just to the east lay hundreds of small islands and reefs that might not be sighted until a vessel was close upon them. The discriminatory pilotage was "extremely annoying" to anyone who was not Spanish, and hazardous to all, Spanish or otherwise. Men serving under the chief pilot, knowing that they had no competitors, went out only when ships were near the channels; "and the winds must be very moderate before they trust themselves to the sea." Vessels were constantly trapped by the winds and grounded on the shores.

Much of this might have been prevented, it was said, had Señor Ronquillo obeyed instructions from his own government. The authorities ordered him to mark the main channel; but, fearing "lest anyone enter without his help" and also without payment to him, the pilot had neglected to do so. When accidents did occur, no smaller vessels were provided for unloading and lightering, so that all or most of the cargoes were lost. Moreover, the twenty-four men under the chief pilot, serving on a military basis, could not resign except at a time when the demand for their services was light and they were out of debt. And the chief pilot was "careful to keep them always dependent on him by furnishing them with the strong liquors which they consume in great quantity."

With the opening of the American regime conditions changed, and for the worse. A system of Anglo-Saxon privilege and neglect replaced the Spanish. American chief pilots took the salary and hired deputies to do the work—usually the cheapest available talent, paid as little as it could be prevailed upon to take. The period was a tumultuous one, with piracy at its height in the Gulf, the disturbances of the War of 1812, and the later uncertainties. It would perhaps be kindest to observe that the profession took the color of its environment; the first quarter century or so of American dominance marks the low period of pilotage in the Delta.

The pilots' hangout at the Balize drew individuals of a character conservatively described as "mixed"—ignorant, venal, culpably indifferent. They had lived on the fringes of many civilizations and occupations; they were men expelled from armies for misconduct, deserters from other services, shifty-eyed, shifty-fingered fellows hated by the river people. The Balize blossomed as the scene of hell-ripping good times for the unsqueamish, a combination of dive, bawdyhouse and hideout. It was known as the wildest, rawest place in all Louisiana; and considering the accumulations of lower New Orleans sink-holes with which it competed for such a reputation, one cannot but marvel at the rich variety of human iniquity packed into so small a space.

Every week or so saw a body, or several of them, stretched upon the broken boardwalks. An official sent to the place seldom returned with anything but confusion to show for his trip. Most of the inhabitants of this Balize had a well-developed aversion to witnessing anything. Non, non, we were somewhere else. . . . Swearder God, mister, nobody seen who done it. Maybe he did scream, but it's loud around here that time of night. . . . Me, I think he just fell over and bled to death, natural. . . . And when a man disappeared, those who knew him could hope perhaps that he had been shanghaied; this was the gentlest of the fates one met at the old Mississippi mouth.

Meanwhile, it seemed that almost anyone could become a "deputy pilot." Men with little or no experience took over the guidance of vessels and promptly grounded them. It was not their fault, they then insisted. It was always the river. It refused to behave, that was all; and the pilot was ready to beat the stuffing out of anyone that disagreed.

Finally, in 1837, even tolerant Louisiana decided that it was time to take action. Too many pocketbooks were being hurt; the legislature was prevailed upon to order a clean-up. The system of "deputy pilots" was ended. Hereafter there would be fifty or so branch pilots of equal standing, all of whom must meet certain requirements. Scales of charges were fixed, bond demanded of each man; and the pilots must take up posts in the Gulf and meet the incoming ships. A new type of individual came to the Balize, from the French, Spanish, Tocko, and other families of the Delta, and from elsewhere as well. The Atlantic coast, England, Sweden, and other places provided recruits, and after them arrived a number of "Frenchmen from France," as the Deltans put it to explain that they did not hail from Louisiana. They were officers who had served extended apprenticeships at sea, among them captains of vessels that had long used the river; and they had incentives now for doing a good job. They included men of education, of high standards of conduct, and the Delta benefited from the influx. The reform made it, more than ever, a place of meeting and mingling for people of all countries.

And new women were at the Balize, the wives and daughters of the branch pilots. They walked about the mud bank, saw the wrecks of the former buildings, and with their men they worked to improve it. Like Pauger and his helpers on that long-past occasion, men dug sand from the river to raise the low places. Sons and husbands were sent to the swamp for bright-flowering plants, and among the cottages, brilliant borders of flowers soon shone in the sun. They demanded policemen to keep order; they put up a school and created a meeting place with a reading room. The old residents would have snickered and shaken their heads at such goings-on. One visitor reported: "They have reclaimed with infinite labour from a waste of waters in the heart of immense marshes, of treeless plains, of swamps sweeping on every hand, a spot of dry earth upon which a neat village has been erected. . . . Society and civilization have grown up at the Balize."

Self-conscious about their status, the new pilots were scrupulous in their behavior, and not less so in their appearance. They adopted a uniform rather like that of an undertaker: stiff-starched shirt, high collar and black frock coat! So arrayed, it was hard for a man not to exude self-respect.

A few of the arrivals had trouble in accepting their surroundings. A gray-haired woman in black, with Vermont in her face and in her heart as well, would sit for hours at her window and blink at the line of waving grasses—always the grasses and the yellow waters. She was thinking of the firmly outlined rocks and the clear streams of home; and she was asking the Lord for patience. How could she and Jonathan ever fit themselves to such a scene? Eventually she and Jonathan left. Some of her sisters were of more pliable material; they braced their shoulders and ultimately they learned that this place and people were not as "different" as they had thought. They mastered approximations of the Latin tongues that they heard; in weeks of high water they took in frightened, sallow children of the marsh, and they came to like the sturdy, gentle-faced Grand'mères who were their nearest neighbors.

But it was, I gather, the adjustable Irish and their pink-cheeked, quick-tongued wives who did as much as any to work out another life at the Balize. They found peace in this isolation, and security. When they saw gumbo on the tables of the French, they asked what it was, and cooked it at home. They discovered how to prepare crabs and shrimp jambalaya, with bayleaf, spices, and all. Always devout, they installed shrines and pictures of the Virgin on their walls. The women persuaded their husbands to take messages to the priest at his station up the river. If Father would come the next week, please. . . . The boat would go to get him and would take him back. They had everything ready. Father Robert Wilken notes that on one occasion the hospitable pilots decided to hold a "grand ball" to welcome a priest due for a mission. The women explained that this would be setting an unecclesiastical precedent, and the idea was dropped.

The Balize became a thriving village with a population of eight hundred, three stores and a dry-goods establishment. In time it could display a mark of high civilization—a shining shell road in the midst of the grasses.

Then the Mississippi played one of its jokes, and the Balize was doomed. The point of settlement had shifted once or twice in the colonial period, as troubles developed with the sites. Now came a greater change. The river crevassed to form an additional place of discharge into the Gulf; silt began to fill the main eastern outlet. Year by year ships turned to different entries; the pilots reluctantly moved away. For a decade or so a dwindling group stayed. Houses blew down and were not restored. As in other localities where the river ceased to build, slow subsidence of the ground followed. The marsh and the Gulf waters slipped nearer, and after the Civil War the last family went away.

Today the Balize is no longer marked on most maps. The Delta has reclaimed it from man. All that remain are a patch of reeds only slightly higher than the surrounding wastes, and a narrow waterway overgrown with wild grass. The former path of empire has become a stagnant ditch. But the shell road holds intact. It can yet be found, if the searcher will take a shovel and dig four feet beneath the greenstuff.

Not far off is a place of the dead, a marsh in which stand a few dissolving tombstones. Covering a period of about a quarter century, they tell another part of the story of this respectable, quieter settlement on the Gulf. Some did not leave the Balize.

"William Halliday. Born June 3, 1837. Died March 30, 1841.

Son of Robert and Mary Halliday." Mary Halliday, twenty-two, had seen her boy placed in his small box beside these waters before he was quite four years old. Three years later Mary Halliday herself was lowered beside him. Susan Mitchell, wife of John Perrin, went earlier, at eighteen. John had a poem engraved:

When one we love is snatched away
By Death's resistless hand,
Our hearts the mournful tribute pay
That pity doth demand.

There is much that asks pity. "Born in Boston." "Born in Savannah." "A native of New York." "A native of Missouri." Several from the distant counties of Ireland. And here is Evelina Lemont, wife of Thomas Ruiz. The end came for her when she was nineteen. But there can be no question that Evelina at least is at home, for the Balize was the only one that she had ever known. Her husband remembered:

Where is she now? Where all must be,
Sunk in the Grave's obscurity.
Yet never, never slumbered there
A mind more pure—a form more fair.
She was—but words are wanting to say what.
Think what a wife should be; and she was that.

Meanwhile, the matter of pilotage on the river was not entirely settled. A committee of the Louisiana legislature at one time reported that the arrangements at various periods had "undergone every phase of change" between a "close monopoly" on one hand and, on the other, a "competition stimulated by individual ambitions, even animosities—a competition pushed to extremes by rival houses." The pendulum swung. After the first rush of reform, businessmen came forward to protest that new and raging antagonisms were almost disrupting the service. In this era of what the Delta calls the "opposition pilots," men strove with fervor against each other. A yawl boat had a pilot and several helpers to row. They were often on the water for several days, scanning the horizons. With them they took food and covering against bad weather. They were tempted to further and further risks in order to win against their opponents.

The unwritten law was that the job of pilotage went to the individual who first stepped aboard the incoming vessel. Sometimes the contest was so sharp that those approaching at the same hour would halt to belabor each other with their oars. Officers of the ship would send down seamen to intervene, or perhaps they would watch the fun from the deck, and then haul aboard the conqueror. A pilot and his men had only contempt for their rivals, and at times the term "cutthroat competition" was not a metaphorical one.

The most celebrated example of such a contest came when, on a day of dark, heavy seas, two pilots reached a vessel from opposite directions at almost the same minute. The first gained slightly; it appeared that he would have the advantage. He arrived at the port side with difficulty and caught at the bobbing ship's ladder. As he did, he gave a cry of success. The second pilot heard him through the winds; he would have to act quickly or fail. Two or three seamen looked down at him. "Toss me a rope, men," he called. The rope hit the water; the second pilot took a firm hold. The ship gave a heavy roll, away from him. The first pilot, moving up the ladder on the opposite side, was delayed as the high wall careened over him, while the pull of the vessel, with the helping hands of the seamen on the rope, lifted his rival high in the air. By the time the first pilot reached the deck, the enemy was there, wet and triumphant.

The pilots formed companies, heightening the rivalries. At last one group purchased a seagoing tug, the *Jennie Wilson,* and her owners could take their pick of the trade. This seemed opposition too formidable for the others. Not long afterward a general pilots' association was formed with the *Jennie Wilson* as flagship. Put into operation in the 1870's, she stays in service today. Remodeled from time to time, new engines installed, she is said to be the oldest pilot boat in use anywhere. The tug has seen the profession undergo a further quieting process, but it is still far from drab. It continues a business that constantly flirts with danger. Only recently great vessels have been caught by contrary winds at the river mouth and sent spinning to their doom. Steamers have fought like animals trapped in a pond; and regularly the Delta women have looked on as their pilot-husbands won praise for heroism.

By general agreement, the pilot remains a riproaring guy. By and large he also keeps his rank as the best-paid man in the Delta. It is part of the code that he be carefree, a quip on his tongue, a practical joke hatching in his head. (There are, to be sure, exceptions.) A crony grins and declares, "Tha's a pilot for true. Jus' like his Papa. Set up the drinks, the Capitaine say' a roun' for ev'body. . . ." A pilot is a fine man to have as a relative. He ought to be good for a touch on sight, for Christmas presents, christening gifts, and favors from the politicians.

Above all, he carries on as a trencherman in the grand manner. When a woman of Plaquemines tells a guest, "This is good salmon, chère, jus' like what the pilot' got at their own table," all know that it is fine food indeed. The pilot fare partakes of the Delta's French tradition, sauced and seasoned with earnestness and resource. A fire always burns in the kitchen at their stations and over it bubbles a pot of coffee. This is the blackest, the most breathtaking brew prepared in any section of Louisiana. Non-natives, unprepared for the first mouthful, turn red in the face. Most Louisianians, after one cup, glance around for the next one.

Thus it is that if a Deltan finds a friend behaving above his means, ordering things that he cannot afford, he tells him, "Stop acting like you think you a pilot!"

The pendulum has swung once more. The pilot of today belongs to one of the most strongly organized groups in America. Those who take vessels across the river's place of meeting with the Gulf form one association; those who guide them from that point to New Orleans make up another. In effect, practically all sizable ships passing through the Delta must use a member of both associations. In the case of the bar pilots—those at the river mouth—the company has an investment of several hundred thousand dollars, and fees are divided every month. If a pilot retains a moderate portion of his earnings, he should find himself nicely off by middle age. His work is arranged so that he is on duty for two weeks, off the next two. No longer does he need to live near the river mouth; when his stint is over, a fast boat takes him to the nearest point of land and an automobile transfers him home. Some pilots own businesses; a number of them are comfortable property owners of New Orleans. They have come far since those wild days of the last century.

To become a pilot is not an easy matter. The aspirant must pass examinations after serving an apprenticeship. But that is only part of it. The number belonging to each association is limited; only when a vacancy exists will a new pilot be admitted, and then the members must ballot to decide whether he will be taken in. Dynasties have grown up with the years. A member can plan with some certainty on a pilot's career for his son; he voted for the relatives of his associates, and they will vote for his. "There is nothing mysterious about the way it works," one explained. "Everybody is interested in his own family." Only when conflicting claims offer themselves do disputes arise. The properly connected young men apply and wait their turn until something happens. Then comes a "tap day," when members meet to consider the new applications. In the pilots' settlement, prospective members drink nervously of their strong coffee, fidget and watch the windows behind which momentous decisions are being made. The masters emerge. There is a silence, an exchange of glances. A name is called. The sweating, smiling youth who steps forward will become a captain, with all of the perquisites, to be pointed out wherever he walks in the Delta.

Despite the modern touches, the pilot follows the tradition of the man of the sea, remembering all of the incredible things that he has seen and telling them with salty detail; and he is an artist in the big joke, the mendacity that recounts a wild yarn with the most guileless of countenances. Whoever visits the headquarters has his recollections of the tales the pilots spun to him, of porpoises that form precise lines to guide the ships into the channel, of twenty-foot snakes that wear down the boardwalks with their movement across them, of strange pelicans whose powers of vision are breathtaking.

The pilot lights his pipe and settles back: "There I was that day, fishing off the pier with a line tied around my wrist, and dozing a little. Not much luck. Then all of a sudden a big, big gar grabbed at the line and jerked me right out into the river. I tried to get loose but I couldn't. It kept pulling me down the pass. So I just kept my nose and eyes above water and let it go ahead. Two miles out in the Gulf I hailed a ship and it picked me up." Observing that he is appreciated, he waves a hand: "See that bare patch of mud over there? We had a lot of rice planted, and it was heading up fine. Then one morning we found our whole rice field moving away. We had made a mistake, put that field on an alligator's back! Yeah, they come big down here."

The Balize has given way to Pilottown, an amphibious settlement a few miles above the broad Head of Passes. Customs agents, fishermen, and trappers share with the pilots the collection of single-storied wooden buildings that make up the place. It can be reached only by water. The stilt-houses face a board roadway, which is sidewalk, heavy traffic route, and meeting place. For some time before the pilots' families moved away, the wives and children led a cheerful existence, visiting each other, taking afternoon walks over the boards. The residents for years have included a few elderly people who remember the Balize and its demise. When I was there the last time, a number of the families had never been more than a few miles away.

Here, among the gulls and the leaping porpoises, the pilots watch the waters and the wide skies and keep their assignments. The pilots' names are on a large board, each a separate shingle. All serve in order; a man tells at a look how near he is to his turn. He may loll about for a day or more, playing cards, listening to the radio, or sitting in the sun. During rough weather, when ships struggle in open Gulf, seeking sanctuary, calls may be almost unremitting.

At Southwest Pass, through the howl of the elements, I hear a signal. The young pilot who knows that his name is next, glances up. Quickly he throws on his coat, raincoat, and boots. His assistant helps me to do the same, the door is opened, and we are all but flung back by the onrush of wind and spray. Outside we seem lost for a moment in a gray-blackness of night and rain. The pilot turns me about and we head toward a light at the end of the wharf. On the way both of us slip, and once my foot goes over the plank. But the pilot has my arm in a secure grip. We step aboard the tug; safe from the hostile waters, we shudder for a moment in a warm, well-lighted room, then gaze through the glass at the rage over sky and sea and land. The throbbing engines are ready; we start at once.

The vessel is sturdily built, but this is a pounding sea, and we lurch heavily as we nose into the waves. The foam strikes against the windows; when it recedes, pellets of rain beat down with angry insistence. Each time the tug lifts into the air, we catch a point of light, flickering on and off at the buoy ahead; and through the walls come the sad whinings of a whistling device. I hear another sound, a slow moan as of an animal in distress. One of the men in the room laughs: "Only the wind; you don't know a real wind till you've been down here."

We fight our way outward, change our direction, and I make out the half-veiled lights of a waiting vessel, a heavy oil tanker. The tug halts in the lee of the tanker, and we toss about more frantically than ever among the agitated waters. The pilot and assistant brace themselves, step forth into the treacherous dark, and we squint at them through the window. The helper releases a skiff from the davits and in a few moments they are on the sea, the apprentice working hard at the oars as the boat is slapped and spun around. For five, for ten minutes the bark struggles; slowly it draws near the tall vertical side of the ship. Now approaches the moment of greatest danger. A Jacob's ladder has been dropped for the pilot; we make out one or two figures on the deck far above, gesturing to him. With difficulty, the pilot stands in the swaying boat. Between him and the limp end of the rope ladder a wide gap stretches. As a wave lifts the boat, he reaches and misses. The skiff sinks again and he catches at its sides with both hands to steady himself.

The next swell is a low one, and the pilot does not try for a connection. A sudden splash of foaming water obscures the view. As it clears, we find that he has missed another attempt; he almost slips overboard as he falls back. The assistant reaches out and steadies him. A grueling wait follows. The men on the tanker cup their hands to their lips; the pilot seems to be shaking his head. Now a great wave is nearing. He spreads his legs wide, raises his arms, and the skiff is elevated along the steep wall—higher, higher. Two strong hands at last grasp the ladder. The skiff sinks, but the pilot has already begun his crawl upward. The next onrush of water drenches him, his lower body lost momentarily in the churning liquid. He pauses for breath, then continues his perilous climb; arms reach over to assist him.

His companion in the skiff heads back toward the tug, his boat is taken aboard, and we turn toward shore. As we approach the pilot station, we find the tanker behind us, majestic, gliding toward the dim low edges of the embankments at both sides. She moves with confidence, and we know that her officers are easier in their minds because the man whom we brought is at the bridge, watching through the spray, remembering the panorama of the river bottom that he holds in his head.

The lament of the buoy reaches a new pitch, and then through the night comes the sound of the tanker's bell, ringing continuously. The pilot is making a further check of his distances in the channel by listening for the echoes of the clang against the banks. To watch, and hear, this process in action is to feel the pulse quicken. Will there be a mistake, a tiny error in calculation, to bring disaster to a precious cargo? The assistant, rubbing his face with a towel, catches sight of me at the window and guffaws. "Don't worry. He'll make it. That fellow knows this place like you do your fingers. You want sugar in your coffee?"

Over the hot cup, I compliment him on his part of the job. "Ah-ah," he shakes his head. "That's the little, little part. What counts is what he's doing now." He sits in momentary silence as the steam from his plate wreathes his face. He is thinking, perhaps, of that future day when he will be out there, and someone else will be rowing him to the Jacob's ladder.

CHAPTER 11

Harness in the River Mouth

ONE afternoon in the 1870's, government workmen in Pass à Loutre, easterly entrance to the Mississippi, were startled when the contours of the river and its banks began to alter suddenly before their eyes. Ominously the earth rose from below to the water's surface, then higher until in places it was nine feet or more in the air. Here was a frightening sight; normal variations in the banks were measured by inches. The massive lump spread and also moved forward the next day and the next; as the newly-exposed soil dried, it broke into wrinkles, and salt water and streams of gas flowed from it. Engineers worked with dredges to cut down the risings; within a day the same amount or more of earth had taken its place, until it extended for more than a thousand acres.

For more than two centuries men had been witnessing similar changes of varying degrees of violence about the river mouth. The Indians told the first white men of these occurrences; the unbelieving Europeans laughed—to be convinced by their own observations. The ground at these points lifted and fell in a fashion that could not be explained. Anchors, dropped years earlier in fifty feet or so of water, were sent unexpectedly to the surface. In one case a pile of gleaming rock was revealed in the early morning sun. A native hastened over, rubbed the barnacles and discovered that it was ballast dropped there when he was a boy. A year or so later the rotting mast of a sloop appeared obliquely out of the Gulf. Deltans found the vessel and cargo intact. Officially it had been lost, years earlier; they were entitled to whatever they salvaged.

These "mud lumps" of the Mississippi are a phenomenon without counterpart, about which speculation has thrived through the decades. Learned visitors have brought notebooks, dug into the mud, smelled it, taken samples, and come to the most diverse conclusions, some of them worthy of a Jules Verne. Dr. Richard Joel Russell has compiled some of their statements. This was obviously volcanic action, insisted one authority. No, maintained another, it was a matter of gas and oil, bubbling up from deep-lying marine deposits. A third concluded that the lumps came into being in much the same way as did the Alps, raising the prospect that mountains might one day tower at the river mouth. A fourth believed that they were workings of vast underground rivers, moving out of the middle of the continent. Today many geologists agree that the muds ascend here simply because the enormous river sediments bear heavily down upon the soft clays beneath. The clays "flow" under this pressure and break through at the surface. In no other place, it seems certain, do lumps of this kind occur.

Less dramatic, but worse as a danger, have been the long bars at the river mouths. Officials tried for many years to solve this problem, without success. The engineer Pauger had shown long earlier that ocean-going vessels could negotiate the river passes, but serious difficulties were continually being encountered. The river-deposited sands grew higher or lower with successive storms, with heavy gales, even with the seasons. The tide, the volume of flow from above—everything made a difference, raising the bars at one point, lowering them at another. Over a period of years, the Mississippi slowly changed its flow into the Gulf, dropping so much silt in one pass that the opening declined, shifting its main discharge to another, and then to another.

During a century and a half after Pauger, Louisianians tried a variety of solutions. Colonial authorities set up sharp-toothed harrows and pulled them over and over the deposits to force them out. Whatever benefit resulted was short lived. In the American period, about 1837, Congress appropriated funds for bucket-dredging; this, too, had little real effect. Later steam-driven propellers were tried, in an effort to stir up the mud and wash it away. After that, engineers went to the bars with sticks of dynamite. This made a pretty show, killed fish, and sent the terns and gulls flapping furiously away; but that was all.

As the nineteenth century progressed, conditions seemed to grow quickly worse. Ships arrived at the river mouth to find that they lacked two, three or more feet of clearance. Seventeen feet was the greatest depth that men could hope for. They would have to wait. How long? Who knew?—several days, several weeks or longer. The officers could only sound the depths, go back to their ships, and sound them again. At one time in 1859, nearly seven and a half millions in merchandise lay waiting at the river mouths; thirty-five vessels were trying to get out, seventeen to come in, while three had been caught and blocked the best passage. Some never extricated themselves, but rotted in the river.

When sidewheel tugs appeared on the Mississippi, they were hailed as the answer to the puzzle. They would meet the vessels at the bar and pull them across by main force. This method was most successful with the fast clippers whose sharp keels helped them over. The clipper was directed toward a place that had been indicated by soundings as the lowest, the tug drawing it over at full speed. On a day of happy omen, the vessel with its sloping bottom would go through like a knife through cheese; but if a bad choice were made, even clippers were caught.

Soon man made the problem worse. The towboat interests "got together." For a time a ship captain had paid a set fee, and the tug performed the task no matter how long it took. Now new rules were in effect: a hundred dollars an hour for as many hours as were necessary. Every tow owner belonged to the association, and the captain had to agree. As John H. Kennard declared in 1873, "We have a powerful corporation, the Towboat Association, and they do not hold fasting and prayer when they hear a ship has stuck on the bar." W. D. Wetmore, who had served at the river bar, described the situation to the Patrons of Husbandry in that same year.

Sometimes, he told them, a vessel went aground along the edge of the channel. One tug at a hundred dollars an hour struggled for some hours before officials decided that another, and perhaps another, were needed, at one hundred extra dollars an hour for each. Then the captain was informed that a yet bigger vessel was required. Where, in God's name, could that be found? Why, up at New Orleans. The association had one. He could make arrangements with the manager; there was a telegraph over there. (Mr. Wetmore noted that only one line existed, and nobody could use it except for dealings with the association, "as many a shipmaster has learned to his sorrow.") The agitated master was informed that a very powerful boat would be sent at a cost of "one or more thousand dollars." More agitated than ever, but unable to help himself, he agreed. This monster turned out to be only slightly more formidable than the rest of them. The combined services pulled the grounded vessel into the channel, but here it was discovered that the current had made new deposits and the ship was trapped once more.

They could only arrange for lightering, to unload the vessel and reduce its depth. How? (Need the captain have asked?) Back he went to the telegraph to bargain for a barge, which belonged to a member of the managing board. Down it came from New Orleans, removed the cargo; the tugs pulled the vessel along, and then it was reloaded. By the time he arrived in port, the master found that the cost of these operations exceeded the gross amount of the freight! Wise captains would as soon make the New Orleans trip, added Mr. Wetmore, as they would "run into the center of a hurricane."

Despite the doings of the tow-men, the basic difficulty remained that of the river mouths themselves. Here was one of the great engineering problems of the last century. Next to the Civil War, said John Lathrop Mathews, no factor had so great an effect in shaping the transport and commercial routes of the American interior. Had man been able to find a continuous way across the bars, the history of the Mississippi Valley might have been different. As it was, the stream of traffic through the river was being choked. New Orleans seemed headed into permanent decline. The valley people realized that something must be done, and quickly, or it would be too late.

For years Louisianians talked of a canal in the Delta, running in a straight line from river to Gulf, eliminating the use of the river mouths altogether. In the years following the Civil War, feeling crystallized in favor of a four-mile connection on the west bank near Fort St. Philip toward Breton Sound. Army engineers favored the idea, and it seemed on the way to reality. Then, in the early 1870's, Captain James Buchanan Eads came forward, to inaugurate a virulent engineering-financial-personal controversy, and also one of the most remarkable of modern construction projects.

James B. Eads thrived on originalities, unorthodoxies, and criticisms. Born a Hoosier, son of an unsuccessful merchant, he left school at thirteen and peddled apples for a time. The river always intrigued him, and he tried early to find out all about it. Serving as a clerk during the day, he taught himself at night. He became an amateur engineer; he learned some wrong things, some right ones, and proceeded to eliminate the wrong ones by experience. In his twenties he turned directly to the river itself. He was a purser, then head of a steamboat-salvaging company of his own. He worked on the river bottom for years. He used his ingenuity to do what none of the textbook men had done, turning out a remarkable diving bell of his own invention. It was said that with that bell he trudged every foot of the Mississippi's floor from St. Louis to Vicksburg. Whether or not he missed part of the route, he watched the stream in action, and he knew its strengths, its peculiarities, and its predilections.

If Eads were sure of a thing, he was ready to back what he knew against any academician or any Mississippi veteran who offered himself. When the Civil War came, Lincoln summoned him and he turned out a flow of gunboats that won the upper river for the Federals. The timber was not yet cut, nor the iron rolled, when he started, but by using his own methods he launched eight vessels in one hundred days, the first ironsides to be built in the United States; and then he went on to other ship construction. After the struggle, the Missourians were talking of a bridge across the Mississippi at St. Louis. Two dozen reigning civil engineers signed a statement that it could not be done; it was foolish to talk of a structure so wide, so high, in a soil quavering and rockless. Eads announced that he could do it, and did. He sank foundations deep into the earth until he hit a firm base and built from there. Underwater construction involved problems that men had never faced before. He had trouble with a contractor who fashioned a vital link too short for the purpose—a discovery made late in the project's development. Thousands were certain that the whole thing would sink right in front of them. Eads tinkered, altered a plan at one point, dropped one scheme for another, and it did not sink.

He had proved that at last the Mississippi could be bridged. Now he turned to the river mouth and prepared to show that it could be cleared. What were needed, he insisted, were jetties, extensions of the river's natural banks outward into the Gulf. The river had tremendous power; constrict it so that its full strength would pour upon the bars and wash them into the sea. Army engineers fumed at this amateur who was also a civilian. River sages, who held that the Old Man was an unmanageable force and that was all there was to it, sir—were aggrieved. Not less so were businessmen of New Orleans, who asked Congress how it could "contemplate or tolerate the half-insane proposition of strangers who can know nothing of the habits of our inexorable enemy." Didn't Congress know that jetties would "inevitably send back the flood waters like a tide to the very city of New Orleans and beyond? . . . Do not, we pray, permit us to be destroyed." In a word, this Eads was a fool.

If so, he was a monumental one. He made an unprecedented offer to the government, his "no-cure-no-pay" plan. He would construct the jetties at his own peril until he had shown they worked. At Southwest Pass, now the largest and most dependable of the two main outlets, he would create a channel twenty-eight feet deep; the cost would be ten millions. He asked that he be paid the first million only when he had lowered the bar by twenty feet, and additional installments as he provided a progressively greater depth and maintained it for some years to demonstrate that it could be done.

The project was tossed from Senate to House and back. Engineers and junketing legislators conferred, recommended one thing, then another. Finally Eads won the right to take his risk—but not as he wished. He would have to take the narrower, minor outlet, South Pass. If he failed, the impediment to commerce would be that much less. Eads was stumped for a moment. South Pass had a much smaller flow of water to direct across its bar, which was as big as that at the other point. Also, he was certain the outlet was too small to serve all vessels that would hereafter want to use the port. He pleaded; he would do it for only eight millions if he could have the pass he wanted. Congress said no, and Eads, worried but still determined, signed the papers. He would have to work harder and shave everything the thinner.

The Deltans could have told Eads a variety of things about the river outlets. At many points above the Head of Passes, along the narrowing earth of the Delta, the river refused to break through the thin edgings of ground. But as it approached the Gulf, they said, it began to "act like crazy." They had seen a once-great passage shrink until it was now open only to skiffs and small luggers; and they had watched a canal grow to a hundred times its size in a single season.

On the west bank, a few miles above the Head of Passes, is the Jump, near which the present-day settlement of Venice has grown up. From early Delta recollections, a shallow opening cut its way here into the Gulf. A man had only to stand back a foot or so to leap over it—hence the name. In 1839, high water arrived, and the river found this an inviting sidepath. Water roared in, deepening, spreading until it ripped out a passage a quarter mile wide, sixty feet into the ground. As the Deltans say now, if you want to get across you will need wings. This miniature Mississippi poured out millions of tons of silt, building a shoal area and then marsh on all sides.

Others recount the story of Baptiste Collette's Bayou, across the river, named for one who once lived here. In former days this streamlet was so minute that a man paddling along it felt the curtains of wild cane meeting over his head. He had only a half mile to go before he reached the Gulf. Then one day—the year is in dispute—the river discovered it, and before long it was a third of a mile across, and building land out into the blue waters. Like the Mississippi itself, it broke into a series of arms, spreading its thickening deposits farther and farther. In probably less than a half century, it has extended its soil and half-soil for five miles.

To the south, two girls could say that, practically alone, they had given the Mississippi another outlet. Martha and Anne Cubitt cut a short ditch across the bank to make it easy for their father, Dick Cubitt, to pole through with his boat. Pushing aside the driftwood, they used their shovels to start a trickle of water on its way. Soon they had a little current; the neighbors called it "Oyster Canal." The Mississippi helped the girls. During the high water of 1862, the river rushed heavily through to create a new passage. Today "Cubitt's Gap" has built up seventy-five square miles of ground.

And now this man Eads was going to try his hand at making the river behave!

On a warm morning in 1875 the Deltans hurried to their levees to behold a small fleet on its way—a floating pile driver, barges with equipment and food, barges with workers. The newcomers inspected this place that was to be their home for years to come. In some cases it would be their grave, but they saw no hint of that on this bright, brave day. This was an odd country, all right, but a feeling almost akin to that of a crusade was growing up about the venture; the men knew that others were snickering or wishing Eads in hell, or at the river bottom itself. That old fellow and his idea had something that took hold of a man and made him want to carry it through. The workmen liked their job.

Living for a time on flatboats, they set out to build quarters for themselves and their equipment. Far down South Pass sprang up Port Eads, a place with few neighbors except porpoises and alligators. The jetty workers became part of the history, and also part of the population, of the Delta. Of many grandfathers, it is said with pride, "He worked for Ead'." Events are often measured "before the jettie'," or "after Ead' came." Eads remains a hero, like some of the early pirates, or Beauregard, or the grandpère who caught a 250-pound turtle.

Young engineers scrambled over mud lumps, chased the awkward pelicans, and ran lines through the quaking prairies. Some broke into a sweat when a female 'gator with young hissed at them, and boasted of their escape. Natives who lived alone in thatched huts watched this behavior and told their aquatic hogs that all this foolishness would never amount to anything.

Along the river bank, workers pulled away at the slight willows wherever they found them. Eads had decided to use these by-products of the Mississippi's flow as a major item in its curbing. While the floating pile drivers sank posts into places for the outlines of the jetties, wide timber ways rose at the edge of land, and men struggled to "weave" huge mattresses of the willow brush. The slight woods bent easily as they were crisscrossed, but Eads knew that they were tough and would hold well. Each mattress, or mat, had a firm wooden base, and was braced and cross-stripped; it was one hundred or so feet long, two feet thick, thirty-five to fifty feet wide. When a mat was finished, it was towed out and sunk with heavy rocks. One was placed above the other, with the rock between and on top; each was narrower than the one beneath. Thus double, man-made levees were extended slowly through the water for nearly two miles and a half into the Gulf.

Troubles were not long in arising. To obtain funds under his hard agreement, Eads had to pay high interest rates and borrow heavily. In one case he promised a ten percent return, plus a profit of one hundred percent. At intervals he had to turn to various persons for emergency loans to prevent collapse of the enterprise. During another period payrolls were held up for two months. The men were summoned; and they agreed to stay on the job.

Construction itself offered discouragements. As many had predicted, the river and Gulf snatched angrily at the mats when they could. A heavy gale tore off top layers; piling collapsed, and Eads' helpers had to devise ways to prevent repetition of such incidents. He must proceed with every possible speed; he could take no time to ponder refinements. Also they must work at the upper as well as the lower part of the pass; shoals spread above like those below. A further danger offered itself there. While he was building constrictions at the bottom, might the stream adjust itself simply by sending more of its flow through the other passages? To prevent this from happening, small dams were erected to close off some of the lesser outlets. At the Head of Passes they built deflections to push the water in the desired directions. Eads deepened the flow here, made it shallow there. This, in truth, was tampering with the river.

Now men began to sicken in this sun and air. A doctor was in constant attendance. Yellow fever hit suddenly; work had to be suspended, and Eads lost some of his most expert assistants, who like him had learned the job by experience. Despite everything, the project progressed. Early in the following year high water arrived. The crews watched in apprehension as the yellow tide snarled about them. A thing was happening that men had never witnessed before. The full force of one of the river passes, pouring downward, was finding serious obstructions at each side. Would the Mississippi smash the jetties, send them spinning in pieces? Clouds of churning mud rose. The river was fighting, and the jetties were answering. Soundings indicated deep gougings at one place, quick deposits at another. Suddenly the soundings showed a sharp downward trend: eighteen feet, nineteen, at some places twenty-one! But could this be depended upon? A test would be made, Eads decided.

It might have been more prudent to wait, to check, ponder, and recheck. But stories were being spread that the jetties already were complete failures. One hostile official made his own soundings at a certain point, found a depth of only twelve feet, and decided that a new bar was forming. Eads was positive that this was the last part of an old obstruction that the river was now cutting away. But the report was in circulation over the country; all of the work was in danger.

Eads had a friend, Captain E. V. Gager, who operated a well-known passenger steamer from New York, the *Hudson*. If it went through, the nation would know and applaud. If the *Hudson* stuck, the word would spread with equal or greater rapidity, and Eads would be ruined. But Captain Gager had confidence. Eads said the *Hudson* would go through; then, by the eternal, she *would* go through. The captain put everything in readiness, shook hands all around, and turned to the pilot. Straight for the bar, man!

Straight for the bar it was. The pilot's eyes darted left and right, then ahead. The rest gazed forward, then stole glances at their neighbors. Had they hit something? It was only the imagination of one of the group. The jetties now extended on both sides; the *Hudson* advanced toward what had always been the crest of the bar. At any moment now might come a drag, a grating pull from below. It did not come. They hit deep water; the test was over. There would be more troubles, later; but Eads had shown that he could do the job.

Within a few years, a channel thirty feet deep had been obtained and Eads' followers had another last laugh. The South Pass route, as he had feared, was soon crowded beyond capacity, and Orleanians assured each other that all of this should have been done in the bigger outlet in the way Eads had first proposed. And so Southwest Pass saw jetty construction after all, but by the Army engineers themselves. Though these jetties were of greater size, their plans followed Eads' in the essentials.

As work ended at Port Eads, the bustling community declined. Today only a small cluster of trappers, oystermen, and boatmen for the pilots remain there with their families. A lighthouse rises, gleaming white in the sun, a comforting, sturdy sentinel in bad weather. A few children play about the water, and waves splash over the lines of broken rock that mark the jetties' progress into the Gulf. Thrust out into the water, almost lost in the grasses and driftwood, Eads' old town is one of the loneliest spots in which I have ever found myself.

There is now another settlement at the lower end of Southwest Pass—Burrwood, home of the United States Engineers and their helpers. To this advanced point, guarding the main passage in and out of the river, the government brought vast supplies of concrete, wood, metal, and other materials to build up a stable, sanitary town, a kind of model community with painted buildings, well-mowed lawns and cement walks. A mile long, almost as wide, Burrwood is spotted with the shadings of thick rose bushes, the whites and heavy scarlets of oleanders; and tall palms sway in the Gulf breezes, to give the place the touch of a colonial outpost on some South Sea island.

Regularly from Burrwood move the survey crews, to check up on the river. Small towers rise along the channel; week by week, year by year, khaki-clad men visit each in turn, climbing over slippery banks, falling over grass-and-rock edges. The lead-and-line drops into the water for the readings. Marks go down on pads; notes are taken to the office, where draftsmen fill in maps with incredibly minute detail. Is she silting up a little here? She's down, though, on the other side. In the central headquarters reports are compared, decisions made, and vessels start out to make the changes that the engineers order. A seagoing dredge, radio-equipped, tears large mouthfuls of dripping mud from the bottom, drops it into the hopper, and moves out to deposit the silt beyond the river flow.

These men joke and swear at the river's idiosyncrasies. They have acquired a philosophy of their job; they are a little proud of the Old Man's steady arrogance, his refusal to obey orders. The Mississippi, they will tell you, has never been fully conquered. Man will never know all of its secrets. Sometimes, in a manner that cannot be explained, it will pile up silt six feet high, and a year of work may be required to restore the former levels. Eddies behave in mysterious fashion; "sucks" drag skiffs and heavy logs far below the surface. A buoy anchored in thirty feet of water at Southwest Pass was reported one morning to be sinking. In three days the river had torn a hole one hundred and four feet deep. For three months the hollow continued, though another buoy a short distance away was unaffected. Then the hole quickly disappeared.

Though it seems longer, only seventy-five years have passed since Eads made his changes. Engineers keep a wary watch; they maintain the jetties; they cut away recurring obstructions; and some wonder what this scene will be like another seventy-five years hence. The jetties stretch far out into the blue water, thin, disappearing lines to the south. Pelicans wheel low to take sad stations on the last wet pilings. Out of the sky swoops a single man-of-war bird, and the gulls screech away into the distance. In the late afternoon, the air and water change to a heavy, leaden hue, and a cloud covers the setting sun. The waters are beating wildly now at the grasses and the rocks. Man's alterations on the Mississippi are to stand yet another test.

PART III

SHADOWS AND TURBULENCE

CHAPTER 12

Death of an Era

FOR a century and more, since those sugar experiments of Mendez and de Boré, the great cane plantations had maintained themselves in the Delta. But gradually the pound of the rollers had been lessening; the gray plumes of factory smoke behind the levees had thinned. With the 1900's an ominous cloud had moved over the horizon of the men and women who made their living from this product of the soil. The Delta, where sugar cane first became an important crop, was on its way to collapse as a sugar center.

Why that happened is a subject over which the older natives will argue long and differ bitterly. Each has an explanation of his own, and is scornful of that offered by his fellows. The reason is not a simple one, but a complex of many factors. The Delta had originally thrived because it possessed several advantages. It was near the heart of the sugar system, close to the capital city of New Orleans. A succession of growers worked at the fertile soil with skill. But imperceptibly the area was losing its margin of difference.

The Sugar Bowl of Louisiana enlarged, spreading up the river and to the west beyond the Mississippi. The length and breadth of South Louisiana lay ready for the cane. The Delta could offer only the narrow ridge of its peninsula into the Gulf. In other places the plantations were growing mightily in scale; so, too, were the central factories. Operations were becoming mechanized, increasing in scope; and the estates below New Orleans, large as they seemed, lacked room for expansion. They stretched for miles along the Mississippi; but toward the back, as always, there was only so much space before marsh or swamp was reached.

The proximity to the great city was coming to mean less and

less. New waterways were being opened up, and steam vessels or railroads could take the produce from other sugar fields to New Orleans almost as quickly as it could be moved there from the Delta. At the same time, other forces were at work, forces whose real nature has not been perceived until recent years, whose full effect is not as yet known. Through much of the Delta a process of gradual sinkage is taking place, a settling of the soft silts and vegetable remains. Some of this is the subsidence of the earth which, since the levees have been built, is no longer renewed by annual deposits of silt. In addition, say the geologists, the river has been depositing billions of tons of silt toward the Gulf, to create an immeasurable downward pressure upon the surrounding surfaces. The land to the east and west of the Mississippi is thus being "tilted" by slow degrees. Islands are falling beneath the surface, and the lakes and Gulf are reaching always inward.

Men noticed that the ground at the back of their plantations seemed a bit lower. At one spot it was beginning to be wet where surely they had found it dry the previous spring; at another the water stood inches deep, though it had barely covered the soil until a year or two ago. The planters frowned, erected back levees or strengthened older ones. They dug more canals, installed new pumps to draw the water out. The subsidence did not of itself mean an end to the plantations in most places; but additional precautions must now be taken, to add heavily to the inconveniences and to the costs of operation. The regular cultivation of the ground became more difficult, because the earth "compacted" and lowered slightly as a consequence. And the brine found other ways to enter, penetrating beneath the embankments from time to time, so that when the sun beat down scale-like deposits of crystallized salt were formed.

"When I saw that, I decided to leave," a man now in New Orleans explains. "I could deal with everything else—enemies in business, brokers, labor. But not the Gulf of Mexico." Others clung; everything that they owned was sunk here. The family would have to reduce its scale of living; there could be no trip to the Atlantic coast this year; and regardless of what anyone thought, the box at the French Opera must be given up. Yet each year saw a still harder struggle against competition up the river and elsewhere. Any factors that were against the interests of the Louisiana sugar man—tariff change, demands of workers for better pay—were felt to that much greater extent by the Delta owner. He had additional weights to carry. Sugar was becoming for many a crop without profit.

Some establishments continued a precarious existence. The first large expenditure that was called for, and they must shut down. A sugar house burned, or the winds did heavy damage. A group of serious-faced men rode down from the city, to spend an hour or so in an inspection of the scene, while the family waited on the gallery for the decision. The slow steps of the master, as he escorted his guests back to the house, gave the answer. It was over, their stay in the Delta. And the word went up and down the river: Another one gone.

"Whole plantations"—meaning the machinery required to operate them—were taken away by steamer to new places along the river, or to Cuba and the other islands, Louisiana's competitors. Among those who watched were often an aged Negro man or two who could recall another day when vessels had puffed down the Mississippi to bring this same equipment. They had been young and spry then, the material new and shining. Now they and it were well worn; but for the steel and the wheels there was still a use.

The line of owners thinned, until only a few were left, their buildings fading, one wing closed off, then another. In the early 1920's, disaster struck the sugar business of the state. Disease almost cleared Louisiana of cane. With the introduction of more resistant varieties, the crop came back; but it did not return to the Delta. The acres that once grew the big grass now produced other crops, or nothing. During the past few years a group of growers tried to reintroduce sugar. With government help, they imported seed cane and equipment. The fishermen, the trappers, and the truck gardeners looked at the tight, waving rows and wondered. The patches were minute in comparison with the acres of earlier years. But it was cane, and to the old people who watched it lifting and falling in the wind it brought memories. The first of the crop came in; it was taken to New Orleans, then up the river to a refinery. The double freight bill sent the expense higher than any possible profit; the rows slowly yellowed and rotted where they stood.

At the edge of a large lagoon a man points out the boundaries of what was once a well-cultivated stretch. For some years, through the dark, soil-steeped liquids, the outlines of abandoned furrows could be made out; now they, too, are gone. Near a sagging back levee stands a small wreck, the frame that housed a powerful drainage machine; the waters that it once held back slip about and through it. A seventy-year-old Deltan nudges my arm: "See that place way out there in the water? When I was eighteen I walked with my uncle there, and the crops rose higher than his head. Now they hunts ducks in the same place!" He is silent a moment, then he asks, almost to himself, "Did any of us ever think this could happen?"

All that is left of the cane factories are the chimneys, thick brick spires reaching into the sky, still the tallest objects between the river mouth and the city. Of the boxlike buildings that always flanked them only an occasional wall stands, unsupported, useless. The chimneys have not been worth the trouble of removal. Scattered about the Delta is an irregular procession of these monuments to the former regime. Along their sides climb thick vines, sometimes so concealing them that they appear to be swollen bushes extending toward the clouds. They were built well, for a future that has had no wish for them.

Here and there a number of the houses have held on, and well-to-do men who purchased them have worked over them with paint and brick. But gone are the wide green acres that gave plantation life its purpose. The new owners visit on week ends or stay for a while; a caretaker is left in charge at other times. The refurbished establishments, with a bit of additional ironwork and new windows, shine pleasantly in the well-maintained gardens. But I remember what an aged mulatto woman, possessor of a sprinkling of white chin whiskers and also of a shrewd perception, said of one of them. Sitting under an oak, using her snuff, she poked her cane in its direction and laughed: "Jus' like it laid out for a wake, ahn? Dress' up pretty, and people sit aroun'. But it ain' alive!"

More often the searcher finds only a burned fragment or a

cracked shell of the mansion. Nature is taking it and its surroundings back from the intruder, man. Each season sees a further advance of the green tentacles of surrounding growths. Tropical plants slide over the walls and the sagging door frames. Into fields which have lain fallow for several years moves the advance guard of a new forest, the twisted cottonwoods and myrtles. The trees drop leaves and moss in thickening layers, and out of the rich base other vines and creepers spread quickly, to make gains and then consolidate them. The rainy season, even a single prolonged downpour, hastens the process of wreckage. The drip of the dews and the wet deposits of the fogs warp the woods; as they disintegrate and dissolve, they become lodging places for creeping things, lizards, chameleons, ants, insects, the small and restless life of the half-tropics. A French mother will warn her children: "Keep away from that pes'-house. It's a zoo!"

Of the formal gardens, set out with care, only traces survive. The bricks that lined a curving path have been removed. Delicate imports have been choked by grosser plants, but some survive in changed forms—carefully tended flowers gone wild, mixing with the commoner breed. Among the stiff-fanned palmettoes rise blazing tropical blossoms, crimson, deep orange, splashing purple; and above it all the live oaks, proper fathers to this tangled profusion, lift their ropy arms.

Urns and statuary have broken, to rest on cracked sides in heaps that may be the middens of Delta civilization for future inquirers. In one case I uncovered the upper half of a garden figure, a classic cherub in marble, with formally curled hair and a plump hand holding draperies. The face had now a greenish tinge; the acid fingers of Delta nature had been at work. It was the most aged and the most malevolent cherub that the imagination could conjure up.

Though the masters left, many of the servants did not. They clung on in the same small buildings that had been theirs in slavery and post-slavery days. The Negro quarters, rows of faded red brick huts with unpainted window frames, have seemed the most stable, the most permanent part of the plantations. They have become small villages, and as such they frequently keep the names of the dead owners. For miles they are a roll-call of departed glory. They will, perhaps, be the last evidence to prove that here rose a place of magnificence among the fields. And surely there is irony in that.

Prime among the sagging victims of these years of change stands Orange Grove, a study in incongruity along the Mississippi. The scene is St. Bernard parish, not far from English Turn. To reach the main building from the road is not easy; a path must be cut through undergrowth. Some, seeing Orange Grove for the first time, have said that they did not quite believe it. Once complete to final details, it remains a three-storied array of pointed gables, sharply sloping roof lines, tri-sectioned windows and ornate, carved cornices. In its setting of live oaks, water lilies and banana plants, it stands forth as an exercise in heavy whimsy—an English-Gothic manor in toto.

The castle is nearly a century old. Thomas Asheton Morgan was a descendant of sturdy fighters in the American Revolution, but his own interests went directly back to the mother country. For his home he imported piles of materials, hand-pressed bricks, tiles, lumber; and he knew just what he wanted done with them. The neighbors blinked at the emerging lines of his medieval structure. They gaped at the formal English gardens with the summerhouse near the levee, at the several fountains and, not least, at the stained-glass windows with the Morgan coat-of-arms above the front door and that of the Asheton branch over the back.

Defying all South Louisiana custom, Morgan built a large basement, with thick brick walls and arches. He might have one of the dampest spots in the New World; but he would have his basement. A friend suggested that in this climate a porch was almost a necessity. Morgan ordered an enormous gallery, ponderously arched, columned, and ornamented.

Acquiring a neighboring plantation, Morgan called it Caernarvon after an old family estate on the other side of the ocean. The vicinity in time received the designation of Braithwaite, and to another property was given the title of Kenilworth. Visitors eventually commented with a grin on the use of these British names so near to old English Turn. Morgan went ahead in his own style, and a lavish and individual style it was. He is remembered by the Deltans in large part because of his ideas about baths. He devised a method of providing private hot water facilities, which some have said was unique for its period and place. A furnace was set up on each floor; into every room led pipes to a basin at which the water could be drawn. When the occupant was ready to wash, he notified a servant who worked at the mechanism outside, and after a time, wonderfully, a man had warm water in his room. Some came especially to see the remarkable sight.

For all his Anglican inclinations, Morgan was a strong advocate of the national government. When the Civil War broke out, he suffered the ill-will of fellow plantation owners by speaking for the Union. In 1867 he sold the plantation to Louis Fasnacht, originally of Switzerland. By contrast Mr. Fasnacht was a Southern sympathizer, who had struggled hard to manufacture a military balloon for the Confederates. Relatives recall how the women of the family contributed petticoats and old dresses and sewed them together at the inventor's orders. How well the garments negotiated the air currents is a question.

It was during the Fasnacht period that Orange Grove received its name. On the property a thick line of the trees grew up, nearly two miles long. When visitors left they usually took away small baskets of the fruit as souvenirs. The good-humored Fasnachts enjoyed entertaining. Callers came by barouche, victoria, and buggy, or on flatboats towed down from New Orleans, with musical entertainment en route. Accounts describe peacocks in the gardens, a neat windmill near the summerhouse, and lighted Chinese lanterns among the trees, casting illumination alike on Tudor roof and Louisiana cypress.

But the life at Orange Grove grew less easy. By 1885 the Fasnachts gave it up. An English syndicate acquired stock of the St. Bernard railroad, and decided to make other investments. To the sugar men of the vicinity the United Railway and Trading Company made a proposition: It would put up a new mill, the greatest that the parish had ever known, if they would use its facilities. They consented; the firm acquired several large holdings in the area, and then began an experiment, not always happy, in absentee ownership.

Every year with the grinding season there arrived a mild-mannered fat man in a bowler hat, who "said very little and that to just a few people"; who observed carefully and wrote things in a notebook. The season over, he shook hands gravely and returned to England. Some months later, in every case, the officials sent a brief message of felicitation on the season's success, or an equally brief note of a change in management. Less regularly, without warning, two dry-mannered, dry-skinned individuals stepped off a train. They would look at the books now, please. They looked, exchanged whispered questions and nods, then ranged over the scene. How many head of cattle were there in the stables now? Six months ago? Two years ago? How many pieces of equipment? . . . The workers quivered at the sight of these relentless inquisitors. A resident manager who proposed mild amenities—a luncheon, two tickets to a theatre—was repelled with a look. Bribery, it was clear, would get him nowhere.

Sometimes the British owners were resolutely determined not to assent to local methods. For a new plant, Louisiana friends advised a heavy piling foundation, always used in South Louisiana. The company replied that so unorthodox a procedure would hardly be necessary, thank you. Soon the wall began to crack and sink in two opposite directions. Hurriedly, at great cost and some hazard, new foundations were inserted and heavy chains installed to tie the sections together.

About the settlement of Braithwaite ("Brait'waite" in local parlance) the population grew until it reached fifteen hundred. A bag factory, a commercial alcohol plant, and other enterprises made their appearance. From the rice-growing borders of the river, and from the marshes, Delta natives were drawn to the spot. Yet the sugar refinery, heart of the settlement, was losing. The planters kept their word to take their products to it, but they themselves went out of business one by one. The sugar plant closed; the other factories continued. Then successive levee breaks practically washed out equipment, or clogged it with sand and other deposits. The owners in England showed concern over the location, and complained that the parish officials, impoverished by the decline of the plantations, were imposing excessive taxes. One establishment, then another, closed, and Braithwaite was on its way to dissolution. Today it has the air of a ghost town. The population has dropped to less than two hundred and fifty; small buildings stand tenantless; those who have stayed scrape along at farming and anything else that offers itself, and remember better days.

Dominating the creeping decay is Orange Grove. Some time earlier I had known it when a friend planned a restoration. I returned after five years, to wonder first at the still-towering strength of the walls, then not less at the results of the buffetings it had received. Vandal nature and vandal man have scored heavily. The overpowering gallery vanished long ago, leaving only gaping wall holes into which the heavy supports were once fastened. Carvings of wood that had clung for years along the sharply-pointed roof line—these went in a storm. The imported roof tiles were replaced by corrugated tin; even this has not held, so that each rain sends down a flood to work further wreckage. Twice the building has been threatened, when adjoining properties caught fire. Sparks destroyed a small corner of the rear section. The neighbors say that nothing is lucky enough to escape three times.

From inside, even on a summer day, the mansion exudes a clammy breath of decay. The sunlight pours through the windows, but there is gloom about everything that it touches. Finely-fashioned diamond window-panes are gone; visitors who wanted anchors for fishing lines ripped out the lead. Double window frames, six feet across, have been yanked from their hinges, a few to lie among the vines below, others to serve as firewood somewhere else. Marble fireplaces have been removed, parts of them put to work as headstones for graves.

Yet the Deltans have not done as well as wind and water. Streaks and jagged cracks spread along the walls. "That one come after 1901 . . . 1893 done that. . . ." The natives count the stages of Orange Grove's damage by the storms and floods. As we walk about the echoing hallways, bits of plaster fall; in the partitions animals scurry noisily. "Watch out," my guide warns. We duck, and a flight of bats wings past.

Through a hazardous rear entrance we descend into the dank basement. My guide grasps my arm to prevent me from falling into a cavity in the floor. He snickers: "Treasure hole." Seekers of gold have come often to this place that has seen everything, perhaps, except pirates. Some say that there was a reason, a secret reason, why Morgan built a house with a bottom section like this. Men have come here with "magic pointers," wands and electric devices, and quarreled, and accused one another of trickery, of removing the gold while their partners were away. And others will come and search again.

We leave the basement for a view of the river. From a high attic the broad sweep of English Turn is in sight. The trees of the opposite bank offer a dim blue background to the closer foliage. At this same place the Morgans and the Fasnachts must have watched the slow parade of the ships on many occasions. I realize for the first time how close we are to the Mississippi. A woman in a yellow dress paddles in a skiff, and we hear her call to a child on the bank. What has happened to the long sweep of trees and floral plantings before the mansion? The native shakes his head: "In the river; and the res', she is going quick."

As sugar declined, another crop slowly advanced itself, that of citrus fruit. The orange was introduced in Louisiana when the early Jesuits imported a few sweet seedlings. The plantation owners in the Delta acquired sour as well as sweet varieties, first as decorations about the gardens, later as a crop of sorts. But the growers found difficulties. Visiting Pláquemines in 1847, R. L. Allen observed that the orange trees bore well but that after a few years disease reduced them. "Every known remedy has been hitherto tried in vain," he reported, "and as a last resource the limbs have been lopped off and in many cases even the trunk cut down to the ground to give a fresh and more vigorous growth that might possibly resist attack." Maunsell White informed him that in one year his trees yielded more than a thousand dollars; shortly afterward he had to slash them to the trunks.

And orange-growing fitted poorly into the sugar scheme. A plantation owner had concerns enough with his cane; when his prospects seemed good, he was always tempted to devote every inch of space to the big crop itself. A mile or so shifted to anything else might mean thousands of dollars less at the end of a season of fine prices. Until after the Civil War, the oranges continued a minor venture. Gradually other Deltans came to realize that a rich source of return lay near them. Some of the many Burases around the town of Buras set out new trees. A number of the Dalmatians joined them. The Italians in their luggers spied the golden globes of fruit shining in the low-hung orchards, and took the produce up the river.

New Orleans gave the oranges a quick welcome. Of all parts of Louisiana, it now became clear, the west bank of the Delta produced a superb citrus fruit; the orange culture of Louisiana would center here. The Deltans of the lower sections took advantage of every foot of their narrow soil, increasing their rows, extending them everywhere. They spread their plantings far down toward the Jump and the hunter-fishermen's town of Venice, then to the back wherever it was dry. They worked hard with their hoes, they struck at the encroaching grasses and other pests, and they succeeded handsomely. Then, toward the end of the nineteenth century, they suffered a sudden blow. One terrible year of frost and most of the trees were wiped out.

But they learned. They turned to a more resistant, hardier growth, the sour orange, for a rootstock, and on this they grafted the sweeter fruit. They experimented with mandarins (the "kid glove" variety), with satsumas, kumquats, tangerines, and grapefruit, from Italy, Japan and other places. One grinning Deltan showed me a tree on which he had grafted six distinct kinds of fruits, of as many different hues. A certain amount of crowding was necessary here, but they found that trees planted too close together produced limited quantities of fruit. Ever since then a gradual thinning out has been taking place, but the Delta citrus growths are still tightly packed.

In time the traveler walked along roads lined on both sides with the dark-leaved trees, heavy with their burdens. They surrounded the small houses back, front and sides. In the spring the white, star-shaped flowers blossomed about the galleries, and over the river and the ponds and lakes at the rear floated the heavy perfume. In the fall, the Deltan had only to reach out of his window to pluck what he wanted.

For most, oranges did not change the earlier ways of living. They remained only one of the seasonal crops. The owners of the small acreages did a bit of farming, raised rice, looked for shrimp, and hunted animals. When a man was away his wife and children looked after the grove. Methods of handling and shipping remained somewhat casual. The Italian luggerman appeared early in the year, to make an offer. He paid half in advance, half when the oranges were ready. At a proper time he appeared with ladders, sacks, and a force of helpers, to "break the crop." The loose oranges were piled up near the lugger and poured into the hold, to remain there for days under a tarpaulin. At the French Market, the vessel drew up and the fruit was dumped out again. Part of it went in hampers to the Market itself; peddlers took what they could get, to sell at the rate of a penny each. And much of the crop was taken to warehouses, boxed and marked "Choice Florida Oranges." Florida was organized; the word would sell produce where "Louisiana" would not.

The problem of freezes had largely been settled; that of blights had not. These were imported along with the citrus growths from Japan and elsewhere and thrived in the mellow Delta air, to bring the crop almost to ruin. State and federal agricultural officials moved down, to destroy miles of trees. Furious Deltans watched agents use axes on groves that they had expected to see produce without interruption for all of their lives. One or two threatened to shoot the interlopers, and ended by firing bullets into their own brains. But the situation improved. The Deltans set up packing sheds, washed, polished, and packed their fruit; grading was introduced with benefits to most of the growers. A number of extensive enterprises were developed, by Dalmatians and Italians in most cases. But to a great degree the crop continues that of the smaller operator, and as often as not he is a Frenchman.

The "Creole Sweet" is thin-skinned, juice-packed and aromatic. The "Louisiana Navel" grows to such size that it is sometimes mistaken for a grapefruit. The Deltans labor earnestly over their trees. Toward their oldest, favorite ones they show an affection close to that which they have always held for their boats. They talk happily of the procreative properties of the more ancient growths, of the way the next line must be coaxed along, of the size of the fruit. They prune away dead branches, spray with dusts and mixtures against the small mottling marks that indicate the beginning of disease. They move about under the trees with boxes and clippers, picking up the windfalls and carrying the produce to the sheds.

Buras is the citrus center, with groves extending above and below it in an almost uninterrupted line, branches touching from tree to tree. A few yards from the eddying Mississippi, behind the road that parallels the river, the eye catches the glint of the rich gold oranges, the pale yellow-greens of the grapefruit and the blood tints of the tangerines.

There are thousands who do not miss the cane.

CHAPTER 13

Rage in the Skies

THE month was September of 1915. The Delta baked pleasantly in a summer that gave few signs of ending. Over the tepid silver-blue bays about the river mouth the gray shrimp leaped in the slanting sun-rays. About their camps among the hills of burning-white oyster shells the Tockos sang as they moved their produce; it was a good season. The French tested their animal traps and sipped a bit of orange wine while they planned their annual visits to the marsh. This was the storm month, yes, when the old people always looked for trouble from the Gulf; but it seemed as if they would miss it this year, ahn?

The hot, golden days went on. One night the Deltans woke to a rattling against their windows, a beating and rushing among the thickets of willows at the river edge. They slammed batten shutters, closed doors usually left open to the air, and slept again. They rose to a rainswept morning, but none worried. This was just a lil' squall from below. Before noon the sun broke out of the clouds, and the children ran about the levee again. The next few days dawned bright and glinting. See, it was what the Americans called false alarm.

Then some noticed the river level. Up for this time of year, non? Eh, the wind was from the south; when she changed, the river would drop down again. You watch. But the air currents altered, and still the Mississippi rose, oddly, unaccountably. Out at the bays and Gulf edges, the oystermen and shrimpers found the waves up a foot, then two feet and more. Now the wind was bearing directly out of the north, and the river still lifted, higher with each day. The fishermen kept at the caulking of their vessels, the women at their net-mending. Down the Delta a message filtered, carried from where the recently installed telephone lines left off. The people in New Orleans said a storm was on the way, and many along the river were going into the city. But in the lower Delta little concern was felt. We'll be safe here on the river bank where it's highest; this ain' anything bad. Jus' a few scared folks. Those nearest the Gulf, and to the rear, heard nothing of any warnings.

They did not know that the worst tropical hurricane in the history of Louisiana, which had known many and terrible ones, was howling upon them from the south.

The twenty-ninth of September came grimly. The sky was an expanse of dun-colored clouds that hung low and sped by as if whipped. The wind pulled and tore first from one direction, then another. Streamers of rain beat against the grasses of the levees, poured into the house yards, filled ditches and sent swift currents gurgling to the back sections. Canals were soon overflowing; some who paddled cautiously from the river through these passages stopped on reaching a certain point; what had been green marsh was now only gray-blue lake with small points of grass waving wildly above it. At the old drainage pumps men labored for a time, then gave up. The water was advancing too rapidly from the low sections. And along the bays and canals to the back, others stared in surprise as the sea moved to the top of their shell mounds, then crept up and up along the stilt-legs of the camps.

A few made their way to the Mississippi to perform forgotten chores, attaching their boats bow and stern along the banks. Never had they seen the river itself so threatening. The Gulf invaded the stream; the water, a mad and writhing expanse, showed a sea-green tinge. The air had almost the same strange coloration, a half-luminous, foreboding shade that touched everything. The spray rose heavily; for long minutes it was impossible to see more than a foot or so away. Here and there the air currents gouged at the water itself, lifting layers to send them scudding ahead. The men did not stay long at the river banks; they hurried to their homes. Outside, bracing themselves, they inspected the poles and other supports that they had installed years ago to protect their houses. When they gazed up at the skies from these chores, they were not reassured. All morning the shore birds had rushed by in low flights, giving cries that had almost a note of human terror. Now came a sign that they had been taught to recognize as a final warning: far up, black and solemn, winged the hardy man-of-war, or "storm," birds. When they headed steadily inland, fury was not far behind.

Inside, a husband found his wife kneeling before a holy picture and a saucer in which tapers flickered. In the halflight the children huddled large-eyed on the bed. Buckets were in place to catch the water, but the floor was thoroughly wetted nevertheless. The mother crossed herself, and asked, Could they leave? Maybe they might flag a boat? He shook his head. They could only wait.

The wind changed to a high-pitched wail, like the despairing cry of a doomed people. From the back of the house came a sudden heavy thud. One of the girls screamed, and the mother held her to quiet her sobs. It was their back room, that they had added last year. Up and down the river, small buildings, galleries, and side sections were beginning to go.

Noon approached, an hour of blackness. Food waited, but none touched it. They heard the torment of the trees outside, the cracking of willows and cottonwoods; against their walls crashed objects whose identities they could only guess. At the window a crack developed and a thick stream poured in. They tried to work upon it; the whole framework, sill and all, was wrenched from outside and sent flying off. The rain beat in without hindrance and the wind, now an icy blast, blew out the tapers. The mother continued to pray.

Over the mounting rage of the elements whispered a small gurgle. Water was lapping somewhere, insistently. With trembling hand, the oldest boy pointed to a corner; a stream was slipping inward from below. The water had reached the level of the house. The father went to a drawer, brought forth a brace and bit and went to work to bore a hole in the floor, and then more of them, to let in the water. This would steady the building; otherwise it might be pulled off its pilings at once. For miles along the river and along the canals, other Deltans were doing the same thing. The water bubbled up in pools, and families climbed upon tables and beds, to watch with a kind of fascination.

Down at Burrwood, the Engineers' station at Southwest Pass, word spread that the hurricane would hit in the immediate vicinity that day. Two heavy government dredges were ready; men loaded their carrying tanks with water so that the vessels would sink deeper, and then double-anchored them in the center of the pass, to prevent them from being driven upon the banks. From every direction appeared fishermen and trappers with their wives and children. Their skiffs and yawls inched toward the dredges, fighting swells in which they bobbed like bits of paper. The engineers' crews stood on the slippery decks to give a hand. Care must be taken lest the frailer boats break apart in a moment against the thick sides of the dredges. The crews held planks between the vessels to form swaying bridges. They tossed ropes, the natives fastened them to their waists, then crawled across to safety. Some slipped into the upreaching sea, but in every case a rescue was made. Then the small boats were turned adrift to be washed away or ground to pieces against the embankments.

Abruptly, about one o'clock of the dark afternoon, hell hammered down. From the Gulf, up the river, came a savage roar. With the winds moved some of the highest tides ever known in the area, gleaming, foam-topped towers of water, five, eight, sometimes thirteen feet tall. Behind the first rolled another and another, advancing with a power that wrecked almost anything in their path. For two uninterrupted hours the wind at Burrwood raged at 107 to 108 miles; then it went to 124, and at one point showed the terrifying figure of 140.

Thrusts of air tore at the barges, making many drop to their knees and cross themselves. In one moment the water leaped in weird formations; in the next, the wind bit deep and the waves opened wide. Under the crash of churning waters the heavy vessels shook and lifted and lowered. The refugees slid about the decks. But the dredges held.

Over the narrow peninsulas of earth to both banks of the Mississippi the waves advanced quickly. For miles all land was lost. There remained no distinction between river and Gulf; all seemed a single sheet. The only protections were the higher tops of the natural banks or the artificial levees along the river; on these the tidal waves and the wind set quickly to work, tearing, crushing. Mile after mile of the mud embankments crumbled; at one stretch nearly twenty miles of earth disappeared in a few hours.

Old men saw tall trees under which their fathers had played bending now to the ground, their branches pulled all in one direction like the loosened hair of a woman. Winds struck at century-old live oaks, long the sturdiest of all obstacles, and cracked them apart near their bases. The roofs of houses were whisked off, their walls swept away one by one until the families within had only the floor to cling to and were themselves washed away. Floating logs became battering rams, smashing in sides of buildings. Other structures were forced, almost intact, from their pilings, and rolled about in the waters until they fell to pieces. One house "leap-frogged" another, to smash into a third and kill all within it. People marooned in their houses made rafts of their doors and wooden bedsteads and held to them as water filled the rooms. When it raised them to their ceilings they climbed into the attics. They heard cries from outside that might be human or animal. It made little difference; these were the sounds of the lost.

In St. Bernard parish small homes had been growing up on the sites of abandoned plantations. New Hope was a collection of cottages and a two-storied grocery that served the environs. Three weeks earlier George Thiel, an elderly fisherman, had moved to New Hope, investing his life savings of four hundred and fifty dollars in one of the houses. With him and his wife were his daughter, his son-in-law, and their three children. The Thiels, like their neighbors, had full confidence in the strength of their walls; hadn't the builders given good assurances?

In the early afternoon the houses went all at once, swept from their moorings. The people who had taken refuge in the grocery prepared to leave. Thiel managed to herd his family and the others into a gasoline launch that he normally watched for a city sportsman. They clung, wet and desperate, inside the vessel. Their surroundings were a half-open sea; the wind grew rapidly worse. At least they could try to steer to a safer place. They were tossed and battered about until, suddenly, the boat was lifted and whirled in the air. All fell into the beating waters. In the deepening darkness women and children gasped and screamed to the men. Old Thiel and the rest swam frantically, calling, feeling for their families. One saw his wife and their two young boys, clutching tightly to her. Starting after them, he cried out as a heavy log struck her head. She went down at once, carrying the children with her. He dived to find them. A friend picked him up shortly afterward, semiconscious, and alone.

Most of the party, including all of Thiel's family, were drowned. A few found their way back to the launch; Thiel huddled in sorrow at the wheel. They were being swept slowly toward the open Gulf and death. The vessel leaked badly; by eleven that night it was sinking, but in the center of a mass of drift. The group crawled precariously to a log, and clung there for the night, as the winds bit their faces and the salt burned their lips and torn hands. About them swarmed thousands of mosquitoes, adding to their agony. Hours later saw them within sight of a high roof. It was the New Hope grocery. It and its occupants were unhurt.

In another case three women and their husbands left their homes as the water drew closer. They crowded into a single skiff. The waves tore about them, more and more dangerously; toward them came a floating housetop. With their oars the men snagged it and scrambled out upon it to test it. It was secure; the first of them reached over to the women. A sudden current struck the skiff and it overturned. The men leaped into the water. One glimpsed his wife, caught at the hem of her dress. Screaming, she was swept by him. The others, thrashing about, heard the shouts of the women, then nothing. They eventually fought their way back to the housetop.

Yet strange rescues were accomplished. A bent, gnarled Negro, who needed two stout canes to walk, went forth into the howls of the elements, and survived. He was Edward Moses, a former slave, reported "between 105 and 120 years old"; he said he remembered the Battles of New Orleans on this same site. Once of gigantic stature and almost superhuman strength, he was described as the father of "progeny which were purposely numerous"; these many children "commanded a fortune, while he himself was too valuable to be sold." Now white-haired, bearded, he lived with his frail, elderly wife in a cabin.

The place fell apart quickly, but they managed to extricate themselves from the wreckage. He held to his two sticks and told his wife to take his arm. The wind was tearing down trees a short distance away, and the water was rising to their knees and above. But the old man knew this terrain from daily walks; he started out and maintained his course, taking slow, careful steps, calling encouragement to his wife. From time to time they could go no farther, and waited behind one of the stronger oaks. They slipped, and one helped the other up; so they advanced, he like a black statue in the whirling waters, she like a wraith clasping to it. At last two Spanish fishermen caught sight of them and picked them up.

Oyster fishermen of Plaquemines perished by the score as their flimsy structures tottered in the back camps. In the Bayou Cook area, a party found the waves too high and left their lugger for a hut on stilts. One gust tore the building away, leaving a single stout timber. For nearly twelve hours, as the winds pulled at their wet clothing and the waters crept up with each hour, they kept their arms tightly about the support, and they lived.

In the neighborhood of Doullut's Canal, William Christein decided that his house would go in a few minutes. Leaving everything behind, he took his family to the Hingle store near the waterway. Just as he reached there, the front levee began to fall away. He knew that the store would soon be taken. He rowed his family in a skiff across the raging canal to a small hotel, then returned to persuade those at the store to follow the same plan. They agreed, but the canal was now a wild river. They could not risk it.

Over the canal near the river bank stretched a narrow, unprotected railroad bridge. Men, women, and children fell to their knees to crawl, grasping to the rails to prevent the mounting winds from blowing them off. One girl slipped toward the side, but held with one hand until an uncle caught her. In the middle, a man cried out; a box car had been deserted on the track just ahead, and the winds were driving it upon them. They could not hope to retreat in time. Just as it reached the bridge, so near that they could hear the screech of the metal, the car hit a switch and hurtled in another direction.

Yet only a short distance away the fates were ruthless. A

twelve-year-old girl raced toward a place of safety as the water rushed toward her. Her friends called encouragement; she had only a few more feet to go. Then, in the furious wind, her long dark hair, blown in every direction, suddenly caught on a wire fence. She halted, pulled furiously to extricate herself, and a wall of water swept over her. Another woman found herself alone in a cabin with her three small children. The place floated from its blocks. She carried two to the slope of the levee and went back for the last and oldest one. When she returned, gasping with the effort, she looked toward the river—to see that the embankment was gone. The hand of the Seigneur was heavy that night.

Meanwhile hundreds of luggers in the river were being sunk or crushed to pieces against the levees. Those who had anchored vessels in midstream saw them rocking fiercely, then moving slowly up the river, crashing into others. Vessels along the bank were lifted and deposited on the other side behind the levee; almost miraculously, many escaped damage in that fashion. Everywhere livestock was drowned. Cats, dogs, and other animals sought refuge on floating logs and parts of buildings, to be carried long distances before their supports overturned. In the lower Delta, cows that had been grazing on one bank of the river were swept into the water. They swam or were blown across the stream. As soon as they felt themselves on dry land again, the terrified things went mad, attacking all within sight.

Up at New Orleans, center of the weather-warning system, staff men shuddered at the reports that came in. In charge waited Dr. Isaac M. Cline, one of the important figures in the history of American forecasting. There were reasons why he did not underestimate the powers of a hurricane. In the Galveston tragedy of 1900, he had lost his young wife when their house collapsed under them, and had fought for hours to rescue his children. Since then he had given all of his time to a study of the tides that would indicate the approach of such disasters. Receiving reports of the rising of the waters down the Delta and elsewhere along the Gulf, despite the clear skies of the few preceding days, he had given sharp and specific warnings. All who took his advice saved themselves; thousands moved out of danger; and it was in great part due to his actions that the loss of life was not greater than 275 along the coast between Florida and mid-Louisiana. Early on September twenty-ninth, impatient transportation officials were demanding approval of their arrangements to proceed with service. Some planned to send trains across exposed trestles. To them "Doc" Cline had a clear answer: Do it and they would have the blood of many people on their heads.

New Orleans was hit directly. City lights went off; the place was without power for nearly three days. Parts of the outskirts were under eight feet of water. Three hundred people huddled in the well-anchored Federal Building, sleeping on the floor. Hundreds of roofs were torn off; in the harbor, tugs were sunk and vessels dashed heavily against the wharves. Scores of minor injuries were reported, but in the city proper only two died—hit by flying glass and other debris.

A railroad express, packed with passengers, arrived at the river bank on schedule a short distance above the city. The winds had not reached their full fury; the transfer boat was ready for the crossing. The train coaches were shifted to the boat as usual, and two tugs left with her for a quick run. Hardly a hundred yards from shore, the air currents struck the vessel broadside, and it careened. The tugs worked furiously, but they could only slow her down. Along the river she went, helpless in her struggle. Other vessels managed to get out of her way; she missed several of them by only a few feet. The terrified passengers found themselves out of sight of land, surrounded by a thick wall of rain and mist. The winds tore more than ever about the clumsy boat, threatening to send her crashing into the docks. Finally she was caught in the mud; the tugs released her just in time to escape being crushed by her weight.

The officers of a delayed steamer, the *Creole,* decided to take advantage of a lull. She was the sturdiest ship of her kind; everyone was certain that there was nothing to worry about. Only a few individuals canceled reservations. At ten o'clock, colors flying in the wind and rain, a band playing, the *Creole* headed into the Delta. This was a lark, some said. Look at the rain—almost horizontal, and the way it had just torn the tin roof off that shed! From their vantage points, they smiled as they saw occasional figures bent forward to face the gale.

The high spirits began to sag and fear to take their place. The ship bucked, rose high, then sank low. The wind, which had been about forty-five miles an hour, stepped up to sixty, to eighty, to ninety. Music played, but none danced and few listened. Some became ill and went to their cabins; others were afraid to do so. The vessel was heading directly into the hurricane's heart. Mounds of waves reared into the air; through the spray, passengers could watch the river as it attacked the levees. Wreckage was being pulled into the stream and sent pounding against the steamer. The wind's shriek came through the thick panelings and above the music. An officer estimated that the air currents were moving a hundred miles an hour. Why didn't they turn back? one asked. That was out of the question; they could only forge ahead.

A woman, looking through a window, cried in horror. Among the broken sections of wood and the carcasses of animals, she caught sight of something else—a human body. A man pointed to the other side, at the bank—two prone figures, one contorted. Suddenly they were in the worst area. Through the swirling air and water, atop houses near the broken levees, they could make out people of all ages, huddled together, waving their arms in supplication. A church went hurtling by them; it was the St. Peter's mission at Ostrica, the Dalmatian settlement. A man slipped from the top of a building; whether he was rescued, they never learned. "We could only watch," said one of those passengers. "There were those people, dying about us, calling to us, and we could do nothing." Eventually they tied up in calmer waters, but they did not forget what they had seen. Theirs had been ringside seats at this pageant of death.

That night the Deltans realized that the worst was ended. The wind tore by but now it seemed more a dirge for the lost than a threat to the living. A wan moon came out, to light up a scene of wreckage. Chill air bore down on the ruins over miles of water that did not leave, or lowered its level only gradually. For hundreds, there was no food; worse, no pure drinking water. Most of the survivors possessed only flimsy clothes and no means of lighting fires. They covered themselves with nets, with flour sacking, with anything they could find. Those in the marooned houses at least had some protection. The rest were trapped along the wet mounds of broken levees or the edges of bayous and canals. On all sides lay dead fish, dead cattle, snakes, and muskrats. Many places were coated with a thick, greasy mud, and the waters deposited bits of green, broken as if some animal had chewed them and spat them out. The people on these spots of land caught at logs and built them into tepee-like shelters, in which the sick crouched. Some of the women lay there as they nursed shivering babies at their breasts.

Rescue and assistance came only slowly. Roads were washed away; railroad tracks had been taken at some points, and the water was yet so high that it put out the engines. Boats came down the river, but travel along the side and back passageways was frequently impossible. They were badly clogged, their courses often changed overnight by the forces of the wind. When some looked at the remains of the levees, they wept. The view was expressed that the protections of the lower river were forever gone. They would not, could not be repaired. It turned out that these prophets were in error.

Relief workers were startled at the damage and not less at the want. At Empire, where once there had been eighty buildings, only twelve stood. At Olga, two houses were left. Food was needed, clothes, cooking utensils, bedding. One vessel that was expected to serve half the lower coast stopped at the first settlement and used up its supplies in a few minutes. On foot, in skiffs, by horse, people arrived to plead for help. They stood there and they cried as they told of the condition of their families. Some were quieter, because they had lost everything. At Ostrica, Mrs. Louisa Franklin had little to ask. She had just buried her two children. One had drowned; the other died of a broken neck. Mrs. Dora Morales wanted only a bit for herself and a friend or two. Every relative that she knew was missing—twenty-two of them.

For days the waters brought in bodies or parts of them from the south and from the bays to east and west. Miles out in the Gulf, ships came upon skiffs bearing the shrunken forms of men whose glazed eyes told something of the terrors that had passed about them. Behind the boats usually moved lines of dim, dark forms in the waves; the sharks had been awaiting the final moments.

Some lived but never recovered fully from these days. They sat among the willows at the water's edge and talked endlessly of the way the houses seemed to shudder during that morning, and how they found themselves holding to something as they floated on the surface. From the swirling grayness of this September of 1915 they could not return. One small Frenchwoman knew that her son and husband were not dead. Their bodies had never been found; she insisted that they were somewhere not far off, waiting for a chance to get back. Her old man had told her that he would come home, hadn't he? For five years she went to every vessel that tied up along the Mississippi. Did they know Auguste or Ludo? She was always certain that the next ship would bring them. Finally, dying, she called a cousin. Let there be no mistake now; the tombstone must not say she was a widow. She was the wife of Auguste. How would he feel when he came back and saw that on her grave?

CHAPTER 14

Silk Shirts and Shotguns

THE 1920's were days of happy spree to countless citizens of the United States; and the Deltans, who had often lived by serving the desires of others, profited by catering to the greater gaieties of their fellows above. American women wanted all the furs that their purses would bring them. Americans, men and women alike, wanted the liquor that the Prohibition Act declared illegal. At least as well as any part of the nation, the Delta could provide both commodities.

For many there ensued a period of happy new tastes and the means of indulging them, of echoing laughter over the dark, rippling waters. But in some cases newly acquired riches brought greed for more, and hostile men faced each other over the spoils. Bands shot it out from points of vantage, and bodies sank slowly to resting places under the rich blue irises and the lightly swaying lavender hyacinths.

In the case of fur and also of rum, a frontier territory accommodated itself to the wants of a more "stable" civilization. For many of the Delta people things were much the same; outsiders managed them, directed them, and took the bigger part of the profits. Eventually it all changed; but the Delta remembered. It has never quite recovered from a number of lessons that it learned during these years.

Annually the men had gone to the marshes and swamps for the mink, otter, raccoon, marten, and muskrat. It was what the Frenchmen called "a nice lil' revenue, yes." A man might bring in a few hundred dollars a year, a sizable addition to an income always figured in small amounts. He and his helper—a relative or a friend—ranged freely over the green-grown, water-marked lands back of the river. When they had all they thought they could dispose of, they split and went home. A traveling merchant appeared in a lugger, or the storekeeper would make a deal. It was all casual and frequently uncertain.

The animal that was most plentiful—the fast-multiplying muskrat, whose mound-houses dotted the marsh—was in least demand. This short-furred creature had to compete in the shops with the great, lustrous skins of Canada and Alaska and Siberia. The buyer would give the Deltan nine, ten, and eleven cents a muskrat pelt, and explain that he did it mainly because he knew him. Ma foi, Justin, you should see the faces of those men from the North when I show them the rat skins! How much more mink you got? Certain Deltans, concentrating on the main opportunities, said that the muskrats were "not worth spitting at," and they grumbled when one wandered into the traps that they had set for something more profitable.

The major market of the nineteenth century was the Old World; few Americans owned furs. After 1900 the situation altered. The northern places began to exhaust their fur supplies. Simultaneously American women, reading their magazines and their books, decided that they must have such elegancies. Buyers remembered Louisiana and the Louisiana muskrat. Furriers experimented. The animal's pelts are of several hues; cut apart and combined by shades, they produced garments of silver or gold or deep brown. The muskrat coat, disguised by other names, came into vogue as a lower-priced article within the range of thousands, housewives and working girls included. Buyers from New York and New Orleans converged on the Delta to take towering quantities of the muskrats. As they matched bids, prices rose with each year, to fifty cents, to a dollar, to two dollars and more. The trappers shook their heads in wonder and delight; men who knew the marsh as they did their side yards turned their knowledge to quick advantage.

Now they were earning money beyond their previous imaginings: three thousand dollars for a man who had never held three hundred at one time; four, five, in some instances more than that. Nowhere was the change more marked than along Bayou Terre aux Boeufs, the settlement of the Isleños in St. Bernard parish.

Until shortly before the beginning of the present century,

only one or two houses here had been of wooden construction. The rest were palmetto-roofed, mud-walled, with mud floors. A few French families went to the Island, but it and its ways remained strongly Spanish and lightly somnolent. Yet with the years had come new influences. These people, who had lived by the soil in their original homes, had turned from it. The corner of land that they occupied toward the lakes was part of the area in which the ground was sinking rapidly. The successive storms and floods were too much. "It's no use," one Isleño told me. "What we plant one year, the water takes the next. I kept up till my field was wash' three times in a row. That was enough for me." By degrees the Isleños were falling into a listless poverty such as even their distressed forefathers had not known.

Then fortune struck with the twenties. The Isleños were in the middle of a thickly endowed muskrat territory. The men might trap for three months and enjoy the rest of the year talking to their friends as they lay on their galleries. They became trappers "and nothing else." The Island bloomed with new houses and with paint, in shining saffrons and purples that appealed to the Latin eye. Saloons installed bright signs, and new boats tied up at the wharves. Salesmen from New Orleans delivered automobiles and left with the cash in thick wads. Several who had never donned anything but marsh boots still did not put on shoes but drove their Chevrolets without difficulty. Their calloused feet had no trouble with the brakes.

Yet the flush prosperity was uneven. For one who earned thousands, a dozen received a few hundreds or less. A bad choice of a location, sickness during the season, or accidents, and a man had to worry hard about the future. Money gravitated into a few pockets, and bosses rose. The level of existence for many stayed as low as the land itself. In the shadow moved children whose legs were pencil-like, whose eyes were lusterless.

Those with ten times their former income discovered that, within a few months after the season's end, they had less than ever. At the stores and bars of the Island, games went on, night after night, that rivaled some in the big establishments around New Orleans. At their Spanish game of cacho or at craps, the Isleños won heavily and lost heavily. A hundred dollars a shot was frequently the rule; veteran trappers say that more money shifted pockets here than at any other place of any kind below New Orleans. Muskrats uncaught changed hands four times on the eve of a season; a man with two thousand dollars and a boat lost both within an hour, then won them back before dawn with his neighbor's car in addition. Big-shot gamblers were drawn to the place from the city. From time to time they lifted their eyes to find a knife glinting in the light and to hear a muttered accusation of cheating. But outsiders seldom took this risk; the tempers of the Isleños were well known.

The women did not complain at this uneven life. Their husbands were the masters; the wives kept to their duties, prepared their strongly seasoned food with whatever ingredients were available, and waited for their men to return. Trappers who drove luxury cars still resided in houses with strings of red and green peppers on the porch and enjoyed long siestas on the steps as had their fathers. And day by day the white-haired grandmothers and the swarthy children dropped their nets and fishing lines into the slow waters to help supply the table.

An unpleasant rumor spread one morning. Strangers were at the courthouse, asking questions; they were claiming part of the marsh that people had trapped all of these years. Before Dios, to think that men could own ground that was practically in the Gulf! Next thing, they would say the sea was theirs. It was all crazy stuff. Alas for the Deltans, the strangers were far removed from insanity. If there were so much reward in the marsh for some, there might be as much or more for others. Lawyers had been studying the statute books.

The Deltans had always looked upon the marshes as the property of anyone who wished to use them. They were not entirely right. Under the Swamp Act of 1850 the federal government had given the title of many such regions to the various states. Louisiana in turn passed on many of them to private individuals; and these generally neglected to pay the low taxes assessed against them. A great part of the property thus went back to state hands; eventually Louisiana granted considerable sections to the public boards of the parishes. Into this situation of mixed ownerships was injected the bonanza in furs. Men who had ceased to concern themselves over these acreages suddenly remembered them. Newcomers, from New Orleans or elsewhere, made discreet calls on this or that political official, and companies were formed in which officeholders were known or unknown partners. Now, it was announced, the land belonged to the companies. If the trappers wanted to use it, they must give over a certain percentage, thirty-five percent or so, to the firm. Over the Delta appeared signs: No Trespassing.

The trappers looked at the signs, spat on them, and went ahead as they had always done. The marshes, with their labyrinths of water trails, seemed impossible to police. Even if the "owners" really owned them, how could they keep people out? The owners went to court. Judges ruled for them. Guards with guns made their appearance, but they met difficulties. A Deltan, slipping through the spider web of canals, heard a motorboat far away, ducked a few minutes, and returned to his trap line when the vessel disappeared. Once he was out of disputed territory, who could prove where he had trapped? For better or for worse, one muskrat skin looks much like another.

The companies thought of another source of assistance, the federal government. They obtained injunctions; now the trappers would be defying Uncle Sam. To hell with Uncle Sam, said the trappers. They were more frank than wise. Fights broke out with federal deputies. The companies imported new men from other parts of Louisiana and put them to work under guards. The trappers' wars of modern Louisiana were on. Deltans discovered that "scabs" were taking much less than had been offered the natives. Resentment grew by the hour.

Bands of Deltans descended on the flimsy tar-and-wood houses of the interlopers and broke them up. Their enemies crumpled under pistol fire and lay moaning among the grasses. Scrawled notes were found in tin cans when the newcomers returned at night: "Bettr Be Gon Wen We Get Back." The federal government made arrests, and the owners obtained more injunctions and more guards.

Changing their tactics, the trappers formed "associations" of their own. Some of the parish officials moved to their side, and leases were signed between trappers and land companies. Overnight, factions of the trappers charged furiously that they had been tricked, that such leases had been transferred secretly to undisclosed persons. There followed more ligitation, near-riots in the court corridors, and more shootings. And rival groups of capitalists came forward to compete for the land. Some of the ground that had reverted to the state for nonpayment of taxes was claimed by the former owners. The state legislature obligingly adopted a law permitting original owners to get the lost land back by paying past-due taxes. This also brought collisions; the quarrels now had three or more sides. But through it all the trapper himself suffered while others grew rich.

A climax was imminent. Word passed that one of the companies in the vicinity of the Isleños had "decided not to play around" any longer. It hired new men who were used to trouble, former Texas Rangers. Drawling men with broad-brimmed hats and tasseled boots were driven to the company headquarters. Newspapers in restrained language described their leader as "a seasoned soldier of fortune." Trapper spies reported something else: the arrival of heavy supplies of ammunition, and stories that the newcomers were going to "move on the Island to wipe it out." The tight-lipped Isleños looked at each other; they would not be caught by surprise.

On the morning of November 17, 1926, thick gray-blue fogs from the lakes crawled over the oval of land that is the home of the Isleños. The scene had a tense, unfamiliar air. None left for their usual chores in the marsh; they sat or stood together in groups, talking in low voices. Few of the children played at the rim of the light green waters or ran about their narrow front yards. The women washed their clothes near the galleries and talked: Sí, sí, it was a dark day. Maria, how you think the season—

The wives fell silent. A white shape was emerging from the swirling mists along Bayou Terre aux Boeufs. They knew the lugger, but there was something different about it now. Eight or nine people, among them the former Rangers, looked out with pointed pistols. Two machine-gun muzzles poked from the window. The women shrieked to the children. The men on shore stepped closer together, then dropped to the ground behind the brown bank of the bayou. Both sides were still.

Just what happened next has never been made clear; but over the marshland echoed the crack of gunfire. One volley followed another; an interval of silence, then more shooting. The gulls lifted their black-fringed wings into the sky with frightened cries; then all was quiet on the Island. The lugger lay motionless at the bayou edge, its gasoline tank punctured. Bits of oil floated over the dull water, and as before the bayou was stirred only by the gentle wind. In the lugger cabin a man leaned against the wall, right hand resting lightly on the butt of his pistol, half-drawn from the holster. He was dead from a charge of buckshot. Six others of the party sat or lay on the edge of the Island, bullets in their arms or chests. A last member, his shoulders peppered, scrambled into the marsh.

By the time outsiders arrived to investigate, the Isleños stood before their gates, arms crossed, sharp dark faces fixed in sullen attitude. The red-eyed, apprehensive women stared from the doors, their children about them. Bits of the story came slowly: "They shot first." . . . "We have right to defend ourself and our little ones." . . . The other side placed the blame on the Isleños. No, those on the boat had had no intention of attacking: "We were only going to the company's place. . . . We never expected anything like this."

The incident received bitter attention. Imported trappers fled; roads were guarded to prevent the escape of any from the Island. Officials could fix no individual responsibility among the several hundred Isleños. The differences continued through the ensuing years, with compromises, new outbreaks, killings. Through it all the line of "No Trespassing" signs grew over the grasses and the water edges.

Trapping had become a matter of monopoly holdings. Never again were the men to know the old free range of the marsh. The Deltans have not learned to cooperate among themselves to build up strong compensating organizations; they have tried to hold on as pioneer people in a setting dominated by an economy of a later day. The rich returns of the twenties have passed. The market dropped with the depression of 1929 and though it picked up later, the price per skin has not reached former peaks.

Annually the Deltans take their families in pirogues or luggers back to the marshes for several months of intensive hunting. They set up crude cabins at the borders of the nearest natural stream, and then they cut narrow runs of their own, along which they will push-pole their way. They, their wives and children have worked long in advance to test and grease the traps; and now the family settles down for the hard, wet days ahead.

First the trapper looks for "the signs," watches for muskrat homes, for the tiny water paths followed by the animals, and the grasses that are their favorite foods: three-cornered grass, cattail, wild cat. He will set his traps in continuous lines, which he will follow day by day. The law prohibits the trapper from baiting them. But he does not need to do that; he "knows mus'rat." He sees where the rat has been eating, where he has swum or crawled in the past weeks. The water must be brackish, but not salt. Too fresh, and the muskrat will be inclined to move. A dry season, bringing the saline mixtures far up into the marsh, will also make him retreat.

Locating his lines, the trapper will cover the implement with mud so that it does not shine; he will place it where the muskrat will be most likely to pass, and then he will thrust a long cane into the ground, to mark the location of each trap for his own guidance—a wise precaution. Then he is ready. Morning after morning he will rise before dawn and slosh out with his sons along the path of his traps. Part of the route can be covered by foot; other sections, more treacherous, can be reached only by water, and many times even the most skilful finds himself sinking up to his waist. He gathers the animals, tosses them into his pirogue, halts occasionally to skin them, and works steadily to reach the finish before the quick winter dusk is upon him. Some days he will come home panting under a heavy load; again he will bring Maman the news that his catch was "low, low." The rat is a night prowler and unpredictable. Some evenings the grasses will be alive with the animals; again, obstinately, they will stay out of the open marsh and out of the traps. A warm, muggy night, and the trapper will be morose. One with a pleasant bite in the air, and he will sing songs that his Père taught him.

Maman, the smaller boys, and the girls will remain at the cabin, helping to clean the last bits of flesh from the pelts, stretching and drying them. The landowner or his agent will move in and out by lugger, to check on the take and to bring food for which the family pays, so that it will lose no time in a long trip back to the river. The business continues to be one in which the middle man wins. Some trappers think that they have found a way out. Arguing that they will be bilked in any case, they fail to give in many of their furs. They bootleg them to others, they poach, they hunt before the legal season and afterward.

The Deltans automatically resented Prohibition. They could not understand it; as one put it, some of them regarded it as a crime directed at them, more or less personally. For years they had been fermenting their orange wine, which could be at least as potent as whisky, and selling it to visitors who liked it. Now the visitors were liking it more than ever. Home owners added to their orange barrels and their side income. Hundreds of Orleanians drove along the dusty Delta roads for the wine; many first came to know the place during Prohibition days. The dry kind of wine helped make an excellent martini; retail bootleggers carbonated the wine and sold it as champagne. The Deltans occasionally expanded their supplies and experimented with stills. When a government agent crossed the parish borders, news flew down those long roads. More telephones had been installed; a few children running with the message from the end of the lines could move more quickly than any agent. The goods were whisked into the marsh or the river, the sacks tied with a rope to the wharf pilings. The snoopers found only the smell of the luscious stuff, and they could not confiscate that.

These, of course, were minor doings. With the early Prohibition years the Delta provided one of the great American arteries for transfer of foreign-made supplies. Easily accessible to Cuba, Central America, and the West Indies, it afforded good anchorages, a balmy climate for operations during most of the year and, not least, those thousands of water inlets. The federal government could not install an adequate patrol here; in the words of a Deltan: "That would have taken a nice piece of the United States Navy."

New Orleans was never a place that embraced or even comprehended the law against liquor. At one time it was recorded that about 2500 persons were at liberty with suspended sentences of a year or more. (Lesser penalties were not counted.) One enforcement officer was fond of estimating that spirits could be purchased with a degree of ease at three thousand places; considering the city's size, this was not an unimpressive total. Others thought the figures conservative. Through New Orleans, meanwhile, moved a wide stream of contraband from the Delta up the valley, to east and west.

At an early date outsiders appeared in the Delta, to look up friends, to stand at the bars for a time, and then call one or two outside. Did they have good luggers? How about making a little extra money—just twenty-four hours' work at a time, easy, no trouble with anybody? The minimum amount offered was one hundred dollars; before long it went to five hundred or more. If any accident occurred to the boat, the owner was well reimbursed. The higher-ups remained liberal. After a run or two, a fisherman became a dependable ally, who would drop anything (including, it was always said, the embrace of his favorite girl) for an assignment.

At Nassau and Cuba, at points on the Mexican coast and in British Honduras, liquor for the United States was loaded into large vessels—"mother ships." Radio played a role. Private stations, and sometimes commercial ones, sent out codes telling men in the city and the Delta where the "mother" would arrive, and when. After a time the federals deciphered the messages. The runners passed along the word: Add so many figures to those that came in, and there they had new locations. The federal men hastened to the scene and found nothing.

The "mothers" were careful not to venture within the American shoreline; as long as they stayed outside, the government could not touch them. Some went to the river mouth, but eventually their main stopping places were about the Breton and Chandeleur Islands, used by the pirates of other days. For one period the main passage became Bayou Bienvenu, the same waterway which the British followed for the Battles of New Orleans. Agents of the liquor organizations drove to the Delta, met their native friends, and the party set out quietly. If neighbors asked, they were off on a fishing jaunt. But few inquired; almost everybody knew, and almost nobody cared. It was a way to earn a living, wasn't it?

The smaller boats met the "mother" and "milked" her to their capacity. She could carry up to 3500 or 4000 cases and sometimes she was approached by one vessel after another. Participants tell of days when several "mothers" hovered about Breton Island; on one occasion of joyous recollection, no less than twenty boats darted back and forth. The supplies could be cached in the marsh or near certain well-marked trees. Passenger cars drove up, to be packed tightly. Oil trucks were also used for purposes of disguise; or the stuff was neatly wrapped in packing cases, as canned vegetables or fruit juices. But generally large plain trucks were waiting, set for a quick dash into downtown New Orleans.

The dry agents were only an occasional danger. The great hazard were rivals in the trade, hijackers who understood routes and methods. As a natural development, protection was required. Men who knew how to handle their guns went along, one quick-moving automobile for each truck. They had their orders; they shot fast and well. At the start these were Orleanians or importations from Chicago and the East. Afterward Delta boys, whose relatives were piloting the boats, wanted to know why they were not allowed along. It seemed only fair to the home people; and so a number of promising young gunmen developed. They wore silk shirts; a youth who could read only with difficulty had his initials embroidered on his sleeve. When a man pays more for a shirt than he had previously earned in a month, he is proud of the garment.

To be a liquor runner, that was not a disgrace but a mark of daring. It had a near-heroic appeal. Children followed him with their eyes; girls knew him for a gay one, with nice spending money. Occasionally he was sent to the penitentiary. That was sad. Such a fine big man, too. It was always the nasty lil' guys what got away, ahn, chère? That one there, he been to Atlanta. He ain' no small potato, no.

When an especially important shipment was due and the federals were unduly inquisitive, an operator made a "fair proposition" to a Deltan. If he would draw the dry men away, appear at the proper moment and let them tail him, he would be cared for. In case they got him, things would still be all right. He would collect a salary for every week in prison and more later. It was an offer that found takers.

And now the Deltans heard the frequent roar of guns and

knew that it was not the noise of early hunters in the marsh. They did not get up and investigate; it was not their concern. The next morning they saw a place on the road where gasoline had spilled, as if from a broken tank, or the charred carcass of a machine. A Delta boy did not return from a run, and for days afterward his pale mother and sisters cried to themselves. That was all; people thus engaged did not run to the authorities with such matters. One candid official shrugged: "Me, I am a servant of my people. They elect' me to carry out their will." And then, it was a federal law, wasn't it? Let the government enforce it.

The trade organized further. The road along the bulge of St. Bernard toward the lakes was rutted by this night traffic. Casual drivers were surprised when untalkative men halted their machines for inspection. So the federals were at work? Ultimately they discovered that these were runners or hijackers, posing as government agents. Intermittently a passerby ran into a fusillade that sprayed his car. But most natives knew better than to go driving about at night; that was inviting trouble. Meanwhile the big shots knew "just how far to go, and where not to go," as a retired operator told me. A maxim of the trade was that a liquor-runner would kill a hijacker, but never an officer. It was not good business. Yet the boys could slip up.

Such was the case one morning in April of 1923, when the sheriff of St. Bernard and several deputies received a tip and took stations near the Violet Bridge. Shortly after five o'clock, in the fragant Delta dawn, a truck hurtled along the shelled highway from the lakes. The driver slowed up, but a swifter passenger car swung ahead. Two deputies went down. One had his left side almost torn away; the other's face and brain were filled with lead. The car escaped, and the officers died in twitching torment. As the news filtered out, men came from all parts of the parish with their guns. Sides were taken, and civil war seemed close.

Officials traced the particular shipment of liquor from the Gulf through a canal. The manager of a packing plant along that waterway was summoned. Yes, he had given the keys to a gate on the canal highway to a man whom he named; that was all he knew, he said. Talk of higher-ups grew general. As the manager was questioned, hundreds gathered at the courthouse, and cries of "Get a rope!" reached the pale man. The sheriff brought him to the terrace before the courthouse. The crowd listened as the sheriff talked softly: "Tell who they are, for God's sake. . . . You know you're lying." The throng added its comment. The manager winced, but shook his head. The sheriff led him through the crowd to the home of the first dead man, where the women stood about the coffin. "Will you let him lay there, shot dead like a dog? You're going to protect rich men that caused it?" The manager looked at the figure among the yellow roses of the Delta, covered his eyes, and turned away. The victim's son reached out: "Lemme have 'im. I'll make 'im tell!" The manager was led to his cell.

Within a few minutes, the bells tolled and the funeral procession passed. At each window of the small, vulnerable building which housed the prisoner a lantern was fixed to prevent escape, or entry. The sheriff brought the manager forth again, and they sat on the terrace. The sheriff whispered: others came closer. At last the man, in tearing sobs, threw himself on the grass: "I wish to God I'd killed myself before I got into this!" He talked now. He had lost everything in a flood; he needed money. Someone had come to him. And he gave names.

Eight were arrested—fishermen, trappers, a truck farmer, several notorious characters of New Orleans. An indictment charged an attorney, who was also levee board secretary and one of the rising political figures of the parish, as accessory before the fact of murder. He disappeared, to remain away for a time, returning to say that he had been a victim of politics. The cases hung on, with one or two convictions. The accusation against the attorney was quashed, and not long afterward he was elected district judge.

For years the traffic continued; the only change seemed its enlargement. Soon one of the greatest enforcement campaigns in the history of the federal law was conducted against New Orleans and the Delta. Here, said agents, flourished the "wettest spot in the United States"; one newspaper, not without a bit of local pride, termed it "the liquor capital of America." A whole army of agents was called in; in one day a series of raids brought forth a million dollars of liquor. Federal warehouses could not hold all of it; an agent from Maine exclaimed in bewilderment: "I never *thought* there was that much anywhere."

Near Pointe à la Hache, a supply of contraband worth \$100,000 was uncovered; more than seven thousand gallons of alcohol were concealed in one spot among the grasses. Newspapers received tips that hijackers planned to take it all from the federals while the latter were removing it to New Orleans. The full force of agents was mobilized in Army trucks, each accompanied by guards with sawed-off shotguns. The impending encounter along the Delta levees was heralded as "the Second Battle of New Orleans." Nervous moments ensued when several Army trucks were stalled. The whole train halted each time, and officers with machine guns prodded the cottonwoods and the thick bushes. The convoy arrived safely.

About the same period, an eighteen-year-old St. Bernard youth engaged in the trade halted and tried to hold up by mistake a party of federal agents. The two groups fought it out, and the agents won. The would-be hijacker insisted that it was an honest error; he had taken them for his competitors. Later, several Delta deputy sheriffs were charged with impersonating federal officers in a pursuit of liquor for reasons apparently not official. Again, a member of a Delta police jury (governing body of the parishes) was found guilty in federal court of a Prohibition violation. And a particularly lurid episode elicited testimony by dry agents that a few members of the New Orleans police force itself, carrying riot guns, had escorted shipments from the Delta to the city, protecting them from attack!

Developing their own camouflage, Deltans moved supplies to the metropolis along back inlets or on the river, under layers of oysters or shrimp. In a number of incidents of which they can boast, a hearse moved slowly along the road with sorrowing friends in accompanying cars. The relatives carried flowers and guns, and the coffin held a particularly expensive grade of champagne. "If they had got us, we really woulda mourned!"

A high moment came when a Delta sheriff was indicted by a federal grand jury, together with the government customs collector at New Orleans, for conspiracy to import liquor. Three deputy sheriffs and three former city police officers were charged in the same supposed plot to smuggle 4250 cases of spirits from Havana. The customs officers were declared to have provided information as to the whereabouts of federal launches so that the runners could avoid capture, and the sheriff's forces were accused of conveying the goods. The sheriff said it was only politics; the case did not come to trial.

Chinese constituted another article of contraband. Before Prohibition and after it, unknown numbers of Orientals were slipped into the Delta from places to the South, usually Cuba. It was an especially dangerous trade. Some refused any part of it, but the price was so good that a few found it worth the peril.

Only infrequently were Chinese runners trapped with their goods. When capture seemed near, the crews behaved much as had others a century earlier in these waters, when the cargo was also human, but black-skinned. Throats were slit and the victims tossed quickly into dark waters; or they were placed for "concealment" in sealed barrels and dropped overboard. Rumors of these practices spread, but Chinese, pathetically anxious to reach the United States, were willing to risk almost anything. They or their friends paid high; they suffered tragic hardships to reach the runners; then they remained packed for days in the stifling holds, waiting, waiting. A runner recalled the era with a wry face: "There was always something peculiar about the stink of the ship after we'd carried them that way—like nothing else I've ever smelled."

In a number of cases the operators brought the Chinese up to New Orleans in daylight, counting on a brazen front as the simplest way to avoid suspicion. They were taken to French Quarter stores in great containers labeled "Dried Shrimp." Or they were hustled into cars, to lie tightly together on the floor for a bumpy ride. For a time, when one Delta big shot saw another roar up the road, he guyed him, "Whatcha got there, ma frien', Chinee?" When the other man went suddenly white, he knew that he had hit the truth. One retired operator, in an expansive mood, recounted the occasion on which he hurried his batch of Orientals to his marsh hut and handed them shoe-polish. If anyone asked, they were going to be Negroes. They must have been a strange sight, these Afro-Asiatics. But they went uncaught.

Supplies that were yet "hotter" intrigued men possessed of a particular daring. Opium and other drugs were in very heavy demand by some sources; the penalties were also very heavy.

The goods were dropped by one vessel at night with floating markers while a second one waited just within sight. Once picked up, the forbidden material was ingeniously concealed. In small, well-wrapped packages, the stuff was sometimes handed to unsuspecting and unsuspected duck hunters, to give to friends in the city. And the runners chuckled at the federal watchers.

Those festive days are gone, but many have not forgotten. Money never came so quickly; and though there were chances to be taken, it was a swift life, and entertaining. Former leaders have died, and the once young and silk-shirted are middle-aged and wear cotton. One asked me with a touch of wistfulness if I thought the Second World War or the post-war period might encourage people to try Prohibition again.

CHAPTER 15

The Twice That Rescued New Orleans

THE Mississippi was "high, high"; men gazed at their levees and wondered. Outside New Orleans the whirling yellow tide, heavy with the springtime scourings of the continent, reached nearer to the top than at any time in the memory of the elders. In St. Bernard parish the residents had been giving special attention to their high, green-clad embankments. On April 27, 1922, officials completed a tour of inspection; they met no signs of weakness, no disturbing trickles at the landward bases. Delta people went to bed that pleasant spring evening without anything unusual to concern them.

Shortly before three o'clock the next morning, a member of the levee patrol passed near the old Poydras plantation, about fifteen miles below the city on the east shore. The night was clear; the restless water gurgled close to his horse's hoofs, but no closer than it had come for a day or so. Another long watch was nearly over. Bien. Fifteen minutes later a truck farmer drove by the spot with a wagon load of vegetables for French Market. He heard a deep rumble, like far thunder on the Gulf. But it seemed somehow close at hand. His eye caught a movement of some kind; in a moment the earth of the levee "seemed kind of pushing out, toward me." Great handfuls of soil shot upward. Out of the mound poured thick mud and grass, and a spout of water. He spurred on his horse; already the earth about them was covered by a thin stream. The rumble became a roar; looking back he could make out a kind of waterfall over what had been the slope of the bank.

Men raced from their houses. Levee going, fast! Some did not require notice. One resident, who lived nearly a quarter mile away, was wakened by an unaccustomed noise; when he reached his gate, water was in front of the house. Crowds hurried to the scene, then drew back as the earth on each side of the crevasse cracked before them. The water was moving in a deeper, more threatening flow with every few minutes; now it was a violent torrent that meant death to anyone who approached too close.

By dawn workers with trucks, wooden pilings, and heavy sandbags were at the break. Engineers made a quick inspection, then shook their heads. The river made a bend near here, and the flow rushed upon the crevasse with a plunging force accumulated in a straight sweep of several miles. The breach could not be closed; all that they might do was to "tie" the ends in an effort to keep it from widening. The new current moved eastward toward the Gulf; a belt several miles wide was soon to be covered—some of the best truck-gardening land in the South.

Hundreds were looking toward the river in dismay. In the distance they heard the water on its way; within a few hours the land was darkening before them, as a line of wetness crept in their direction. About their yards the chickens were flapping, jumping up the steps or to whatever higher roosts they could find. Dogs scratched at doors, horses and cows shifted about in alarm. Over the fields the moisture trickled between the pale green rows of lettuce and cabbage. Farmers ran about frantically, pulling up the vegetables, tossing them into baskets. They were in a losing race with the Mississippi. As they worked, the lower leaves began to disappear, then the whole heads. Before many of them could reach the end of the first line, all was under water.

One farmer had been planning for a week to harvest his produce. Each day he had looked at it, growing bigger in the balmy, dew-covered morning, and had decided to wait a little longer. Now the river swallowed his livelihood. In the house were seventy-five cents and a few pounds of flour, for eight people. What was to be done? He gazed down again at the water, and knew the answer. Already it was up to the doors and a trickle reached into the kitchen, which rested on a lower level. An official approached in a boat. They were right in the path; they had better go, certainement.

With trembling hands the family gathered its things—bedding, clothes, food, the picture that Grandpère had left; then they realized that they could never take it all. The big skiff was drawn from under the house. They could make two trips, said Papa;

that way they could take more of it. But Maman was crying now, the bitter tears of a woman who must leave her home. Her aged mother sat in the corner, saying her beads, talking between prayers about other, earlier occasions that had not been entirely different. The children drew up about their mother, frightened by her weeping, and the older girls pleaded with her and tried not to give way themselves. Now, Maman, it will be all right . . . It will be all right . . . The baby watched unmoved, chewing the shrimp that had been handed him to quiet him. Papa announced that as soon as he had put them all in a safe place, he would come back to guard the house. Maman cried harder at this. Non, non, he would die. The building would fall, or he would catch a disease in this terrible wetness. Well, they would see, Papa tried to comfort her; the boat was ready now. Eh bien, it might be worse, may-*be!*

Setting forth gingerly, he rowed to the front gate, carefully opened it, rowed through and told the boy in the stern to close it tightly. Then he advanced up what he judged to be the road. As the family drew away, they could hear noises within the house. The water was beginning to move their belongings about, knocking them over. It was a sound that made Maman shudder.

First they must get to the levee, always the highest place. On it, some distance from the break, they would be safe until someone came. Maman whispered that maybe if they jus' stay' there a couple of days, the flood would go down. But when she and the others listened to the pound of the water through the opening many yards off, they knew this to be a futile hope. Sitting on the levee top with the baby, Maman gazed in silence at the opposite bank. In the gathering twilight Papa observed that yesterday, just about this time, he had been telling his neighbor what a good growing season it would be.

Emergency shelters were being set up along the upper borders of the parish. Motorboats, luggers, and barges moved out to pick up the people. Many had to wait long hours, a damp day and night, before help approached. They sat about fires or under thin sheets; if it rained, a family could only try to protect its youngest members. Whenever a boat approached, the men waved their arms and called for help. Often they were told to be patient. A message had arrived that groups of families were marooned to the back; or there was a sick man, with his family, alone in a threatened home; the boat would be back. The flood was rising. Near Lake Borgne eighty people huddled in a few shacks; scores had crowded into several of the canning factories, seating themselves first on benches and then on tables as the waters lifted.

The spreading waves now approached the Gulf, moving across ponds and bayous, overwhelming canals and their bridges. They added a paler coloration to the green-black liquids of the swamps, then swept over the marshes and into the blue salt currents. As they went they brought ruin, at least temporarily, to hunting and trapping grounds and to oyster beds. The fishermen toward the lakes were accustomed to frequent intrusions of salt from the sea. But this silt-burdened stream was worse than any that they had known.

Owners of small properties sometimes gathered with their neighbors and tried to build levees in a ring about them. After twenty-four hours or so, the river was casually washing it all away. A baker, turning out thousands of loaves for the flood victims, kept his machinery running for several days, until suddenly the protection fell apart and a sheet of water broke in. At another point a factory force of hundreds labored at the borders of a man-made island in the yellow sea. No sandbags or other materials for building a levee were at hand; some were on the way, but meanwhile the men must struggle as best they could, using shovels, scraping up the earth with buckets. Once the water reached the delicate equipment they were striving so to protect, they knew it would be out of commission for months. Their energy was desperate; hour by hour they kept at it, halting only for brief intervals of rest on the ground.

The women stayed at the men's sides. The flood crept higher, an inch or two at a time. At dawn one morning they realized that hope was lessening rapidly. A section six feet long began to give way. All hands rushed to the weakened spot and saved it. Then the men scattered again, each to his section of the mud wall. "We prayed, over and over, for them to send fresh help," one worker sighed. "We knew it was promised, but when?" The water was edging to the top; here and there it slipped over in pale streamlets. Still they worked, panting, sweating, silent. Then down the river came the dim outlines of a boat with relief—supplies and eighty or more additional men.

But they were too late. The water was topping the levee at all points, and it was crumbling. "Make for your houses!" The men ran, and the river poured after them. Soon it was five feet high, and over everything. Those whose quarters had second stories fled to them; some were so exhausted that they fell helpless upon their beds while the women furiously packed what they could. Further orders came: they must go at once; the pent-up strength of the current was terrific. They left most of their belongings behind.

Meanwhile cattle faced danger up and down the river bank. Thousands headed to the main levees and a precarious refuge, while others moved ahead of the water toward the lakes and their doom. Some fell into hidden canals, to drown in their exhaustion. Stinging swamp flies and mosquitoes concentrated upon frightened animals and they stampeded. Men went out in barges to round up as many as they could; accidents multiplied; barges carrying men and cattle capsized with heavy losses. Vessels advancing toward the back areas were forced into the Gulf by the surge of the river waters. At the front, the break still grew. Already a third as wide as the Mississippi itself, it dug forty-five feet into the ground as its force struck immediately behind the levee. The crevasse created a peril for ships in the river. Even in midstream, pilots felt a pull to the side, and smaller ships fought hard to prevent being sucked into the hole.

Up in New Orleans, people told each other that the crevasse at Poydras had been a godsend. The volume of water withdrawn from the stream rapidly lowered the level at the city. The Delta, whatever the feelings of its people, had rescued the metropolis. But those among the eddying waters could only say, as did one while he watched his house disappear, "This flood, she is the poor man's hell."

Terror and need were destroying ancient hostilities among the animals. Wires, fences, poles, and chimneys were packed with life of all forms. Wherever trees or bush tops remained above water, things that flew and things that swam made their way, to rest there together: rails, muskrats, and rabbits; herons and chickens; possums; and everywhere snakes, crawling over branches, coiled among the leaves. A creature followed its enemy with bright eyes in which two fears met. One was greater than the other, and the antagonists remained, shifting restlessly to hold fur from contact with scale or wing—but alive through it all. Houses became animal quarters; the refugees pushed their way through broken windows or through doors forced open by the water. Raccoon families took places on beds and inside stoves. Snakes wrapped themselves about the sills; and among them flew bedraggled birds.

Other creatures crept along the last ridges of land above the water, or swam about for hours, seeking a stable footing, to climb at last, almost dead, on logs and other debris. The natives were amazed when rabbits and furred animals crawled up the sides of their moving pirogues. Deer stealthily approached the levees; families who slept there discovered marks to indicate that they had not been alone during the night. The animals kept outside the light of the fires, and then swam away with the dawn, to reach shelter elsewhere, or to drown.

One woman found a forlorn, frightened bird—a rail—following her about the levee. It was silent in its terror. Somehow, it had chosen her as a friend and pattered behind her everywhere she went. At first it darted away when she tried to touch it, but eventually it let her stroke its back. It stayed with her until long afterward; then one morning it was gone.

Most Deltans did nothing to injure these fellow victims. But eventually they saw thousands of muskrats within range, on driftwood or atop their tiny house-mounds. The state conservation officials urged them not to kill the rats and lose their "seed stock," but to help save them for future seasons of growth and reproduction. The authorities floated rafts covered with the rich three-cornered grass and other foods of the rats, and many were thus preserved. But men were greedy. Over the Delta sounded the report of many rifles as the furred things were taken, regardless of size, age or condition. The muskrat crop was drastically reduced at its source; the Delta economy would suffer from this blow.

For more than two months the people remained away from their lands. Ultimately the waters receded, and the natives filtered home, to gaze about them in astonishment. Over everything lay mud, deep and rich, already sprouting bits of green, with yellow wildflowers here and there. Fields rose a foot or more higher; behind obstructions, miniature hills had formed. The men worked with shovels to spread it evenly over their land; the patriarchs nodded their heads and quoted their fathers' stories about the thick base of new wealth that a flood would always leave. But there were less happy discoveries. The sight of the houses was dismaying. Galleries hung loosely; windows and doors were warped so that they would not shut. One Deltan came upon his place yards away, in a friend's rear field, and dragged it back with the help of the neighbors. Some, less fortunate, could retrieve only broken boards.

Wherever a home was spared, the women dug through mud to reach floors. They made other discoveries and cried "Passez!" to the unwonted tenants. Birds left nests, snakes their skins. Occasionally there followed a lively chase after a raccoon or a possum, and the family had a pelt or a meal. They could do with both. The larders were low, the reserves down to nothing, or worse—a heavy debt. All natural forms—oysters, furred animals, and the rest—were sadly reduced. Eventually, the conservationists might declare, the enriched soil and the deposits would provide a source of renewed life. But for a long time to come, things would be hard, yes.

The date was now 1927, five short years later—the year that has been termed the grimmest in the history of the valley. Unprecedentedly heavy surges of water were rushing into the lower river. Upstream levees were breaking; thousands were fleeing their homes in districts that had never known serious flood. New Orleans was frightened, more frightened perhaps than at any previous time. Few Deltans appeared fearful on this occasion. Their upper levees had been rebuilt and strengthened; the banks would hold.

At the city thousands of sandbags were stacked along the river. Engineers did not like what they saw. Hundreds labored in the sun; still the stream rose, and the crest was not yet in sight. Some recalled the way the levee down at Poydras had broken without warning in 1922. It might happen like that at New Orleans, any day, any night. Nursing units, first aid, and emergency police were organized; but the men and women on the streets asked for more than that. Ways *must* be found to save the city. Millions in wealth were endangered; a population of a half million was alarmed.

A note of hysteria entered the voices of the people behind the levees. Confidential messages were conveyed by city officials to the Governor and to the United States Engineers in general charge of the river protection. Reports spread by word of mouth. Yes, there was a way to protect New Orleans. . . . The Deltans realized suddenly what the city had in mind—the Delta; specifically, a crevasse to draw the water out of the Mississippi just as the last one had done, a man-made break below the city! It was the interests of a metropolis against those of the farmers and fishermen. Washington was even then being asked for permission.

The Deltans cried out in astonishment. It would be a shame, a crime in the sight of le Bon Dieu! Who did those people think they were that they could act like this to others? Let them watch their levee'; we watch ours. Oui, they got fine house' and nice thing'. We got ours, too. Faces grew sullen, and eyes bitter. It was bad enough when it happened by itself; but for somebody to come along and make a levee go! The men talked of forming lines at the parish border and shooting it out with any who tried to get at their embankments.

The city's representatives worked hastily. The peak of the river was coming; they could not delay much longer. Emissaries went to the Delta. Look, everything would be arranged to lessen the blow. The city agreed to give full compensation for losses; merchants would put up the money. Central headquarters would be set up at the Army Supply Base below the city. The Deltans could even remove their furniture and it would be stored and ticketed with their names and addresses, see. The children would go to school; city ladies would cook meals for them. Stage shows every week, a daily newspaper for the family. Wasn't it all fair?

The Deltans listened and said Non. Would you give up your house and everything you got, mister, for somebody else? New Orleans knew about the trappers' fights; well, they would be picnics compared to what would happen now! Delta officials sent committees to New Orleans, telegrams to Washington. Couldn't something else be done, in God's name? They had just recovered from the last flood. Appeals failed. The water swirled higher by the day; the city's pressure grew.

Then Washington gave its approval. Soldiers assembled and a decision was reached to blast open the levee at Caernarvon, not far from the previous break. The Delta officials gave in. A farmer shrugged and nodded. Trappers and fishermen muttered, and walked slowly back to their homes. The Deltans gave way because it was all that they could do. "We got pick between pay crevasse and crevasse without no pay. We better take pay."

The women thought of that day of the last levee break. When it had to be done so fast, and unexpectedly, it seemed easier. Now, though they could take everything, the weight on their hearts was greater. A few hurriedly dug up their vegetables for a quick run to the market. The remainder left behind their partly ripened crops; they would now feed only the river fish. Trucks and wagons called for their belongings, bearing bright banners on their sides: "Flood Relief." "What flood?" demanded unreconstructed Deltans.

An intense woman, wetting white lips with her tongue, talked as many others thought. Shutting her gate, she told the Army driver: "I don' think we'll ever come back. We been here so long. My own Mère was born here. . . We had to leave at the las' break, but when we got back I fix' it nice. We even put an inside bathtub. Now they say water might take the whole place. I guess you ain' never had somebody move you out like this?" The soldier said he was sorry. Her husband took her arm and led her away.

It was an exodus of men and animals, trucks piled with tables and vases, blankets, boxes, and chairs; rattling cars, people on horseback, on muleback, a few driving oxen before them, others with chickens in coops, or hogs and cattle. They left their animals at Jackson Barracks just below the city, and pressed on to the great building in which they would stay. If they wished, they could board with relatives; at the last minute some chose this rather than the life that would be so different from what they had known. The men and women carried their small bundles, the children their pets—cats, dogs, turtles, tame ducks, a baby alligator. Well, here was where the party broke up. Merci, we keep in touch with that office like you say. We will get along, we guess. Now, Marie, you ain' crying again?

A few refused to go despite everything. Let the water drown them if it wanted. Toward the lakes a number of the bootlegging operators were reluctant. With everyone watching, it was impossible to move their commodities; none had any thought of deserting such valuables. In at least one instance, a rescue barge brought a large quantity, covered with fish. Most of the men stayed, with guns close at hand.

As the time for action on the levee arrived, the Army checked every vehicle entering or leaving the east side of the Delta, turning away thousands of the curious. New Orleans received high governmental officials, engineers and construction authorities, to observe a feat of extraordinary interest, comparable after a fashion to that of Eads in the last century. On April twenty-ninth at midday a tense group watched. Negro workmen prepared the soil, sank dynamite into the holes, and connected the fuses. A roar, a small puff of smoke and dust, and only a thin stream or two. More dynamite, and another tiny flow. Again and again, and the Mississippi refused to break through as men ordained. Deltans made remarks in French, in Spanish, in Italian, in Slavic. One winked and snickered: "The river, she fool New Orlean'. She don' wan' run out, do she?" An officer looked down in red-faced disapproval; the Frenchman laughed again.

A call went up to the city for more explosives, as America waited to receive the news. Eventually it worked; the opening broadened, and the current threw out the mud in several directions. The dull hum changed to a growl. Here came the Mississippi; let her roar! A Delta official spoke solemnly to all who listened: "You are witnessing the public execution of a parish."

In the city there was jubilation and there was thanksgiving; among the Deltans it was heartbreak. One of the truck farmers shook his head: "This was the twice that we rescue' New Orlean'." The damage spread downward across the Plaquemines parish line; the flood was worse than the last, and its effect more than physical. As some predicted, they did not return. Compensation was provided, but it seemed to slip away before the families knew it. Certain ones profited; the average man, considering the disruptions and their aftermaths, came out the loser. Many who went back attempted farming again, but often they felt that their hearts were "not in it any more." They shifted to fishing, to shrimping at the Gulf fringes; or they took odd jobs or went on relief during the depression that struck shortly afterward. Welfare records contain repeatedly the words, "Tried truck gardening again, failed. . . ." "Does not wish to make attempt a third time. . . ."

An observant merchant, who lived in the Middle West during the drought and crop failures of the 1930's, says that he found among such Deltans the same dejection, the same conviction of helplessness, that had spread among his own people. One St. Bernard man asked me, when he finished a recital of those years, "Eh, whatcha gonna do?"

CHAPTER 16

"La Politique . . . She Stink, She Stink!"

For exactly one hundred years, outsiders have heard of the Delta at intervals as a place of public affairs with an overripe odor. In 1844, Plaquemines parish changed the political history of Louisiana and won a new kind of national fame for itself. Its leaders used a device which, one might say, first mechanized elections in the state, resorting to the steamboat as a means of turning out voters.

Until the 1840's Louisiana had been generally in the column of the Whigs, the organization that in its day had become in large measure the party of property. An oft-quoted jibe of the opposition was that one Whig knew another "by the instinct of gentlemen." The Democrats formed what was then predominantly the organization of the new and rising fellow. Into the state were moving thousands of settlers from other parts of America, yeomen, small farmers, and laborers. In New Orleans many immigrants were joining the poorer natives of the country to clamor for the ballot. The earlier pattern of Louisiana government, it need hardly be emphasized, was something less than sympathetic to the common man. The franchise was rigidly restricted in the aristocratic tradition. If an individual could not show that he possessed property, what interest had he in public affairs? Yet the lesser people insisted on pressing forward; rabble-rousers like that Jackson in the White House were stirring them to vulgar hopes and impudent demands.

With the year 1844, Whig faced Democrat in an evenly balanced contest for the state as for the nation; the presidential vote was to be one of the closest in American records. The Delta parishes of St. Bernard and Plaquemines were lumped with New Orleans and other adjoining localities to form one unit. The Whigs controlled the city machinery, and practically all the rest of the district. The Democrats said that they expected to be cheated of their proper ballots by the Whig managers. The Whigs fought against the Democratic tendency to attract the newcomers, especially the newly enfranchised immigrants. Regularly at the polling places the cry rang forth: "Clear out the Irish and German so-and-sos!" The booths were cleared, regardless of law.

This time the Louisiana Whigs seemed fairly confident. But they forgot Plaquemines parish. The opposition was in control there, under the leadership of a stout Democrat. The division had a comparatively small constituency—a few plantation owners, a handful of trappers and hunters. Yet the Whigs underestimated the opposition. The state Democratic leader was John Slidell, a commercial lawyer, not an earnest equalitarian but an astute observer who could follow a trend when he saw it. Mr. Slidell and his assistants were probably no more blameworthy than the officials of the other side. But they appeared to be more ingenious, at the least.

The law of the time required no "local" registration of voters. Within a district, a man could report to any polling booth that he wished. Fertile minds went to work on these facts. Early on the proper morning two steamboats, the *Planter* and the *Agnes,* churned their way downriver. They were filled with good fellows from New Orleans, Democrats all, who would use their American privilege of voting where they wished—in Plaquemines parish. The good fellows cast their ballots at least once; a few sour sources later claimed that some did it at three separate places to make sure their will would be expressed.

When they learned the results the Whigs gasped. The party's newspaper asked its readers to bear with it until it regained its "faculties." In Plaquemines, for the previous four years, the Whig vote had been 40, then 93, then 36, then 37. For the Democrats the balloting had begun with 250 in 1840, then gone to 179, then to 310 and now, marvelously—to 1007. The latest Democratic vote in the parish was larger than the white male population of all ages when last counted! Even in the fruitful Delta, inhabitants did not multiply so quickly. And the difference between this newest Democratic vote in the parish and its previous high figure—lo and behold, it was almost the identical state majority for the party. The two steamboats had won all Louisiana for the Democrats. Denunciations and investigations followed; the election stood. And for years "Plaquemines" remained a term of derision, and a "Plaquemines count" meant a piece of bold manipulation.

As time went by, Deltans improved on this example, manufacturing constituents without outside help. In 1896, a casual observation was made that 1200 more ballots were recorded in the same parish than there happened to be voters. In 1930, St. Bernard had a registration of 2454; when it went to the polls, it recorded itself as 3979 for Huey P. Long and 9 for his opponent. In one part of this exuberant place, the grand total of population, white, Negro, infant, adolescent, male, female, reached 912; of this number, 913 exercised their prerogative. In the following election the parish eliminated the blemish of those nine negative ballots by casting a completely unanimous vote for its champion! The enraged oppositionists were told that they must have put their votes in the wrong box.

Shortly afterward the federal government grew inquisitive. A friend of mine was at the sheriff's side when an assistant brought the newest figures—about 3000 for the right man, about 20 for the other. He jibed at the sheriff, "Looks like you're slipping." Twenty adverse ballots—they were not at all in the Delta tradition. The sheriff smiled: "Times are changing. Nowadays you got to let people vote the way they think!" The feeling has been general in Louisiana that not only the people, but many of the muskrats as well, vote the way they think in the Delta.

Feudal from the start, the design of such matters in the Delta has changed little. For years each parish has had a master, who was district attorney, or sheriff, or judge. Government, like other things, was from above. Education came late, delayed in part by the natural difficulties of the surroundings. An inquiry showed that about 695 out of 700 voters in one ward signed with a mark—a state of affairs which served to simplify things for the man at the top. Yet, though there may be little understanding of governmental principles per se, there is sharp attention to la politique—more than that, a frenzied, almost hysterical absorption in the subject. Day in, day out, Deltans think about it, talk about it, plan for it. An amazed non-resident, after his first visit, told me, "I think there are more politics than people down there."

The present century has seen this concern grow more, rather than less, avid. One factor has been the series of heavy blows to the Delta economy, and the consequent dependence on other means of livelihood. The institution of the political big shot, who finances the purchase of a lugger or gives a handout, has grown with the years. Even when roads were extended, political inbreeding did not disappear. The Deltans take delight in intrigues small and large; they whisper and they confer, they laugh and they boast. Eyes sparkle with plans; old men slap palms against foreheads, blow lustily on fingertips as they differ; for mile after mile, there is argument and argument. Ah, but non. It is not so. But yes, I swear it before the Virgin. That man stole fifty dollar.' May le Bon Dieu strike me dead as I eat this gumbo. . . . It is no place of pale distinctions, of delicate balancings.

Here in the Delta, single groups of enterprising citizens are able to maintain their grasp upon public funds for phenomenal periods of time. Dynasties flourish for twenty, thirty, forty or more years. The natives often say: "Let one set get in, and it take ol' hell and high water to get 'em out." An entrenched clan can be harder to dislodge than the levee of the 1927 flood; the dynamite must be heavily packed and strongly charged.

The finger of the boss inserts itself into practically everything; if the finger does not like the feel of what it finds, the clenched hand beats down. A man will not necessarily deal with the grocer who gives him a lower rate; he will go to the one that the master favors. When he must buy a new boat, it will be of a certain make, obtained from the proper salesman. One thoughtless fellow acquired his vessel through a cousin in New Orleans, who represented another firm. On his return, a message awaited, and a stiff dressing-down. If the boat were not sent back and one of the other type acquired within forty-eight hours, he and two of his relatives would be out of jobs.

That both relatives were employed in private industry was a point over which no one raised a question. The operator of a shop or factory knows what the boss wants, and also what he himself wants—peace. He will think twice before he disregards a suggestion that this or that man be dropped for "disloyalty." His licenses can develop flaws; his establishments can become public nuisances overnight. Or his customers will slip away; whatever service he offers, he may find that people do not want it. A man seen entering his business premises will receive ominous looks, and a "report" will go in. A child who ventures there will get a warning lecture outside: "I know you' Papa, and you gon' get whip' good!"

The system has its positive side. Support your candidate properly and you can plan your next four years with the virtual certainty that you will have a public job, and work or not as you wish. The notion that a man must perform duties here to draw a pay check is, of course, fanciful. If you like, you can send a son or nephew for your envelope. In an emergency, around voting time, or flood water, your presence may help, but then, too, it is not essential. You may provide a proxy. (To be seen at work may be beneath the dignity of a proper jobholder.) If it is ruled that you must carry out your duties, this is an arbitrary abuse of power by an immediate superior—certainly a breach of trust.

Other benefits can be equally concrete. Some years ago one parish boss called upon various well-placed backers. He had a few friends who were poor fellows. The others wouldn't mind giving space along the river for some houses, would they? Rent? These were *poor* folks. He wanted them accommodated. The squatters-by-edict caught wood from the Mississippi and built neat houses on the lands of the others. After some time they came to regard themselves as owners of the sites as well as the buildings, and they still occupy them.

For a long period any small industry moving into the Delta knew that it would have to reach a clear understanding with the master and his friends before it would be "allowed." Sure, the company could use the owner's son and a few of its own forces from other places; but the rest, they would be men sent around by the boss. Sure, if any of them did damage, or couldn't count right, the company didn't have to keep them. The boss would send replacements. During one phase the attitude of a reigning organization practically halted all movement into the parish by outsiders, job-hunters or job-givers. The boss wanted the status quo; he was not especially interested in additional establishments. They might upset things; they could also compete with his own line or two of trade.

Within recent years new types of mass industry have arrived, following the discovery of minerals in the two parishes. The corporations insisted on bringing in a certain number of men whom they knew from elsewhere. Ultimately, in the important cases, agreements were reached; the political organization was to provide a certain large percentage of all employees. If the company did not want trouble, it complied scrupulously with the arrangement.

The past decade in Plaquemines has brought changes to make the heads of less agile politicos swim. In the early 1930's the parish was at low ebb. The plantations were gone, the depression was gnawing; officials had to scurry for payroll funds. Suddenly came the mineral discoveries—wealth such as had never been visualized, and taxes to match. In 1932 Plaquemines had a budget of only $35,000 or so; in ten years this had gone to $425,000. Not many American counties can record such a proportion of increase. Those fortunate enough to be in office at the time could not be blamed for realizing that here was the stuff with which to cement themselves into blissful, perhaps permanent position.

It became difficult to find a family or a branch without a connection to the public payroll. The range of posts grew intricate—supervisors of front levees, supervisors of back levees, drainage foremen, parish mechanics, supervisors and engineers, oil gaugers, and many others. In later years, complications developed when all too many rushed to the payrolls. Could the jobs be curtailed? What's the matter with you, man; you got a sunstroke? Instead, governmental functions could be curtailed to maintain an undiminished array of jobholders.

A friend took me to a badly clogged waterway, where fish were dying and bridges sagging. He gestured: "Haven' kep' this up lately. Added four new inspectors, and didn' have enough money lef' for dredging." His voice held no resentment. "But what about you people that live along here?" I asked. It turned out that several of them, including my friend, belonged to families that had received the extra jobs. It would hardly have been graceful to complain.

The new industries whose funds provide most of the taxation carry on quietly, complying with suggestions. Usually they show little concern with the way the parish is operated. Their main interest lies in keeping the company's levies, in official phraseology, as " reasonable" as possible. As a result of this windfall of industrial money, the local electorate pays less than it otherwise would. Officers with understandable pride set up billboards proclaiming theirs "the lowest tax rate in the state." And everybody is pleased, except the opposition. One furious man of the other side retorts, "Why, with all that cash coming in, we people shouldn't have to pay a penny. They ought to declare a dividend out of the company taxes, and pay *us*—so much a head!"

The rivals struggle on, despite many handicaps, for their chance to get in. In certain parts of the parishes it is possible to be oppositionists and survive. One faction patronizes a store on the left side of the road. The other will use the place on the right, and never can a man transfer his trade without proclaiming thereby that he has altered his allegiance. It is not advisable for him to be seen in too many conversations, however offhand they may be, with an individual of the other faction, even if he went to school with him. No matter how excellent a trapper a Deltan may be, he can never get a lease from an operator of the other side. When a shrimping crew is selected, the boat's owner must check the affiliations of all members. This one says he won't trawl with that one, even if his children have to starve. Within families, splits go deep. One branch joins one faction; the opposition gives a job to another, and estrangement is automatic. Not until I found myself in the middle of such hostilities did I know the meaning of the expression, "They hate like cousins."

Attempts to develop cooperative farming ventures have failed, in part because of suspicious individualism that has its roots in the past; at least in equal part because of this deep-rending partisanship. Is this outfit you're talking about going to be for us or them? Both? Are you crazy? Similarly in trapping, shrimping, and other activities, Deltans have never organized effectively. That the owners and operators are frequently themselves political figures is no small factor. Leaders on both sides know the maxim: divide and rule.

"Unions" have been proclaimed, but cursory questioning shows them to be mere adjuncts of the political machines. Among trappers, a "union" leader has turned out at times to be none other than the landowner himself! In one case, shrimpers combined among themselves and were winning a higher price, when a rival body suddenly appeared from nowhere. Another faction had formed it; and it would take any pay that the canners offered. The original element lost, and the standards further declined. In one or two cases when women set up their own groups at canning places, someone enlisted male union-breakers of the opposition. A few forays, the killing of one or more women shrimp pickers, and matters were back to normal.

Louisianians, who know piebald politics as well as any, have long been open-mouthed at happenings in these problem parishes. Whether it is a matter of some racy peccadillo or of something worse, there is often an almost disarming amorality about the deed. Non, that ain' bad. It's the way you do a thing when you wan' make sure it's done right! Year after year the Deltans have blazed at each other with charges ranging from the merely fantastic and sprightly to the most libelous. Inquiry often indicates that at least half the claims are correct on both sides.

On election day I met a Delta acquaintance. He was up early; had he voted already? Sure, sure; got it over with in a second. As he drove by the polling place, he waved his hand. His friends knew how he felt, and they took care of the matter for him. Others, who also arose with the first light, spent all day in unsuccessful attempts to cast their ballots. Going to the usual location, they found that the officials had changed the booth. Nobody knew where it was now; certainly no oppositionist would tell.

Hours later, they learned that it was far back toward the lakes; they would need a motorboat to get there. After more delays they obtained one. But as they headed toward the spot by the obvious route, it was blocked to them. This was a private canal, open only to adherents of the other side. They had to take a highly circuitous passage, through bays and bayous; when they arrived, they discovered that the poll had just closed—in advance of the time set by law. They could complain, of course. But the committee that would hear them was controlled by the boss; it *was* the boss. In any case, the election was over.

On another occasion, as the deadline for qualifying of candidates approached, the committee did not announce a meeting for the purpose. Daily the opposition demanded that the members set a date. They received no reply; none of the committee members knew anything about it. The deadline passed; then it was disclosed that the committee had gathered a week earlier, after midnight in a boat back of the bays. No other candidates offering themselves, the organization qualified only those of its own faction.

The ruling element takes a step clearly depriving the opposition of its clear rights. The opposition prepares an injunction, setting forth precedents long recognized in the courts. The only difficulty is that the judge cannot be located to receive it and act upon it. No, he ain' at his office. Sorry, he's not home. The judge is in New Orleans. The judge is fishing. Don' know where the judge is. The last day for action passes. The judge, refreshed after a rest, comes back the next morning.

A man is arrested on a minor charge. He will be able to get out on bond at once, of course. Whoever thinks that, does not know the place. The citizen wilts in jail for a week. No one who can sign for him seems to be available. It's too bad, yes. Eventually the accusation, obviously false, is dropped, and he is released. (Sometimes the victim in such instances has to apply to the state supreme court to get out.) In a related case, the grand jury calls a witness offered by an oppositionist. The witness finds two deputy sheriffs at his door; they are to bring him to court. On the way, he says, they turn off the road, one pulls him from the car and beats him unconscious while the other watches for passersby. A report is made that the witness-to-be "picked a fight" with the two deputies, and the witness-to-be does not testify.

Item of informality: The boss of one of the parishes has a tiff with his wife. They remain together, but do not talk for several weeks. He gets even; he orders her taxes raised. She complies with his wishes, and the taxes go down.

On the witness stand a number of years ago, one of the sheriffs was asked about gambling and related violations of the law in his jurisdiction. He made a rather celebrated reply: "St. Bernard is the dumping ground of the city of New Orleans. We get the worst of everything that the city doesn't want. At night we have all kinds of visitors. On my appropriation I can't patrol the marsh, the Gulf, the highways, help the federal officers, and look after everything else. Out of last month's salary I got only seventeen dollars." He concluded, in ringing notes, "You have to have money to be sheriff here, or you have to rob a lot!"

Later a Delta deputy sheriff, who handled all court matters for his office, testified that he himself owned and operated slot machines. The statement drew amusement, but not in the Delta. Why pick on one poor deputy? Who didn't have them? The number of the machines has grown with the years, in bars, groceries, notion stores, garages, and elsewhere. Once a constable went berserk with a hammer. He was tired of seeing the machines everywhere, with children playing them, he declared. Walking into a barber shop, he broke up a supply belonging to the chief deputy's brother; then he moved on to oil stations, restaurants, and other locations. In each case he recognized machines belonging to other officers, justices, wardens, and the rest. At last another official halted him and arrested him. His victims demanded damages for destruction of property.

At almost regular intervals, Delta officials have been called up on charges of misfeasance, malfeasance, nonfeasance; bribery, organization of "crime rings," subornation of perjury, instigation to arson, extortion, dereliction of duty; malpractice, slander, libel, and other offenses. A recent incident led to the ouster of Judge J. Claude Meraux, who was accused, among other things, of corruption, misconduct, and extortion in office, favoritism, oppression, misdemeanors, and incompetence. He was said to have operated a divorce and annulment game, handling scores of cases in which he had no jurisdiction over either party or the causes of action. A deputy testified that the judge approved bills for jury expenses and used the money to buy clothes, gasoline, paint, soap, rope, and other articles.

When an outside jurist acted temporarily in the Delta, he found himself bemused by the state of affairs. He dismissed a grand jury and a jury panel, and he shook an angry finger at the members for failing to do sworn duties, for passing by violations of all kinds. Practically nobody seemed to want justice, said the visiting judge; everybody was out to protect his own side. A newspaper commented, "If the Judge succeeds in getting untainted juries down there, he is a wizard as well as a seer."

The current dictator of much of the Delta is Leander H. Perez of Plaquemines, a man in his mid-forties, of medium height, of plump and square-spectacled face. An attorney and individual of many business connections and many plans, he is of Spanish descent and shows it; he has had a college education and also shows that. (Not the least impressive of his skills is his capacity to correct the grammar of opponents at the bar.) Governors, mayors and heads of corporations have asked his advice and often taken it; in justice to Leander, it should be noted that he has generally received a recompense proportionate to his effort.

A quarter century ago he began a career as a highly obscure attorney at a dusty desk in New Orleans. But it became clear that his field was the Delta, and his best work was not to be done at a desk. His father was a lesser native politico; Leander knew his people and their place. Appointed to a judgeship, he was later elected to it and then to his present rank as district attorney. Today he is The Man of Plaquemines parish, controller and handler of practically all boards, committees, public offices, public officers, and other things public and private. At an early date he aligned himself with Huey P. Long, emerging Kingfish of Louisiana, and learned by observation. He counseled Huey, and Huey several times paid tribute to Leander as one so wise that Huey himself watched him. After Huey's death, Leander proceeded in the Long manner, with adaptations and improvements.

At first glance Leander might seem a misfit in his role; he lacks the hale camaraderie, the big-bellied joviality. He seems more the well-paid bookkeeper of a company than the political autocrat. Unlike Huey, Leander operates quietly, in the wings of the stage. His actors—chairmen, secretaries, and others—have their speeches and resolutions and proclamations, written well in advance. When there is a slip-up it is usually noted that the so-and-so just didn't do things the way Leander said. Some have termed him one of the two or three shrewdest men in the state. Others, paraphrasing a remark of the Kingfish, observe that there may be smarter men in Louisiana, but that they don't live in the Delta. In recent years Leander has resided on part of an old plantation, called, not inappropriately, Promised Land.

Leander's rise to greatest stature coincides with the discovery of minerals in the Delta. At times impolite men have tried to pry into various companies with which the Boss is connected by report. Each time Leander has stopped them. He was largely responsible, through many lawsuits, for the elimination of the Louisiana Crime Commission, formed by the administration which succeeded the Long regime, after the commission began to inquire into Leander's supposed relationships. To date he continues one of the preeminent holdovers of the Long period. Yet he remains a czar whose power is finesse rather than the warmth of personal appeal. He still has the windfall tax money; while it lasts, he can be expected to nourish well the soil of his political growth.

New celebrity came to Leander in Louisiana's "Little War" of 1943–4, hostilities which brought the Delta the kind of notice that Huey himself once achieved for the state. Leander's sheriff died with less than a year of his term to run. State law declares that in such cases the governor shall name a successor. But here was a hostile governor, Sam Jones; and Leander would have none of Jones' appointee. Barricades rose at the courthouse at Pointe à la Hache; armed deputies patrolled the scene. This was in theory a public building, but none could enter unless he satisfied the custodians regarding his attitude toward Leander.

The governor went to the courts; their machinery ground slowly. With its National Guard at the battlefronts (the other ones, in Europe and Africa), Louisiana had formed a State Guard to replace it. Leander decided that if the governor could have troops, so could he. Up sprang a parish Wartime Emergency Patrol. The State Guard drilled and marched; Leander's guard drilled and marched. Now the state supreme court ruled in favor of the governor's appointee as sheriff. The governor "earnestly requested" Leander and Leander's man to give up. In legalistic verbiage they told the governor to go jump into the Mississippi River. Leander's guard hurried to positions at the courthouse for twenty-four hour sentry duty. New barricades lifted; no stranger, no matter how mild he looked, could enter.

Asserting that Leander was defying the courts and creating a situation of "open rebellion," the governor declared martial law in the parish. Leander retorted that the governor himself was trying to "incite riots," and called on his grand jury to investigate the governor. From the district judge, Leander obtained an order restraining the State Guard from setting foot in the parish. He thundered that if the lives of innocents were to be lost, the governor and not Leander would have their blood on his head. The State Guard mobilized in New Orleans; word was current that it would move the next day on Pointe à la Hache. Leander called a mass meeting of all good citizens before the courthouse; the time coincided with the expected approach of the soldiers. It appeared to some that the Deltans would be drawn up as a shield before Leander's military. The latter brandished their guns: "It'll be them or us, and we guarantee it won't be us." To prove that they meant what they said, they fired a shot or two after a reporter and a photographer.

A convoy of the State Guard started down from New Orleans —thirty-one trucks, an ambulance cruiser, and command cars bearing mounted machine guns. While the newspapers carried large headlines, Leander drew forth his own revolver and summoned his forces. Near the English Gothic castle of Orange Grove, at Braithwaite, a Plaquemines outpost had been set up. As the State Guard approached, three parish deputies stepped forth into the road to serve it with the local court order telling it to keep out. The leading cars came to a screeching halt, two officers leaped out, disarmed the three and took them into custody. Their automobile was put into service for liaison work. Scouting parties moved along the levee to guard against snipers or flank attacks; the State Guard rolled on.

A short distance above Pointe à la Hache rose Leander's place, at Promised Land. (For some time, all who passed on the public road had been routed through Leander's yard, for inspection. If they failed to meet approval, they did not use that road.) Today a truck on the road barred all passage; carefully ditched on each side lay other heavy-duty machines. The armed parish men waited. Negro drivers who were delivering oyster shells had been stopped, and their supplies dumped into a pile four feet high, six feet across. A heavy container of gasoline was brought out, and a flaming obstacle crackled. Hesitating, Leander's men watched the approach of the troops, then leaped into their own machines and drove down toward Pointe à la Hache. (One report declared that hunters shooting game in the nearby marsh brought on the nervous retreat.)

The State Guard halted to shovel away the shells and remove the trucks. At the courthouse, promises of derring-do were dwindling. Leander's "mass meeting" had not been a thorough success; twelve people appeared, six of them deputy sheriffs. Some of the warriors walked out of the back door. A passing Army patrol plane and a bomber circled low; the good men milled about in alarm. Leander cogitated, waved his arm, and he and the last of his forces slipped over the levee. The classic Leander had swum the Hellespont for love of a lady; the Leander of Plaquemines disappeared across the Mississippi on his "free ferry," to get away from the military.

Six hundred soldiers took over. Within an hour they had bought every bottle of mosquito lotion in the community and were using it. In a day or so, having exhausted the available cistern water, some were bathing out of tin cups, and saying that this all seemed more and more like foreign duty. The Office of Price Administration announced that the gasoline used to fire the oyster shells had been rationed stuff, and that it was investigating. Each side charged the other in court with conspiracy to murder. Leander added accusations of burglary and kidnaping. The master of the free ferry filed federal admiralty proceedings, seeking ten thousand dollars in damages, saying that the State Guard had falsely arrested him, intimidated, humiliated, mortified, and degraded him, all of which tended to impair the value of his license as a second class pilot.

Forgotten in the many flurries was a Negro in the jail, sentenced to be electrocuted for murder on the morning the State Guard arrived. He missed death, but also his meals for a day and a half. The new officials had never heard of him. Then it developed that the governor had granted him a thirty-day reprieve; this, too, had gone unnoticed. How did the condemned man feel about the reprieve? He didn't know about it. Well, then, what did he think about the scheduled execution? He hadn't been told of that, either. Everybody had been very busy around here, you know.

On the first Sunday that followed, the Guardsmen knelt beside the natives in the little church of St. Thomas, and the Reverend Peter Oswald, S.V.D., urged his listeners to "love thy neighbor as thyself." The forces were maintained for several months, because the state said it feared that if they were withdrawn the appointed sheriff and his men would be killed in the night. These were the months when American and British soldiers were fighting their way up the Italian peninsula, and the Russian Army was moving against the Dnieper River defenses of the Nazis. The sheriff's term expired; the 1944 parish elections arrived, and Leander and his men won all over again.

Despite its less solemn notes, this is one of the gloomiest aspects of Delta life. Some who call themselves realists shrug and say that these people get what they deserve. It is cruel to believe that any set of persons should merit some of the things that have happened here. They have never known anything other than overlordship; one first touch of democracy might bring a number of changes.

CHAPTER 17

Shadings

WITHOUT its people of African descent, the Delta scene would lack something of its gaiety and its warm humors. It would also miss a portion of its sadness. The darker Deltan knows laughter, and he knows tragedy as well, the tragedy that comes of racial minority and also of countless uncertain gradations between two colors.

Many of his fellows have a skin that seems jet-black and shadowless; others show so fair a complexion that none but a neighbor would say that they were of the Negro race. The rest are of every intervening hue, tawny, brown, mahogany, and others. Though most speak English, some know nothing but French. A few use Spanish, and a number of them, like the whites, command something of the three tongues with an occasional smattering of additional ones. And though traditionally they have been Catholics, a large element have become Protestants, "Bab-teestes" in particular, even when they talk French in the pews and bring beads and rosaries with them. Whatever their shadings, these Deltans have exercised a quiet, unending, largely unperceived influence on those about them.

They stem from several groups. Some are descendants of slaves who spoke the language of their Latin owners; others are grandchildren of Negroes brought from the Atlantic seaboard by their Anglo-Saxon masters, who took up only a few words of Delta French. But many of the lighter-skinned ones declare with flashing eye that their people were "free—never slaves, no!" In Louisiana, or in Cuba or the West Indies, these ancestors had achieved freedom and then maintained themselves by their skills.

In the Delta of pre-Civil War days there appeared several planters of mixed blood, whose mothers had usually been mistresses of white men. Acquiring holdings and slaves of their own, such growers led circumspect lives that had rewards but also limitations. In matters pertaining to plantation management, they approached their white neighbors on approximately equal footing. Able in money affairs, they were careful to meet their business obligations; their accounts were kept in scrupulous order. Otherwise, they held to themselves. Their intimates, if they had any, must be of their own mulatto blood. Old parish records show a surprising number of slave owners whose names are followed by the notation, "free man of color" or "free woman of color."

An Orleanian made a number of business calls in the Delta one day during the last century. In each case, as the agent of a merchants' group, he was received with courtesy; he was impressed in particular with the last place at which he stopped. The French-speaking master, white-haired, goateed, met him at the door with easy grace, and escorted him into a drawing room of velvet elegance. A clap of the hands—a chair for the guest, Emilie. Another signal and a second servant appeared—a glass of water now, vite, vite! Still a third servant came with sherry—or would monsieur prefer brandy, perhaps? The visitor finished his transaction and left. That night at a public meeting of the sugar men, in connection with the tariff, he saw all of the owners of estates whom he had met except the final one. He turned to the chairman: Why wasn't Mr. ——— here? The chairman was surprised. The man he mentioned, sir, had colored blood. The Orleanian said then, and says now, "I would never have guessed."

Little by little the mulatto planters disappeared. Some of their children went back to New Orleans or New York or Paris, where they had been educated. Others took small houses along the river, becoming farmers and tenants, or opened stores. After the Civil War, other divisions by shadings occurred. Of those who remained in the Delta, the darker ones stayed in the upper, more settled places, closer to the city, often in the old plantation quarters. The lighter ones filtered into the lower stretches. They spoke French, sometimes Spanish; they had a background of greater experience in fending for themselves than did the former slaves. Toward the Gulf, in the half-agricultural, half-aquatic life of the narrow fringes, no great holdings had ever existed. They found themselves not a rigidly restricted class but one of several varied elements: French, Spanish, Tocko, Filipino, all working at much the same tasks, fishing, trapping, raising rice and a few vegetables.

Here rose casual friendship rather than sharp resentment and division. In most frontiers, the settlers manage among themselves. Along the cut-off reaches few came to point a finger and raise questions about the exact status of this or that family whose wharf was next to another's. The lighter-colored people took to the waters, thatched their roofs with palmettos and sang lively French songs to their children in the purple twilights. When their homes were threatened, all of the lower Deltans fought together against water and storm. And in some cases, as elsewhere, further intermarriage occurred. A number of the lighter-skinned, by industrious application, achieved a fair economic success, building larger homes for themselves, prospering with expanded markets.

But new forces, reaching the Delta in the present century, brought new issues and social crises. The mass-scaled industries introduced their rules: Jobs for the whites, none for the Negroes. Such had been the regulations in other parts of the South; such they would be here. Men who, in the marsh, had labored side by side to support their children, could no longer work together. The lower Delta was being shaped by outside influences into a different pattern.

When centralized schools were set up, officials met and lists of prospective pupils were canvassed. This one, to whom was she related? What did that family do for a living? Would these be inclined to fight back? Such questions were not always asked in words. A quick glance, silence . . . a point was raised and settled. Ensuing scenes were tearful. Non, Monsieur, I am Spanish, I swear it. . . . A whitefaced boy, fist clenched in his pocket, maintained that his family was part Indian, part French. Everybody knew that, oui. You just come and ask at where we live. . . . A hysterical woman beat her hands on a table. It was just those people down the road. They had a fight with us over some duck', and it was their way to get back. An' don' you remember, Julien, the time my grandpère saved your uncle? Is this a way to pay back our family, ahn?

New bitternesses were aroused. Children whispered that this

or that one was "dipped." In a school yard a taunt was passed: "You got a spot!" The usual retaliation was to pick up an oyster shell and throw it at the tormentor's head. Year after year the teachers were to receive anonymous notes: Did they know that so-and-so was not white? In at least one case, the word carried a threat. The parent of one girl sent a message claiming that she could prove another to be "tainted." She had just learned that the child in dispute was about to be graduated with first honors, while her own daughter was second. Now was that right, Mamzelle? The implication was clear. After long thought, the instructor gave the honors to the second pupil. "It seemed, all considered, the kinder thing to do," she said.

For the first time, the Delta saw the phenomenon known as a "color trial." Suits were threatened, and sometimes brought and won. Weeping parents faced each other before judges, and the shouted accusations and whispered denials went into the record. Damages were awarded, and decisions issued that this or that one was, without question, white. The aroused racial hatreds did not die.

Further differences grew, with gradations of caste based on varying hues. (These were not entirely new, but in later years they have strengthened.) On one side were the whites; opposite them, the dark; between them, the middle shades. The whites felt superior to the light-skinned; the light-skinned looked down on the blacks or near-blacks. In meeting places, and especially in churches, three divisions rose—a kind of layer cake of color, whites in the center, blacks to one side, middle-hued to the other. No member of one element could move under any circumstances to an empty place among the next. There would be mutterings, and a fight after or during Mass.

One mulatto group has resented its classification as "Negro" and refused to send its children to the same school as the darker ones. Bitterly, persistently, it has maintained its position against those only a shade too dark skinned. In a community in which the lighter-colored group predominates, the children drive away the slightly darker ones; those must go to a "nigger" school. When a darker teacher is sent to conduct a class for light-skinned, revolts break out. Parents will not permit their children to attend; lines of shadings have been set up for instructors as well as for students. A religious organization made a promising start toward Negro education in the Delta a few years ago; against the inner barriers of color, the effort collapsed.

A singled-storied movie house thrived with a three-section division. Its manager decided to expand, to a more elaborate establishment of two levels. The whites would be downstairs, the others would divide the upper floor, each taking half. Both darker groups resented this; many of the middle element would not be "put up there with the black." The ambitious owner lost much of his trade.

The darker Negro, an earthier fellow, scorns such mulattoes. "Mules, neither one thing or nothing," and he spits when he says it. A mulatto declares with assurance, "But we have good blood, some of the best, n'est-ce pas?" When a mulatto child was born in the earlier day, as the tradition has it, the family inspected closely: "Not a bad lip. . . ." "*Good* hair, yes. . . ." "A nice nose, wouldn't you say?" In certain of the quadroon families of the Delta, a girl knew from her childhood that she must "proteck her skin." She and her sisters wore sunbonnets whenever they left the house, or when they sat on the gallery where the glare was strong. Never were they permitted to go barefoot; they donned long stockings as well as shoes, regardless of the status of the family. Over their arms they drew gloves against the sun. One who saw them walking about in summer with throats well covered by scarves did not conclude that they suffered from colds. When their brothers had hair that was not straight, they cut it short, kept it short, and wore hats wherever they could. All of this, pathetic or diverting as it might be to outsiders, was of course a conforming to the rule of caste that had been ordained by the society about them.

Deltans have charged that numerous light-skinned colored have left the Delta to be accepted elsewhere as white. The stories on the subject are doubtless exaggerated, part of the folklore of the place, but the change has occurred in some instances. In the cities there was no woman from down the road to whisper and remember an incident or a face from the past. Over one who made the decision to "passer à blanc," a nagging fear might hang for years, for all of his or her life. Sometimes, too, a tense moment arrived, when a new-found security was at stake. A marriage impended, or some other event that required a certificate with a word or letter opposite a blank space. The man or woman would slip back to the Delta in the evening, to someone who had been a friend of the family, a former official. One such friend has told of it: "They handed me the paper. They did not argue or cry, nor did I bring up the thing that was in the mind of both of us. I perjured myself like a gentleman, and when I prayed to God, I told Him I had acted to the best of my lights."

A family has been known to divide by gradations of color. With the mulattoes in the church a tall woman looks straight ahead as she says her beads. On the opposite side a darker, hulking man gazes in her direction. She ignores him, though they are first cousins. At funerals among the lighter-hued, a black woman will walk in to take a place. She is received with constraint, but she can insist on her right; she is a niece of the dead man. "Everybody pulls from everybody else," nods a much-wrinkled carver of decoy ducks. "They yank so hard they all fall on their backsides." Upon these feelings of separation, many have played to their own advantage. Here, too, politics has been making itself increasingly felt. The bosses use one group against the next; by keeping each in a turmoil of resentment toward the rest, they win over all of them.

At one edge of Buras and at several other points, the middle groups have separate settlements, to which the darker ones are not admitted. In the lines of plain cottages along the road, all of the residents have straight hair, yellowish complexions, and jet-black eyes, and the faces possess a markedly Latin quality. Sometimes the cheekbone is high, and a sharp nose and coppery tone to the skin give evidence of American Indian in the family. Again, a father or grandfather was Filipino, and a distinct, swarthy type results. These people know the lives of hybrids, with ties to two or more groups and full membership in none. Along several canals the settlements multiply, the level of their existence fluctuating with the seasons, now flush, now verging on want. In the deep, luminous eyes of the healthy children, the shadow of a coming melancholy is reflected.

The dark people live quietly along their river. They are farmers, fisherman, and orange growers. Their wives wield the hoe in the gardens when the husbands find jobs as helpers on the shrimp boats and carriers of oyster sacks. The family enjoys its wine and its fish dinners and seems to have taken on an additional slow somnolence from its surroundings. Few can hope to acquire larger homes, as did some of their fathers; "progress" has further reduced their opportunities. Yet they stay on; they go to their churches, Catholic or Baptist, and they have their dances in their orange-packing sheds. Negroes from New Orleans send down three- and four-man bands; rich, quivering notes ring from the bright rooms, and lights flicker upon the ponds of inky water. Throaty laughter echoes over the levee; nothing has taken from these Deltans their capacity for easy joy.

To the Delta the Negroes have brought their superstitions, largely from Africa, and to them the whites, for the most part the French, have joined their own. A lush mixture has resulted, with members of both races and all shadings enjoying a rich spirit world all about them.

Commonest among the spirits are the revenants, simple ghosts—harmless creatures most of the time, with nowhere to go, roaming about a graveyard, fiddling among the orange trees, or trying, poor things, to sample a few oysters on a reef that they once dredged. A zombi is worse, a ghost with something on his mind. When you paddle through a swamp and see a zombi staring at you from a moss-hung branch, get out of that place, just to be on the safe side. How will you know a plain revenant from a zombi? My Delta friends say that it is simply a matter of personal perception; it cannot be clarified to one who has never beheld either. They can only explain, "When you first get a good look, you'll know the difference, all right!" Many of the poor revenants are only creeping about, trying to find a person who will do a little thing for them, a harmless act that will permit them to go back to their coffins and rest. Usually they want only a handful of salt. But, human nature being what it is, very few people will be inclined to do this for even the most angelic looking of revenants. He might turn out to be a zombi in disguise!

Many places in the Delta are to be avoided because strange things lurk there. For instance, there is Devil's Flat at the river edge, to which the French first gave the title Batture du Diable. Its haunting genius is a soldier lacking a head, a fellow halfway between revenant and zombi. Usually he behaves like a fatherly old man, talking nice as anything. But because he has been good humored, some are supposed to have taken liberties. He will tolerate only a certain amount of familiarity, and then he will explode at you. One drunk offered him a drink, and the old soldier hauled off and slapped him so hard that you could see the marks on his face in the middle of the afternoon the following Thursday.

Loups-garous (loogaroos) are not so plentiful as they used to be, but old people still warn against them. Every once in a while a man or woman is missed. His friends look and look, and always there is a certain animal nearby—a hog that they had never seen before, an odd black bird, a big dog. Eventually they will realize the truth—that thing is poor Emile! Some spirit caught him in its spell, and now Emile is trying to find a way to get back to himself. Or perhaps Emile has been a malevolent being all along, hopping back and forth into animal shape and up to all kinds of devilment that his friends never realized. At any rate, everybody in the neighborhood had better watch carefully now!

Sooner or later, no matter to whom you talk about the loups-garous, you will hear the classic story of the man and wife. Madame A. wondered when her husband stayed away for a week or more in the marsh, but like an obedient housewife she raised no questions. Occasionally she noticed a curiously spotted tomcat slinking around the levee. It peered and peered at the house, as if it wanted to make sure that it missed nothing. Madame A. grew annoyed, and tossed a bit of mud at it. The cat slipped away. The next day it was back, and she threw a stick. Crying, it moved off. The third morning, truly angry when it made its appearance, she advanced with a kitchen knife. It snarled; she tossed the knife, and it cut deeply into the left hind leg. The cat vanished at once. In an hour or so, Monsieur A. came from the marsh, limping, his left foot heavily bandaged. "I drop' my ax on it," he said, and avoided her eye. "Oui," she nodded, and went back to her housework. That cat didn't come back any more, let me tell you!

Things always to be avoided are the feu follets, the French equivalent of will-o'-the-wisps. Actually, they are bits of marsh gas, forming balls of flame, bouncing about the wet edges, in cemeteries, and along the swamps; but do not, I suggest, attempt to impress any superior knowledge of the subject upon a Deltan. (When I did, one fixed me with his eye: Had I ever found it coming after me? When I admitted that I had not, he pointed his finger: *He* had. And that settled me.) Some of the natives are sure these are, alas, the spirits of the poor bébés that died without being christened. Others believe they are merely free-lance villains, on the lookout for any available victim. All of the elderly and middle-aged people have seen them, and they have one bit of advice: If they move after you, you run like crazy.

Men, passing a graveyard at night, have spied little circles of light darting around the headstones, and then run home to creep shaking into bed. Others, catching sight of them at a distance, have stopped only long enough to fix a nail or their knife in a tree, before darting back to safety. A feu follet is fascinated by metal. When one comes at you, your best hope is to sidetrack him in this fashion. A man and his son, rowing together after dark, anxious to get home, suddenly halted at the same time. The father said to his boy, in trembling voice, "Al-*fred,* please to look what back of you!" Alfred was silent a moment, and then he muttered: "Papa, look wha's in back of you!" Each jerked his head about, saw a feu follet balanced on the edge of the skiff, bumping up and down as if anxious to leap upon him; and each jumped into the water and swam home. Just what happens when a feu follet gets you, I have never been able to find out. Come to think of it, I have never talked with one whom the feu follet succeeded in reaching. And it is this uncertainty that makes the feu follet the poor man's terror that it is.

From the 1880's and 90's until a comparatively recent day there grew up in the Delta an organized worship that was a mixture of elements from Louisiana, from France, and from Africa—a system of faith in mediums, with various additions. A sect largely of the mulattoes, it can be traced to a white man. An individual known as Monsieur Trin, who was an attorney in France, apparently a man of some means, was won to spiritualism when a wave of such belief swept the Continent. In Louisiana on a visit, he came to the Delta, gave demonstrations of table-tapping and "converted" many who met him. Soon the vicinity of Buras welcomed a disciple, one Antoine Langevin, an unkempt person of irregular habits. Langevin set himself up in a cabin, and the exciting intelligence spread that he could bring messages from the world of the dead. He sat at a table in a darkened room; from somewhere came knocks and frightening noises. It was the frère of Térence who wish' to speak to him. . . . This was his mère, who die' only six month' ago. . . . The crowds grew.

The belief adapted itself to the environment. On the walls of the meeting rooms hung religious pictures; altars rose with candles and statuary. From remnants of African voodooism, Langevin borrowed remedies, incantations, and other colorings. The priests looked on in disapproval, but he insisted that he and his followers were "Catholics." They believed in the Father, Son, and Holy Ghost, didn't they? But they felt also that it was possible to talk with the dead. Banned from the churches, they prospered to themselves, conducting regular services, baptisms, and burials. Several "cimitières des médioms" were set up about the river banks for the bodies of members.

A number of the mulatto men recall ceremonies which they witnessed as boys: "Sometime' we was invite' along; sometime' we jus' creep aroun' and watch. They was regular séance', like what you see in movie-picture, maybe. Ev'body form in a circle, and that man Langevin, he at the head. He go to sleep, like, on his feet, and people ax question', and the sperrit, it speak through his throat. All sort question'—how you are, what you get to eat now? Once I laugh' and my Maman crack' me on the head. She wan' hear more from her firs' husband, and when I bus' out like that, she had to wait till nex' week to get his ghos' back."

Another peeped at a ritual in the open air, with the members gathered to consider the proper treatments or remèdes for sick members. Before them stood Langevin, again in a trance. Each ailment was taken up in turn. A woman rose to tell of her sister who had mysterious stomach pains. Then all cried in unison to Langevin, "Quelle traitement faut-il?"—"What should the treatment be?"

"Traitement de patate!" The words came in a strange, faraway voice, that of a wraith from the beyond. They meant that a tea must be brewed of potato peelings.

The next case was presented, with an appeal for instructions: "Quelle traitment . . . ?"

"Traitement de ravés!" This was a malignant fever, and it called for a serious remède: tea compounded of large water roaches.

Again a request, and again the medium called the answer, "Traitement de vers!" It was a brew of earthworms. Clearly, the more nauseous the tea, the more efficacious it must be.

At intervals a message went out to the membership: A séance was to be held that night, beneath a high oak, or in one of the cemeteries of the mediums. The men describe the high priest as carrying "a religious book something like Father's across the river at the church," a massive volume with brass clasp which none but Langevin ever opened. It was Le Livre. In the light of the moon, standing beneath the drippings of moss, he let its pages fall and he read strange, impressive words. The denouement was a supplication of departed spirits for guidance and protection. Each member knelt and raised his arms or beat his head: "Ah, Esprit de Memère, soyez bon!"—"Ah, spirit of my Grandmother, be kind!" "Oh, mon Père . . . mon chèr Père au ciel!"—"Oh, my Father. . . . My dear Father in heaven!"

Our informant adds, "Some was getting like crazy-crazy. 'Looka there, there the sperrit coming!' Then they was all screaming and crying and pointing. Everybody was looking up and looking down and looking around. Then a knock somewhere and they yelled and hollered some more. It was a real layout, yes!"

The high priest lived a life of ease among his followers. He decreed regular feasts with brimming bowls of stewed chicken, with wine and other liquors. Places were set for the dead, and they must be served heaping dishfuls. Telling of it today, the men grin and say that though few talked of such matters, some always suspected that Langevin kept the dead people's portions for himself. "You had to clean out the chicken house to please that man." When a person died, the medium said, the soul remained on earth a full week, and must be pleased: prayers for him, words that would make him happy, and above all, food. At least once Langevin was discovered with his hands deep in the gravy after one of the feasts. He explained that he had gone back for a special message from the spirit.

Langevin never needed to ask for money; his followers saw that he had all he wished and more. A slothful fellow, he was supposed never to bathe. He acquired an expensive suit and he did not take it off "till it drop away, practically." By that time his followers had a replacement ready. After some years, Langevin himself died, and whether he could appreciate it or not, a lusty banquet was set about his grave. A few of the mulattoes continued the faith, but finally the last séance was held. The Catholic church took over one of the graveyards; another is deserted, a wet, thickly overgrown spot near the river, which some say is haunted by revenants and a few zombis. A mother tells a mischievous child, "I'll call ol' Langevin from his grave to you." Among the elders, including modern-day churchgoers, there is less scorn than might have been expected: "Langevin smott man. Médiom' not bad, tell you truth. Not bad as voodoo. Different like night and day. . . ." And one wonders what success a modern Langevin might have, with a few new trappings.

Today many Deltans, white as well as Negro, go to the remède-man or remède-woman far more often than to the doctor. He or she is a person with a "gift," a power granted by the gods to heal illnesses simple or serious. He does not sit in splendor or proud self-satisfaction; he works for a living at a shrimp factory or in his garden. He knows how to do certain curing things, he tells you; he will do them for all who call. It is his duty. For his services he can ask no price. If some want to leave a little present, c'est bien.

He tries to heal by teas and other medicines, prayers and incantations. For a sprained ankle or wrist, the remède-man will draw forth a string and, whispering a standard prayer with his own modifications, will tie eleven knots. Within three days, the trouble is gone. For a baby that is having trouble in teething, he holds ready a rattlesnake's vertebra, to be hung around his neck. To "raise a fallen palate," a knot of hair at the top of the head is pulled tight, and salt and pepper is swallowed. For one who injures a hand, a tisane, or tea, of parsley roots is used; applying it, the remède-worker makes the sign of the cross.

Regularly, in most of his treatments, he employs his index finger to make cross marks upon the flesh. It "bring God into the cure." For "sun-pain," or sunstroke, great care and no little skill are required, he says. Salt is dropped into a potful of river water to the accompaniment of prayers. Then the patient is bathed in the liquid. When this has been done three times, he is saved. The remède-man gives clear evidence that the heat has left the patient's head. He places a glass of water over it, and calls the family to see. Presto! Small bubbles rise in the water. Look at that heat pouring out!

There are remède-makers and remède-makers, specialists by inclination or by the demand of their customers. Some give heat treatments, or induce vomiting. Some set bones with considerable effectiveness, or cure simple infections. They murmur messages to the world beyond; they recite the Lord's Prayer and the Catholic Hail Mary in French. Their materials are often plain folk-medicines that have been effective in many places. In serious cases they may cause death or fail to avert it. Again, they or the patient's faith may bring recovery.

Marie is recognized as a leading remède-woman of the west bank. A mulatto of copper skin and straight black hair, she is a plump, serene woman in her fifties. Her father was celebrated for curing children of spasms; he prayed and he purged them. She does much of her work with "waste-away sickness." When a child is weakly, the mother calls Marie. Marie heats a large pot of water on the stove, says her rituals over it for seven minutes, dropping in her herbs and making her signs of the cross without interruption. A few baths in it, she tells you, and the child is pink with health. In the old days she obtained her "waste-away" medicine from the swamp; now she sends to the New Orleans drugstores, and the cost is heavy. She showed me the patented mixture. "Maybe it's the wars; or maybe the docteurs, they put something to make it high for us," she thinks.

Marie has a sister who is best with "sun-pain." Marie once knew that remède "good, good," but forgot it because she did not use it frequently. Marie, in turn, is so expert with "waste-away" that her sister brought her own child to Marie. And how does one get to be a remède-worker? Generally he is "born with the gif'," a veil over the face or another indication. Otherwise, "something happen' " when he is a child; a message is received from somewhere. Even then, a technique must be acquired from one who knows remèdes. There is a certain date on which the art must be learned, St. John's Eve or Christmas. "I could recite it to you all night long," she explained as she rocked. "It would make no difference. It wouldn' do for you or for me, 'less you had the gif' and 'less it was the right time to learn."

In the earlier days, one desiring to be a remède-man prepared himself on St. John's Eve. He made a fire with green moss from the trees, and he jumped through the smoke until he fell exhausted. Then he had visions, got up, and hurried to an expert. If the latter approved his descriptions of what he had beheld, he would now be instructed. Then and today, if a remède-worker is about to die, he has a duty. He will call someone and pass on his secrets. When a remède-man falls sick, the neighbors watch for the arrival of a younger friend. At the sight of him, they know. The poor old one, he is about to leave, and he must now impart his knowledge. Well, this new little willow sapling, he won' be half the man his teacher was.

My friend Marie is an earnest housewife, with a good disposition and thirteen children to mind, hers and her daughter's. While we talked of remèdes and such things several of them hovered about to hear. It was not proper for their ears. She called out: "The only remède for you all, I see, is a switch!" They ran then as they would have done from any grandmother, healer or not.

In this Delta that knows so many combinations of elements, it is not surprising to find that Spanish, Italians, and "Americans" —the Anglo-Saxons—have turned to the remède people. But the influence has gone further. A number of the leading remède-workers are Tockos. They do not confine their skills to their fellow Dalmatians, but cater to all. One is recognized for miles as a maker of remèdes for cows, to protect them against prevalent diseases. Walking about several Delta farms, I found the cattle well shielded. Each animal had a small brown object hung about its throat—its own special remède.

priests influ

CHAPTER 18

Rare Ducks, with Salt

OVER a period of slightly less than a half century, two men served the Delta as priests. Widely different individuals, they had widely varying interests, but to a large degree they made themselves one with their place and people. Each was what the other Deltans call a rare duck, a personage of much salt and some spice—one to make his friends slap their knees, say "Him? Ho!" and then recount a string of tales. Each took a difficult assignment and handled it in his own way. The Delta, as a consequence, is a somewhat different place.

When A. Barthélemy Langlois, a tall, shy young man of twenty-five years, stepped off a gangplank on a December morning in 1857 at Pointe à la Hache, no delegation awaited. It was his first Louisiana assignment. Born in a small community in the department of the Loire in central France, he was one of four brothers who were priests. (His father, who had planned for a time to enter the religious life, had decided that it was not his vocation but had declared he would give this number of future sons to the church.) A. Barthélemy Langlois had come to the Delta with a record of scholarly accomplishment. But neither he nor his priest's robes were objects of friendly interest in this section of the Delta. Only a few years earlier, his predecessor, Father Savelli, had been killed by a furious mob. The new arrival walked into the church, to see cobwebs everywhere, over the windows, among the pews, as thick as crapes. When he opened the confessional, he discovered the dagger-ripped, blood-marked cassock hanging on a hook, where the crowd had left it.

For a day he kept to himself. Surely, some of his parishioners would call. None approached; those who passed looked the other way. "Then I must go to them," he said. He stopped a man on the road. Where was the best place to find them? The answer came quickly, with a grin, "The saloon!" The young priest walked slowly to that establishment. Only the bartender was there, and he was clearly not pleased at the visit.

Father Langlois stepped forward: "Well, Monsieur, I am your new priest."

"Oh, are you?" A pause. The eyes did not grow less hard: "You know what we did to the last one. We can do that to you, too."

"I hope you won't."

"We'll see."

"Well, anyway, will you take a glass of beer with me?"

With some hesitation, the bartender agreed. After a few more exchanges, only slightly less sharp, the man at the bar made a small concession: "You *may* do . . . We shall see." Such was the introduction of Langlois to his people.

Two days later was a Sunday. The priest said Mass to an empty church. The next Sunday was Christmas, and a bleak one for him. There was only one participant at the Christmas service, the priest himself, alone in the newly-cleaned church. By the week after that he had obtained a housekeeper, and she attended. A few days later a well-known resident died, and a funeral was requested. The newcomer worked hard and long at his sermon, to take advantage of this unexpected opportunity. He was rewarded when several diffident men and women stayed behind for a minute or two. A slow fight had begun.

He found the people grateful for help, but hesitant, silent, difficult to engage in conversation. At first he could not understand many of their words, but eventually he surmounted this barrier. Yet even among those inclined to be friendly, he met few with whom he could talk of subjects that interested him. Of all places in America, this was one of the most unpromising for a cloistered youth with the tastes of a classicist. A. Barthélemy Langlois had long hours to himself. He remained indoors between his visits; he studied too hard. His eyes bothered him; his health declined. He knew that he needed a change, to take him in the open.

Now he thought of something that he had put aside. In France, at the seminary at Lyons, he had chosen botany and become an ardent student of the subject. An old professor had taken the class twice a week on walks among the hills; under his guidance, young Langlois had made small collections of the flowers and plants of the locality. Now he looked more closely at the natural world of lower Louisiana in which he found himself. The heat, the pounding rains, the showerlike dews and fogs, produced a wealth of foliage that seemed extraordinary to one accustomed to the ordered fields of France.

On all sides moved varied waters: the silt-thick freshness of the Mississippi; the still, stained liquids of the swamps, and the cool, salt elements toward the Gulf. From the many moistures grew grasses, sedges, and reeds of half a hundred types; lichens and ferns, some lacy and delicate, others hardy and resistant; enormous, fleshlike fungi that multiplied in the crevices of the ground and spread rapidly over root and bark and smooth surface; mosses and trailing greens, vines and flowering plants, thrusting out heavy blossoms of blues and yellows, or spreading light carpets of pinks and purples and cream-whites. He was puzzled at the variations in the waters, fresh leading to brackish, brackish to salt. In some places salt forms were invading and forcing out the others; at other spots the river was making thick new deposits so that freshwater flora were beginning to dominate. Few people had ventured far afield or made any serious investigation. Some had stopped briefly along the river, but they had lacked the opportunity or perhaps the inclination to attack the places beyond, the thick, green-covered ponds, the long reaches of the bayous, the canals that led to cypress and tupelo swamps and the wide miles of the green-gold marsh.

The priest inquired about books on the plants and flowers of Louisiana. His letters came back promptly; there were none. Intrigued, he began to examine the burgeoning growths, and to ask the natives. Those tall purple plants that came with the first spring air, what did they call them? These small flowering brown things, how long had they been seeing them? The Deltans frequently had only looks of blank surprise for him. For some growths they offered their own names. Tha's herbe à huitre (oyster grass); the kind over there, tha's herbe à cayman (alligator grass), and next to it, jus' jonc rond, cane grass. When Father Langlois obtained standard listings of plants, with neat

Latin titles, and tried to compare them with the patois words he was in a quandary. He would have to dig hard. Interest in botany was developing in the United States; there were individuals in other sections who might have assisted. But he was a newcomer to the country and did not know how to proceed. He had a few names of naturalists in France; he would collect what he could, and then get in touch with them.

With his first specimens he met unexpected difficulties. In so humid a place it seemed almost impossible to dry them; only after long trial did he discover ways to overcome his problems. Callers at the rectory during the worst days of July found a hot fire in the living room, and Father covered with perspiration as he worked at the hearth. He acquired presses, blotting papers, and other paraphernalia, and eventually he succeeded. With a sigh of satisfaction, he put together samples of three hundred species, some of them items that had never been gathered before. Carefully he addressed the bulky parcel to France and returned to his regular duties. He knew that it would be some time before an answer could be expected. He would wait; like others in the Delta, he was learning patience.

Months went by; ships passed through the river mouths, up to New Orleans and then down again without a reply for him. Slowly he realized that he would receive none. He never knew what had happened to that precious package. Perhaps it did not survive the sea trip. Perhaps those to whom it was addressed were unimpressed. Langlois? No record. Point of the Ax—what a strange name for a settlement; what a place this America must be. . . . It was a disappointment worse than any that had come to him. He put away his specimen books, and locked his cupboards. For ten years, for fifteen, he forced his attention in spare moments to other things. He read intensively again. But often he found items that started his speculations. Hadn't he come upon a peculiar plant like the illustration in this journal? The description of the Asiatic swamp—how it brought back the day he had called on the colony on the bay! And as he was rowed along narrow canals he still reached out to pluck an occasional wine-colored lily and examine it in the bright sun. Yet he always asked himself if this interest was of any worth to him or to anyone else. He was busier now with his Masses and his visits; he was acquiring additional assurance, and making his way with the people.

A few Deltans, now old, remember him as "very French and very serious," yet a man who could turn suddenly with a quip that made trappers and rice growers roar with glee. He had lost his early austerity; the Delta had taught him much. He came upon a number of congenial spirits. One of the plantation owners on the west bank of the river was Auguste Jean Marie Groleau, whose property lay opposite Pointe à la Hache. The Groleau family received frequent messages and journals from the old country, and the two men talked of their contents, and of the France that both had known. Sometimes, moving among the weatherbeaten houses along the river, he would tell himself that this might almost be a coastal province of the mother nation; and then he would hear a sudden cry, watch a family on its gallery, and know that it was a different place. Yet he spoke English only infrequently; this part of Louisiana did not encourage a "Frenchmen from France" to learn the tongue.

Then one day A. Barthélemy Langlois, after years of discouragement, made up his mind again to study the green universe about him. He purchased a general manual, a book on Southern flora; at least he would have some measure of guidance. He heard of a botanist at a seminary in New York. He suggested a trade, Louisiana plants for others. This time he was not ignored. Learning of a botanical journal, he sent in a belated subscription, checked advertisements, and corresponded with teachers and research workers. And he was afire with his subject. Men who had first smiled now guffawed when they saw him, trousers rolled up, wading, slipping in the marsh, a metal box suspended about his neck. Returning, he handled his collections as if they were rare eggs. He let it be known that he wanted certain plants; those who called at the rectory, those whom he met after services, received requests to bring in this or that item. Some who came to Mass from the back canals and the lakes brought containers that they deposited, with a touch of pride, in the aisle beside them. Everybody knew that they had plants for Father. Sometimes such containers had the wrong specimens, but on other occasions they made the priest's eyes sparkle. It was probably hard now and then to wait until Mass was over to get at a certain flowering growth that he knew one of them held for him.

Those who viewed his collections were, as he wrote later, "much astonished at the quantity of forms I have sent to them, and declare that my region is one of the richest in the United States." One room, then another, of the rectory filled with his materials, his cases and presses. The housekeeper grumbled but the collections grew. On his infrequent trips to New Orleans he was accustomed to jokes about "Langlois and his plant zoo." Priest friends tried to dissuade him from his peculiar hobby. He thanked his well-wishers and went on as usual. He described the vegetable kingdom as "a great book written by God Himself, profusely illustrated for man to use, read, and enjoy." In his research he found "happiness, health," and the French love of work, "l'amour de travail." Suddenly, too, he had more: fame in his field.

He had become one of the important botanists of his day, a pioneer in the wet ground of South Louisiana. Men of science wrote him; he was asked for articles, called upon to give talks, to express his opinion on debated points. Growths that he discovered—lilies, tiny violets, ferns, and others—were named after him; he published the first authoritative catalogue of Louisiana plants. Ironically, messages of inquiry or praise came from France, whose reception of his first exhaustive effort had set him back more than a decade. (Often did he regret that period of inactivity, with the Delta blooming all about him.) His attitude toward what some called his "exile" in this remote spot seem to have been mixed. Several times he was offered church assignments elsewhere, but he preferred to remain here. However, he often felt the isolation. In letters and in conversations he expressed mild regret that he was out of the line of usual communications, that he could see so few of the other botanists of America.

After thirty years, he prepared to leave for a new assignment at St. Martinville, in the heart of the "Evangeline" bayou country of Louisiana. Out of the marsh, from the oyster reefs, from the river mouths, thousands came for his last service, to cry at his farewell sermon, to shake hands with him afterward. He had had his troubles with some of the Deltans, but he had managed far better than had ever been expected. An organization of laymen which he had formed some years earlier lined up and fired guns into the air in salute; and then the priest gathered his plants and his packing cases and went up the river.

His recognition was now general, his church duties somewhat less strenuous. But he had gone from the scene of his pioneering; and in later years his mind turned back often to those exciting moments of original discoveries among the pools and the thick canes of the Delta. When he died his collections of more than five thousand specimens were divided among several institutions in various parts of the country. He may be remembered as long as any modern man who lived among these watery fringes of land.

Thirty more years passed; church affairs at Pointe à la Hache waxed and waned. In the year 1917 another French priest took up an assignment here. He was Father Joseph Girault de la Corgnais, round-faced, forty-eight years old, and the possessor of an energy hurricane-like in its concentration. Not less important as an asset in dealing with his scene and his people, he had a good measure of humor. Born in Brittany, of a family whose members had served for generations in the French Marine, he had worked for a time in other parts of Louisiana, but all of his career seemed a preparation for his stay in the Delta. The assignment still remained one to dismay weaker spirits—a broad, watery terrain, difficult to reach, and a people who were sometimes no less a problem than the geography. More restrained than in the earlier days, the lower section was still not a meek and docile locality. If unconventional gifts were called for, Father Girault was the man to provide them.

The new arrival snapped his fingers at his secular helpers, and told them to take him at once around his parish. He traveled by machine, by foot, by horse and, of course, by boat; he insisted on getting to the stretches farthest back. "But it is raining, Father, and this is the bad season. Hadn't we better wait?" He shook his head: "Can you swim? Let's try to get there." He wore down one helper, another, then picked new ones of muscle and will to match his own.

Doctors were scarce. One day he passed a house in which a man had just cut his leg. "What's the matter, what's the matter?" he demanded as he bustled in. Then he stopped the blood and dressed the wound with skill. "Now you won't need any remède-man," he grinned. It became known that he had once made medical studies; from then on, he was part-time doctor. He set bones, diagnosed fevers when regular practitioners could not be found; he dosed and he purged. He did everything but operate. "But I'm not forgetting the church," he wagged his finger. "What do I get for binding this sprain? All right. Communion next Sunday, all fifteen of you." Once Father Girault fixed a family with his eye, they attended.

If he wanted assistance, he obtained it. A man lay dying twenty miles away. Interrupted at his annual church fair, Father Girault demanded a lugger. When it was not immediately forthcoming, he commandeered one. In other matters he joked, he bullied, and he got what he asked for. If collection plates were empty, he told the parishioners to bring what they had—pelts, rice, oranges. The church would manage with them. After one trapping season he was presented with a small hill of muskrat pelts. He piled them into his car, drove to the Archbishop's residence in New Orleans and declared with a flourish, "Monseigneur, I have come to pay my diocesan fee." The prelate nodded, waited, lifted an eyebrow. "Right out here. Come," Father Girault gestured. The Archbishop allowed himself to be led down the steps. At the car Father Girault flung open the door: "All yours, Monseigneur, all yours." The Archbishop looked hard, sniffed delicately and turned: "It will be all right, Father. You may keep the fee." The priest kissed the ring, said "Merci, Monseigneur," and departed.

Soon he was deciding that without a boat he could never cover his parish. He obtained a spick-and-span motored vessel, the *St. Thomas,* with a shining cross on top. If the people could not go to the church, he would bring the church to them. Some said with humor that they came to dread the sight of the *St. Thomas*. It meant Mass on the spot, with attendance by all within hailing distance. Going to a remote area, Father Girault called for bridal parties, rode all members to the church, and then returned them. When word filtered through of a death, he hurried to bring in the coffin and the family for the rites and then took the people back to the lakes. On both trips, he was ready to save limbs and lives. The boat always carried his small black kit with iodine, cotton, splints, and standard medicines.

At one time a vacancy occurred in the office of coroner. The political factions found someone on whom they could agree —Father Girault. They obtained the Archbishop's approval, and as the Catholic historian Roger Baudier declares, he became perhaps the only American priest to assume such a post. He served also as probation and truant officer of the civil parish. Later the sheriff grew seriously ill, and plans were under way to put up Father Girault for the place—an even more unusual one for a clergyman. But the incumbent recovered.

Father Girault had meanwhile acquired the objects that gave him perhaps his greatest celebrity—his cannons. They were small brass ones that had seen service in European wars. His helpers must have a supply of ammunition, or blanks, ready for instant use. The cannons boomed on Sundays and on holidays, but particularly when French vessels passed. None bearing the colors of his France went up or down the river without proper hail. "Pointe à la Hache, she is the second France!" Père Girault would declare, then set out to prove it. Ship officers came to know the place; unfailingly they stopped and requested a visit from the Père. Complying, Father Girault exchanged compliments, made gallant speeches, and joined in toasts to La Belle France, La Louisiane, and the Delta.

He had troubles with his church building. It burned and there was little money to restore it. "Then we will go to the river like anybody else," he decreed. He and his parishioners fished for logs in the *St. Thomas.* He took saw and hammer and helped the men. To friends in New Orleans he wrote innumerable letters: "We need everything. Give what you can—anything from a nail to a hundred dollars." (Later he no longer set this limitation.) He visited a plantation in its final stages of decay. "You don't have anybody to call to work with that bell," he observed. "I can use it." At a New Orleans pleasure resort an amusement building was being removed. He called on the contractor to ask for the balustrade; it became the altar rail in the new church. Inspecting a hotel undergoing demolition, he saw a dusty telephone booth. Altered, it was the confessional.

In his new church as in his old, informality dominated. Sunday was a busy morning—callers, conferences, other matters. Mass was seldom on time, but the parishioners understood. Father Girault owned a watch, but it is affirmed that none ever saw him consult it. The crowd waited patiently; only when the hour approached noon would one sidle up: "Father, getting late, ahn?" He would shrug, "Well, let's go." While services proceeded, he was a tyrant. A man who scraped his shoes unnecessarily, or a youth who squirmed, suddenly discovered the priest standing beside him. Would they tell him what was wrong, if they pleased? A stranger whose car had a flat tire near the church started to fix it there. Father Girault left the building to descend upon him; as the victim said later, "it was like hell came right out of the ground on top of me." And when a drunk wandered in one day, the priest caught him by the collar with one hand, the seat of the trousers with the other, and tossed him neatly out of the window.

During his sermon, Father Girault ranged the aisles, slapping hands together for emphasis, pointing at this and that member, peering sharply at some openmouthed fellow to whom he thought the matter had particular application. He was a remarkable preacher, unsubtle and highly practical. Many of his parishioners did not read newspapers or books. He talked of international, national, and sometimes of state affairs; he discussed storm protection, sanitation, or any other relevant subject. "You always knew what he meant," one listener recalled. It is especially testified that "at funerals that man was a wizard." When he knew the departed one, no wife or son wept more bitterly; for Father Girault, first and last, was a man of emotion.

Now and then a breathless helper came in during a service to pull at the priest's sleeve. A body was floating down the river. As coroner, he must look into the matter. Father Girault paused momentarily to whisper back, "Throw a rope around it and tie it to something." Or, through the window, he caught sight of an approaching French vessel. A quick nod to his general factotum, and the cannon pounded outside while the service proceeded as if nothing had happened. In either case, as soon as the rites ended, priest and flock hurried to the levee.

A ship blew up in the river, and for long afterward, bodies of Chinese men came to the surface. They were horribly torn, and repellent in decay. None would touch them. As coroner and as priest, Father Girault went to the river, took the victims ashore, and dug graves with his own hands. When smallpox epidemics struck the Delta and most others were too frightened to approach the stricken ones, he went to the families, nursed them to health, or buried them. The American Red Cross decorated him with a gold medal, and the parish added a bronze one.

A man of his prestige and his warm insistence could advance measures at which many hesitated. Father Girault had a strong interest in the Delta Negroes; in the wake of new missions he helped set up schools, cajoled and pushed officials into supporting them, and otherwise looked to the welfare of the darker people. He helped them go to school, he found jobs for them; and every Sunday he drew them to his services. One mulatto showed me a photograph of an open-air altar that the priest improvised, while he was hunting money for a regular church building. It was fashioned from what seemed the only available materials: a coffinlike box, on top of others bearing the faded name of a soft drink, and over it all, a gay awning. The parishioners stood and sat in the grass, or moved to nearby galleries when it rained, and services went right on.

For ten years Father Girault worked furiously in the Delta; then he became ill. As he languished, the French consul pinned upon him the Silver Palms of the French Academy. He remarked that he now had a bronze medal, a gold one, and a silver; the next would be a wooden cross at his head. He predicted correctly. Today a native says, "That Father Girault, he jus' wear himself apart." Another pays him an ultimate compliment: "He had fault', yes, but they were good fault'."

In any case, not many other places could have fostered two such rare ducks, with or without salt, as Father Langlois and Father Girault.

CHAPTER 19

The Big "Little Doctor"

IN HIS late sixties, after a lifetime of zestful preparation, Dr. Hewitt L. Ballowe has become a Delta sage, now benign, now peppery, a great white-haired bon vivant of a fellow. To the manner of the higher Delta born, he knows everything and everybody about him—trapper, oyster-digger, politico, retired bootlegger, alligator, bird, muskrat—and whatever else walks, crawls, or makes noises. A man of tastes and tempers, he possesses high affections and magnificent hates; and to match the latter a vocabulary of joyous invective. He is or has been a surgeon, planter, cattleman, orange grower, Army officer, naturalist, authority on folklore and, not least and determinedly, himself to the core.

The family is part Louisiana French, part Virginian. One of Dr. Ballowe's ancestors was the Colonel Déclouet who sent Andy Jackson that alarming message about the legislature during the Battles of New Orleans. His great-great-grandfather was Auguste Jean Marie Groleau, close friend of Father Langlois. Hewitt Ballowe represents a mixture of many elements, with a high flavoring of his own individuality.

He began life on a plantation as a doctor's son and, he admits, he might easily have gone on to a dull and prosperous existence. He had, he thinks, a highly pleasant childhood, in which he did practically anything he wanted. He hunted, he listened to the stories of Negro laborers, he dug for pirate gold, he went on marsh calls with his father, he poked his long, straight nose into all things and did not mind when it was smudged a bit. "I found very soon," he sighs with pleasure, "that I had good, low tastes. Luckily, I've never lost them." At an early date he was developing, too, a scorn for the over respectable and the over erudite. When he was in his teens, he was sure he "knew a damned sight more about everything than all those jelly-bellied, prissy people." He is still certain of it, and to the devil with any pedagogue who feels differently. Yet he has a firm background of knowledge in a variety of subjects, from rare tropical birds to medieval witchcraft.

The family saw that Hewitt Ballowe received a sound education. He went up to New Orleans to the Tulane High School, to the Tulane College for his bachelor's degree and then to the Tulane Medical Department. In the last institution he had unusual opportunities for observation and practice, including a bout with smallpox that swept the great Charity Hospital and took doctors, students and nurses. In the late 1890's he studied with the celebrated Dr. Rudolph Matas and had the privilege of assisting him in a number of operations. "From Matas I got inspiration," he says. "That and some humility, maybe, and an incentive to study and work like old hell."

Home on vacation at the end of his junior year, he learned that a virulent epidemic of yellow fever had broken out on one of the plantations. His father was in the grip of a serious ailment; the doctorless neighborhood was terrified. Someone thought of young Ballowe. No degree or license yet, but everybody knew he had lots of ideas and a plentiful supply of gall. "So," he recalls with a chuckle, "I was allowed to wreak my wonders on about a hundred people. I still think I had an awful nerve." He commuted by train between his home and the scene of pestilence; after a day, his fellow passengers shrieked in protest. Suppose he gave them the disease? "So they presented me with a private coach—a big box-car all my own, with a rocking chair as an allurement. I rocked and rocked and had me a time. It was the first bribe of my career. And I got it before my license!" The epidemic ended with many recoveries and high praise from the authorities.

After graduation he represented the state Board of Health on ships to yellow fever ports in Latin America. For years he had watched the great vessels feeling their way along the river, and had yearned for the excitement of a career at sea; instead, he languished in ennui. Then he turned to the British transport service; during the Boer War he was surgeon on a vessel carrying mules and men to Natal. On that trip he saw near-mutinies, a fire on the ocean, and other troubles with a crew that had apparently been shanghaied. Then he returned to the Delta, to begin a lifetime of restless activity at the river, along the canals, and back in the marshes. He became the "Ti' Docteur," Little Doctor, as separate from his father, the Big Doctor. The little one was considerably larger framed than Papa, but this was beside the point.

Now he had all of the difficulties of the rural doctor, accentuated and expanded. He traveled about in a rowboat, a pirogue, a launch, on foot, on horseback, in a buggy, and in one or two tense emergency cases, by rickety plane to far places on the fringes of the shore. No hospitals were available; on the long, primitive water-and-land trip to New Orleans, the patient could have died several times. Equipment was limited and emergencies often demanded surgical action without delay. He diagnosed cases in the back rooms of oyster camps, and within the crumbling walls of the plantations; often he used a lamplighted kitchen table for delicate internal operations, wiping the sweat from his eyes and the mosquitoes from his face and neck as he proceeded.

The marsh and river people knew injury in many forms. Arms were pulled from bodies by whirring flywheels on the boats; there were gunshot wounds, razor slashes, terrible hemorrhages that could be controlled only by drastic measures; snakebites, including those of the dreaded Congo, the cottonmouth moccasin; bites of gars and sharks; puncture wounds from the barbed tails of the heavy, flat-bodied rays. Under normal conditions, most Deltans agree, an alligator will not attack a man; but in several cases to Dr. Ballowe's knowledge, a disturbed saurian seized a forearm in its jaws and ripped the flesh away, leaving practically nothing but bare bones. Once a tarpon, the six-foot game fish that frequents the waters near the river mouth and is known for his spectacular leaps, jumped into a boat full of women and children. The great tail maimed and bruised and tore the flesh about him until he found his way out again. "It was not a pleasant case to handle," the doctor shakes his head.

Meanwhile he was occupied, year in, year out, at what appeared sometimes to be his major chore, that of presiding at childbirths. "They seemed to wait for the damnedest times," he snorts. "The minute a storm warning arrived, I told myself—'Oh-oh, they're going to start having them fast!' It never failed." One of his best-remembered patients was Relief Jones, so named because while Dr. Ballowe worked, the winds and waters struck at his mother's cottage. She was sure that the weather would win, and she made no secret of this conviction. When the boy came and the wind went down, she was "jus' so reliefed" that the name for the child came to her, "like that, Docteur."

He has delivered as many as five in a night, racing from one palmetto-thatched house to the next. In one family, he helped a woman give birth over a period of years to sixteen children. (Only one set of twins was included.) For a time he kept a count of the babies; after it reached a thousand, he said "What the devil!" and tossed the records aside. A number of girls whom he brought into the world he assisted, fifteen years or so later, in having their own babies. And then, within another fifteen years, he was called upon to deliver the third generation. "That's when I first began to feel old!" he guffaws.

A strapping Italian called for him one spring night. Things went wrong; instruments were urgently indicated for the wife. He explained the situation to the husband. "Go ahead," the man told him. "I explained that I was absolutely alone, without any one even to give the anesthetic. He looked at me hard. 'You mean she might die?' I nodded. His face worked: 'No, no. She must na die. I will kill myself.' Then he paused and added, 'But before I do that I kill you, too. You are a doctor, and you must save her!' " The marsh doctor went to work. The husband knelt by the bed a foot or so from him. Dr. Ballowe heard the man as he prayed before the holy pictures on the wall, appealing to San Giuseppe to give all the help that he could to the doctor. But in his hand the husband held a knife. Happily for everybody, the doctor saved the patient.

During his early years of practice, an overgrown boy came to Dr. Ballowe's house, pulling a skiff. "You the docteur?" he asked. "Are you sure? My Maman, he say he been four day' trying to have his bébé and he give up. If you don' come, he is die." Dr. Ballowe packed his black bag; the boy took him miles down the river, pointed to a palmetto hut and left. Inside, on a bed without sheet or pillow, lay the woman. "Do what you can, Docteur," she appealed to him. "I have many small children. I don' know what they will do without me, no."

"Where is your husband, Madame?"

"He is gone for visit his alligator line. He say he can' was'e no more time for me."

"Where are the women, your neighbors?"

"They mad with me; they don' come to my house."

The doctor started a fire in the stove, placed his heavy forceps in boiling water, made everything as sterile as possible, and gave the patient chloroform. He applied the forceps; the blades slipped on the head of the unborn child.

"Uhn! He done miss it!" The words came in a piping tone at his elbow. The doctor looked down. A girl not more than six years old had crept in, an interested spectator. On the other side he spied a boy, a year or so older. "Oui," said the girl's brother. "But he is a docteur, him. I bet he don' miss the nex' time."

The doctor knew that his reputation was at stake. He reapplied the forceps with great care; he took every precaution; he succeeded. The boy stuck out his tongue at his sister. "What I told you?" he taunted.

Far down the river occurred the death of a baby at the water edge, a tale told and retold to Dr. Ballowe by all in the vicinity. A young mother stood at a flimsy wharf along the bayou. Her husband approached; he waved an arm in greeting. She held the child up for him to see. The baby laughed in excitement, jumped, slipped, and fell into the water. A great snout appeared at once from beneath the landing. White-fanged jaws opened; there was a flash of cloth and as the mother's rasping screams rang out and the father paddled frantically forward, the alligator disappeared. Others prevented her from leaping in; her husband beat helplessly about the water, wild cries on his lips. All knew that there was no hope.

For twenty years Dr. Ballowe was coroner of the parish and in a place in which tempers flared with the suddenness of squalls from the Gulf, it was not a mild occupation. One day he was notified that a man had been shot to death some distance off. Before he left, the sheriff sent word that he had just been called away; would the doctor please bring the killer in after he conducted the inquest? As Dr. Ballowe's horse and buggy reached the scene, black with people, excited cries met him. He found the body, clasping the trunk of a mandarin tree in the dimness of a citrus grove. Twelve buckshot in the chest, placed in perfect pattern, showed that the murderer was a marksman.

Where was the assailant? All pointed to a little house between two rows of satsumas. He had barricaded himself in, cut a hole in the front door, and as Dr. Ballowe looked, he could make out the muzzle of the gun sticking through it. The crowd mumbled, "He say he shoot the firs' one ope' the gate!" It was a difficult moment. Some of the fishermen looked at the doctor and laughed; others advised him not to try it but to wait for a posse. "I went forward," says Dr. Ballowe. "I wasn't being a poseur. It wasn't courage. I thought I knew my man." Yet he admits to an assortment of feelings as he marched up the path. The gun moved slightly; the man inside held a bead on him.

"Jean," the doctor called out, "stop all this foolishness. You're in for enough trouble without making it worse. If a posse comes your house will be set afire and you'll be shot down. Now I have to hold my investigation. Pass me out a chair and table, and when I go, you go with me."

The crowd on the levee outside, and also Dr. Ballowe, waited in tense silence. The gun shifted. "Oui, Monsieur Docteur," came the answer, in a tone of doubt. The door was unbolted, the man handed out a stool and three-legged table, and shut the door. The inquest ended with the killer still inside. Dr. Ballowe walked to the door; the crowd scattered out of gunshot range. "Come on, Jean. Be sensible." A lean, white-faced man, eyes rimmed with red, stepped forward. The gun was still in his hands, both barrels cocked. The coroner made no attempt to take it from him. "It was better for him to have it," Dr. Ballowe reflects. "That gang wouldn't have hesitated to throw itself on him and tear him to pieces. I knew I was right when we got into the buggy, started off, and Jean whispered: 'Drive faster, Docteur.' We made the trip alone, and in complete safety."

About the same time he was summoned to another outlying section. One man lay dead; the trapper who had shot him was unconscious, with a bad skull injury. "I have to operate, fast, or he's dead, too," Dr. Ballowe informed the family. They nodded, and he began the operation. Behind him he heard a mumbling and suddenly he knew from their faces and their words that the family planned to knock Ballowe over the head as soon as the operation was over, and escape with the killer. And so, with the man's brain exposed, Dr. Ballowe worked with all possible lack of speed. He fidgeted, he fretted over his instruments, he discovered one thing to do, then another. The sheriff, he knew, was on the way. The family came to look, muttered, asked questions. "But I had them," says Dr. Ballowe with grimness, "and I wasn't going to finish until it was safe. And I didn't! As the sheriff's boat came in sight, I put in the last stitches."

For a time he left the parish. Ordered into active service from the Reserve Medical Corps in 1914, he commanded a hospital, acted as field adjutant, signal officer, and in other capacities. He came into contact with Generals Pershing and Leonard Wood and other major figures of the day and had a riproaring time through it all. (When he offered himself for duty in the Second World War and was refused for physical reasons, he made a number of sulphuric suggestions to the authorities.)

Back in the Delta, he returned to his people, the French, Spanish, Tockos, Filipinos, mulattoes, darker Negroes, and the rest. "I like them all, and I learned something from them all," he reflects. Not the least of his friends were the remède-men. They and their art had always interested him. He read everything he could find on strange worships, magic, and cults; and meanwhile he set out to find out about survivals of old beliefs in Louisiana. He always got along with the remède people, he observes.

"I'm not narrowminded. I told 'em to do their work, I'd do mine; and let the best man win." Finding a voodoo bag under a pillow, he did not harangue. "Let's try my stuff, too," he suggested. The workers with prayers and strings appreciated his viewpoint. One healer told me with feeling, "The docteur, he is a good docteur. But I think he also makes a good remède." If you know him well, the doctor today will open his pockets and display a nutmeg in each. "They are supposed to take the pain out of my ancient knees," he smiles. "My favorite remède-woman recommended them. I'm passing up no chances, me."

Sometimes it has been a race between Dr. Ballowe and the remède-man; he admits that a victim has now and then been saved by the quick arrival of the latter. "There are plenty of things I can't understand," he says. "One is the power of these people. I've seen them bring about what looked like cures in cases I thought doomed. According to test-tube analysis, the patients couldn't live. But they did." The healers, he thinks, are at their best in stopping loss of blood. Once during a ball game near Buras, the bat crashed heavily against the catcher's head. Blood spurted thickly from the cut. By the time Dr. Ballowe arrived he found a remède-man there. Wetting his thumbs with his tongue, the healer placed one on each side of the wound, murmured a few words, "and I can swear that the bleeding stopped in a minute or two." Dr. Ballowe complimented him on his skill, but pointed out that the saliva might cause an infection. The remède-man shook his head. "Non, Monsieur Ti' Docteur, no infection." None developed.

Dr. Ballowe received a supreme compliment when a remède-worker called him to assist with his son. As Dr. Ballowe entered, the father, without leaving his patient, called out, "Bon jour. Please, Docteur, to do your best. Docteur, I take the top half. You take the bottom, if you please." Dr. Ballowe found the youth in high fever, suffering from a complication of ailments. If he were to prevent death, he must act quickly to cut down the fever. He used ice and sponges upon the stomach and feet, while the father worked at the head and chest, with appeals to the skies and the making of many signs. The two labored without letup.

Ultimately the father asked in a tired voice, "Docteur, how your end gets along?" "Bien, bien." The father sighed. "My end not so bien. Ah, his poor brain', they look like they want to get cook'. Docteur, please to swap with me?" Dr. Ballowe proceeded with sponge and ice upon the upper body. Before long the father reached out to feel the boy's brow. He smiled: "Docteur, please to take whole boy and make your best if you please."

Between cases Dr. Ballowe was a relentless naturalist. He devoted his spare hours and his vacations to hunts for specimens in the marsh, down at the river mouth, and about the shell-mounds. Repeatedly he knew the excitement of a find, and the satisfaction that followed scientific recognition. He was the first man since John James Audubon to find here a smooth-billed ani, the strange bird that had been thought extinct; he discovered it one day in the vicinity of his home. He was also the first to note the presence of various rare snakes, frogs, bugs, heavy mottled spiders and brightly-hued butterflies.

On other occasions the doctor ranged about the parish with his cronies, occasionally participating in great poker games whose every player might be of a different nationality; sometimes he was to be found at the bars and especially at the "bamboches," gatherings of the men for gay evenings of yarn-spinning. These were meetings about large tables, on which sat pitchers of wine. Women were not wanted; the talk had gusto and, not infrequently, anatomical detail. The songs were long ones, short ones; funny ones, sad ones; about animals, about mothers-in-law, foolish husbands, gay lovers, and wives. Dr. Ballowe, a gallant bachelor then as now, was a leading participant. "I could sing like a nightingale, with a voice rich and clear and true." Somewhere in the program, Dr. Ballowe remembers, when the fumes of the wine had stimulated the imagination, and before drowsiness stilled the tongue, someone suggested the telling of "big lies." These were the Paul Bunyan tales of the Delta. The story-tellers vied to see who could concoct the most grotesque and the most whopping; Dr. Ballowe won considerable repute. One of his best, in dialect, went this way:

"I trap' all day. When I get back to camp, I am blow' out an' hongry. At the camp I ax my wife what he have cook'. 'Not much, vieux,' he say. 'I pick up a few swimp an' crab. With these I have make a gombo.' 'A gombo, chère, is very lil' for a man fatigue' like me. For what you don' kill a chicken?' My wife say 'We have only one lef' an' he lay egg every day. It would be mortal sin to kill a beas' like that.'

"At the same secon' I hear 'qua-ak! qua-ak!' I run, throw open the door, an' what I see? A big rat-de-bois have grab our las' hen by the neck. 'Yas, ahn?' I holler, an' give him a coup de baton what put his feet in the air. 'Look,' I tell my wife, 'le Bon Dieu est bon, oui. I will skin the possum. Zebe in the nex' camp, he will give me bottle wine for the hide. You will cook the meat. With gombo, wine an' it, an' bread and café, we will eat good.' My wife find two-three potato, an' everything come good.

"Befo' we start to eat, with that wine ope' on the table an' that gombo in the bowl, she ope' the do' of the stove to look how ev'ything is go. Maybe you not believe it, but there was the rat-de-bois stand up in that pan! He have eat the potato an' drink the grease. Now he jomp out the stove, he pass between my wife leg, an' on the table. He turn over the gombo, knock over the wine, then he run out the back door, me behin' 'im. Outside was the poor hen still on the groun, his neck all twis', his eye' making comme-ci, comme-ça. That rat grab him as he pass an' run away in the grass. That was not all, no. That night, he go to Zebe' camp an' take his skin from the stretching board an' put it back on. Now that was some*thing,* ahn?"

Then there was the tale, supposed to be a true one, of young Valeton, beautiful Zilda, and old Damas. When the teller began this, someone usually exclaimed, "Old Damas! But he had been a man in his day!"

"Ah, his day was about over, though."

"But occasionally the sky lighted a little, and he wanted to make the most of it."

The story started: Zilda was sharp. She thought she was so smart that no one could catch up with her. She married old Damas with her eyes open, preferring the comfort of his house to the bareness of Valeton's camp. Her stomach revolted against red beans one day and white the next, and she knew that this was what life with Valeton would mean. Now she could select the most expensive pieces of dress goods at the store, and have her pick from the peddler's packs. Yet she wanted Valeton, too. She would have a husband to give her luxuries and respectability, and a lover for her lighter hours. She had succeeded, and in her impudence she used old Damas in carrying out her plan. At night she would say to him, "Chèr, I have to go outside, and I'm afraid of the dark. Come and hold the lamp on the back gallery."

Now, Damas had gotten about in his youth. He held the lamp like a beacon over his head; but he followed the beams with his experienced eyes, listened, and figured shrewdly what was going on. He said nothing for a time, but then he began to adorn the gallery—to please her, he explained. He made little shelves for jars of pretty flowers and climbing vines, nailing them to the posts at about the height that he held the lamp. Then, when Zilda was not looking, he took an old sword with a long thin blade and sharpened the point.

One evening Zilda called him, and he held the lamp as she left the house. He knew that she went into a clump of banana plants to the rear. Waiting a short while, he placed his lamp upon one of the shelves. Zilda, seeing the lamp, sighed happily and felt safe. Suddenly Valeton felt a double sting upon his backside. He leaped to his feet and burned the wind, uttering sharp cries that all the neighborhood heard.

Dramatically, Zilda tossed open her robe de nuit and invited Damas to plunge the blade into her breast. (She thought it was going there, anyway.) Damas only smiled. "I know that I am old," he said, "but I have my pride, and I refuse to hold the light for another man." The next morning he cleaned his pistol and put fresh cartridges in the cylinder. This time he let Zilda see him at the task. She was warned, and she behaved. "And so," Dr. Ballowe chuckles, "they said always afterward that old Damas carried his head high—and Valeton carried the two scars to his grave. Eh, bien. . ."

When you say "Ballowe" to certain of the other Deltans, they look wise and say "Treasure." They whisper several stories, sometimes to the doctor's mild annoyance, again to his wicked delight. Just before the Civil War his great grandfather, fearing Union invasion, decided to hide his money. Taking it from a bank vault in New Orleans, he secreted it in a metal box, surrounded that with a larger wooden one, and buried it somewhere. He is supposed to have told some of the family about it, mentioning the sum of forty thousand dollars; but he did not disclose the place. They all asked. He smiled; there was plenty of time for that, plenty of time. Then in the night, he had a stroke. As he lay on the bed one of the relatives put the frantic question, "Where—where did you bury the money, Grandpère?"

"Vous trouverez . . ." he began, his speech thickening. "You will find . . ."

And then he lost the word, as the marsh people say. The others put a pencil between his fingers. His writing hand was the one that was paralyzed! His eyes tried to tell, his face contorted; and he was dead. "The family had all of the probable places dug up," Dr. Ballowe sighs. "There was nothing." Dr. Ballowe did come upon an old book in an armoire, with a fair amount of bills between the yellowed leaves, of ten-, twenty- and fifty-dollar denominations; that was all. But many are sure that the doctor really found much more, and in the ground, yes—a place that he will never disclose. "Lot of thing' that man won' explain."

When an uncle died, Dr. Ballowe inherited a simple, handsome, white building at Diamond along the river. Some neighbors raise questions about the true source of what they say is Dr. Ballowe's wealth. Inheritance? In a certain section west of the river, various individuals would make affidavits that he acquired his means by discovering half of the money buried by the pirate Johnny Gambi, follower of Lafitte. One man called on the doctor: "Now you know, Docteur, that was a dirty trick you did. You bamboozle' Miz ——— into giving you a map that her Papa had. Then you row yourself alone in a skiff way back ten mile'. A man saw you and follow. You fin' a big chest, too heavy for you to lif'. So you take out the string' of jewely, and doubloon' and bullion, and you pile them on a sailcloth. The man, he look when you swing it on you' back and go to you' boat." The doctor comments, "I thrilled with pride when I heard of that feat, sack and everything else. At my age, and weighing over two hundred pounds!"

The one who called on the doctor had an object: He "knew" that the doctor still had that map, showing where the other half of the Gambi treasure lay. He and his friends wanted the doctor to discover the treasure and, in fairness, give it to the lady. When Dr. Ballowe laughed at the whole wild yarn, he received a warning. He had better stay away from that place. At the first sight of him, at least three individuals would get their guns ready. And Dr. Ballowe says he knows the section well enough to heed the suggestions.

Several years ago Dr. Ballowe decided that he was fed up. "Damn this medical stuff. Same thing every day. I'm going to do something I really want." He typed out a series of stories that were quickly published. Then he sent off for a boxful of typewriter paper and sat down to work. He has finished a novel and a variety of other efforts, and he still strives at his desk. Today he has managed to get his patients weaned away, and he is enjoying himself as much as he ever did.

"Ti' Docteur" is a man of prodigious size, great girth, and a full head of hair, firmly parted in the middle. In white vest, brilliant tie, and lounging costume, he smokes long cigars, cogitates, and rules his property in cheerful dictatorship. He has his cattle at the side, the rolling river at the front, and his ancestors in a graveyard at the back. With him stays his sister, the gentle, delicate-featured "Miz' Alice," a lady of breeding and spirit. She insists, in self-deprecation, that she is "only a doormat for Hewitt"; but it is obvious that she is far more than that. ("Alice has done so much, made so many sacrifices for me," says the doctor.) During one of my visits, the doctor excused himself to call at the post office. Returning, he began to roar as he approached the steps, "Alice, *Alice,* ALICE! Open the door! Unlock the door, I tell you!" I leaped forward with Miss Alice. The doctor was certainly upset; bad news, I told myself. Miss Alice threw open the door just in time to accommodate the doctor's hustling bulk. The doctor nodded: "Thank you, Alice." Miss Alice smiled, "You're welcome, Hewitt." It was just the doctor's way.

A group of children (Miss Alice knows hundred of them) once watched the doctor's behavior in large-eyed wonder, until one critic piped up, "Miz' Alice, he's *bad!*" Some of the neighbors tell you: "Miz' Alice, she's kind of high tone, but the docteur, he's common, common as everybody else." The doctor cherishes this description.

The doctor and Miss Alice like good stories of the macabre, with a wraith or two in them if possible. They belong among those who believe that there may be no ghosts but that if this is true, it is certainly a shame. They collect things mystic, superstitious, and puzzlesome. In a tree near the house a certain horned owl is sometimes seen; Dr. Ballowe is not above the suspicion that he is the reincarnated spirit of a dead relative, and notes that he seems to appear whenever someone in the family is about to expire, as if to give warning. He calls him Grandpère; the owl is supposed to look rather like that ancestor. And Dr. Ballowe's favorite ending to this and other related accounts is, "Of course it can't be true—but it happened!"

Their home, they say, has seen its quota of frightening occurrences. Some of the natives believe that the shade of a woman on whom Dr. Ballowe conducted an autopsy once returned, and screamed all over the place. Also, there was an aunt, the beautiful Melanie who came home at sixteen from the convent. Walking at the levee edge, she found a large apple, still wet with river water. She took two bites from the rosy side, and tossed it away. That night she fell ill; within a day she could not rise from her bed. The apple had been traced to a vessel up the river. Cholera had broken out; the cargo had been condemned and dropped into the Mississippi. By that time Melanie was in her grave near the house. Some of the servants were certain that she often wandered back to the river from her tomb.

About two decades ago another member of the family found in the river the body of a soft-featured girl, hardly more than a child, in a white bridal gown. She was placed in the family cemetery. Before long, of course, they would know who she was and how the tragedy had occurred. Months went by; despite inquiries for miles along the Mississippi, her identity was never learned. The episode was forgotten. Then, one dusk, a farm laborer came shouting from the vicinity of the new grave: "Betaille! Betaille!" ("Beast!")

The spirit had come from a clump of trees—a thing with green eyes, bristling hair and half-human face. Everybody rushed to the spot. Nothing was there, but some were certain they made out claw marks. Later in the week two Negroes, hoeing near by, set up the same cry, "Betaille!" This time the monster was red and shaggy. Men hunted up and down the river without result. For months the betaille manifested itself, always at dusk. When new laborers came, though apparently they had never heard of the incident, they suddenly saw it; eventually the workers refused to till that part of the place. All were sure that the betaille was connected, somehow, with the dead bride—perhaps the spirit of her young husband, who must also have been killed, or the girl herself. Who knew? Only after a long interval did the

Deltans cease to talk about the manifestation. "Of course. . ." Dr. Ballowe shrugs. "But it happened."

The doctor squatted on a log near the small cemetery in the early winter twilight, and looked up at the slowly waving moss. I asked him what he was thinking. He turned his head: "I've lived. I've had a full life. And I'm satisfied. When my hour comes I hope I face it with the courage of some of those patients I've had. One in particular. I asked him how he felt. He told me, 'You're a hell of a docteur. Can't you see I'm dying?'

" 'But you aren't afraid, M'sieu Jacques, are you?'

"M'sieu Jacques shrugged in his bed: 'What good? Die ugly or die pretty, you die all the same.' "

And then we went inside before the fire and sampled a fat bottle of kumquat brandy—prepared twenty years earlier, a brilliant combination of sugar, water and the small, tart, citrus fruit. We talked more about zombis, remèdes, rascals, and magazine editors. The doctor's roaring laugh rang out, startling a small black bird that had alighted on the windowsill. I decided that when I returned twenty years hence, the docteur and Miss Alice would still be there, still savoring the life about them.

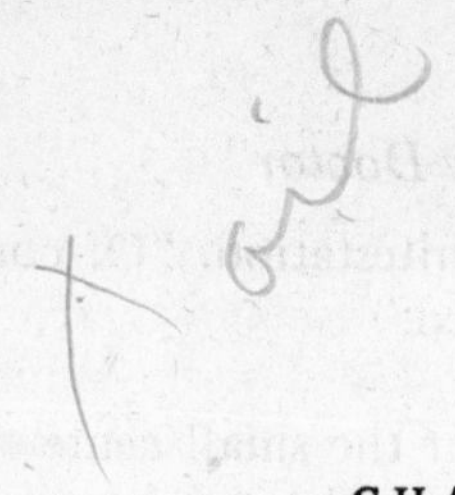

CHAPTER 20

Everchanging, Everlasting

A GNARLED Deltan, half French, half Tocko, piloted our lugger through the gates of a canal at the river edge. As we bumped into the current, a dark shape cleaved the waters—a great oil tanker sliding toward the river mouth. We were silent a moment as the sharp, modern outline cut against the amber sky and the greenness of the opposite bank, and began to disappear below us. Then the oysterman rolled a cigarette and laughed.

"Sure a crazy world, and a crazy land." He jerked his thumb in a half-circle. "Ev'thing topsy-turvy from when I was a boy." His eye was caught by the distant glint of one of the last plantation façades. "That was where you used to get rich—that front ground, the fine top soil. You couldn't hardly get hold of a foot of it. The marsh and the rest at the back—fff"—he made a derisive noise—"you could take it for a nickel. But now! The big money, she's way out there, under the ground, waiting to be drilled up. In the right place you can get more than cane ever thought of paying you. Funny, ain't it?"

There is further irony. For centuries the French and Spanish entrepreneurs passed up and down this area, giving it little more than a side glance in their restless search for precious things of the earth. No metals there; nothing but bogs and birds and fevers. Yet wealth to rival that of the Peruvian and Mexican gold mines lay beneath the wet soil for the first man who would fathom its secrets. Not until recent years did strangers appear in the Delta, to move about the marshes and ride over the shallow bays on errands of particular mystery. For a time the natural assumption was that they were hunters of pirate gold. When rumors grew that they were after oil, the old-timers howled. Oil? How you gonna get it out, you fool?

In strict fact, this terrain presented almost insurmountable obstacles. There were few signs of minerals near the surface, as in other places. The geologists and geophysicists, scouting the area, decided that far below the land and water stood mighty salt domes, thousands of feet thick. About the salt plugs might lie thick pools of oil and deep pockets of gas, trapped there long centuries ago before the river had forced its way into the Gulf. To the Delta went skilled men with dynamite. Burying it under the trembling ground, they sent one explosion after the other into the earth; and they used delicate seismographs to chart the sound waves in their movement through the formations. Comparing the results of many testings, the investigators eventually knew the depths and shapes of the salt thrusts. The oil might or might not be there; when it proved to be, much of the deposit was located far lower than man had previously been able to reach; some of the deepest wells in the world would be needed to tap it. Necessity would breed new devices and new techniques.

Like others before them in the Delta, the oil men became amphibious. To reach the indicated spots, they followed the bays and bayous as far as they could; and then they were forced, at high expense, to dig additional waterways, miles of canals to carry supplies and men. In position at last, they put their equipment to work, only to find it sinking under its own weight. As had the men of the oyster camps, they resorted to pilings, dropping one support close to the next until they had a firm base. Then, after each job of drilling, the derrick was dismantled bit by bit and transferred to the next field.

Eventually ingenious men devised a method of further defeating the topography. A sturdy steel barge was fixed on each side of a derrick and the whole construction towed into place. The barges were then filled with water until they submerged. When they were firmly grounded the derrick was still out of water, and operations could proceed. Work ended, the water was pumped out, and the barges were shifted again.

Strange sights appeared at the water edges: drillings in the middle of the bays about the Mississippi mouths themselves, fantastically long lines of catwalks zig-zagging over the waters, and then the grotesque "marsh buggies." The latter are combinations of boat and automobile, especially designed for this locale, to travel where nothing else can. They consist of a covered platform on wheels with bulging rubber tires taller than a man. The device rides on land and moves like a slow motorboat on the water.

Against the horizon stand the derricks of these oil fields in the waters and grasses, and the operators have one great fear—a storm from the sea that can topple the costly structures in one or two gusts. Everything is buttressed and strengthened, with side pilings and buckles of steel cables; but despite all precautions a sudden blow can wipe out an investment of hundreds of thousands of dollars. Meanwhile month in, month out, machinery chugs about the drilling rigs and crews operate day and night. Over the marshes and lakes is reflected the vivid yellow and orange of the gases, and motor launches drone endlessly as men are carried back and forth. At the wells ten, eleven thousand feet and more of pipe sink into the clays; men test and shake their heads, and continue at work through spreading Gulf fog, through squalls, through days of heat like that of an oven. Then, in a moment, a thick stream leaps into the air. Workers yell. She's in! Number Four's coming through! Capping is started, someone telephones to the company offices; a launch moves off, and word filters among the Deltans.

At other times the trappers jump as seismograph explosions crack over the grasses, and look up from their traps as marsh buggies rumble a few feet away. A film of grease, green and gold, covers parts of the marsh, and the Deltans blame the oil operations for the destruction of some of the natural forms of life. Oystermen offer bitter proof that the force of the blasts has killed thousands of molluscs in their beds. Suits are brought, and conservation officials inquire into charges of pollution and damage. For others, the coming of oil has been a happy thing. They had held to bits of property largely because they found no takers. Now they learned that their ground overlay a rich field, and they could choose among offers.

To these families, the changes have meant undreamed-of luxuries—two-storied houses, trips to New Orleans on the spur of the moment (no waiting until a friend was going in), sometimes even an old plantation house, unless Madame prefers something newer. For Madame oil has brought that most superb of gratifications—a thick fur coat, and not made out of muskrats, either! One matron holds out a sleeve to a friend. Feel that fur; that didn' come from St. Bernard or Plaquemines, no! Other landholders hide maps, reliable or unreliable, that city friends have prepared to show how rich their holdings are, and they wait for the drilling of new fields. Yet these are only a few individuals; the average Deltan has little land, with or without oil, to sell or lease. The greater part of the marshes and shallow coastal waters are in state or parish hands; and even when the land is leased, most of the wealth goes to the outside corporations.

One day tidings traveled up the river that something new and rarer had been struck. Drillers for oil had come upon traces of sulphur. Soon they discovered one of the greatest pockets of the substance in the New World; simultaneously, engineers reported it practically impossible to reach the stuff. The sulphur, far underground, lay at the edge of a lake ten miles back in the tidal marsh—a fibrous mat, virtually floating in ooze many feet thick. But a decision was made to go ahead; the result was one of the most remarkable construction enterprises in the history of the South. Contractors inspected the site in rowboats; prospecting crews placed sections of picket fences in front of them to form bridges over the syrupy wastes. Men worked up to their chests in quagmires, sometimes slipping over their heads; and the mosquitoes and other pests became so bad that they could not continue until engineers devised "blowers"—automobile engines with airplane propellers attached—to drive off the insects.

From the river edge to the drilling place a canal was dug for all of ten miles. At both ends dredges shoveled up sand and mud, which was used to raise wide areas to levels ten feet above their former surfaces. More was needed; complete new bases had to be provided for industrial operations to the back and for a large town site at the river. Tens of thousands of pilings were put in place to provide a firm support. Seventy-five feet long, they dropped unaided for forty feet before pile drivers had to be used to strike a tap upon them. Atop the pilings, heavy reinforced concrete mats were deposited, to create an artificial floor for the settlements. Today hundreds live and work in dryness and safety above the surrounding marshes. Unending quantities of the brimstone are melted beneath the marsh by the pouring of streams of hot water. Raised in molten form, it dries in jagged yellow mountains, to be broken for loading at docks along the Mississippi.

Oil, sulphur, and related industries have brought to the Delta floods of newcomers, rangy, lighthaired men of other Southern states. A large proportion are the drawling men of Texas; and as the Deltans applied the term "Irish" to every levee worker of the earlier period, they use "Texan" (pronounced with a strong French accent) for all of these, including Georgians, Oklahomans, Mississippians and even Anglo-Saxons from North Louisiana. Whatever their origins, the "Texans" have introduced another tempo as well as another drawl. At the bars and restaurants, the juke boxes play songs of the range and the mountains, and the older natives watch in wonder as the slow-talking, quick-walking new arrivals step past them. The oil-rig workers look puzzled at what they find; they know no French and they are not inclined to learn it. They do not drink as regularly, perhaps, as certain of the Deltans, but they save up for a roaring night; and then they make it roar regardless of the consequences. They may not like the Frenchmen, but they do like the French jeunes filles; and over this issue they and the Deltans exchange insults, blows, and intermittent gunfire.

But, like the "old Irish," these "old Texans" are coming to appreciate the Delta; and to it they have brought an increased prosperity. Stores have expanded, and also changed their stocks. Less gumbo, Marie, is what we need; more eggs with ham. Eggs with ham, tha's all we hear now! Reluctantly the owners have informed wholesalers that they will take some of that Yankee slop-coffee, as well as the good stuff that their old customers want. Would you believe it, I thought that large big fellow would choke las' night. He wouldn' finish his cup. Said he couldn' breathe after he took it, and he ask' for whisky instead. Ain' this a funny country, I tell you!

Relations between the new industries and the Deltans have been mixed. The companies claimed that the natives were "unenterprising" and "undependable"; also, it sometimes seemed, the free, individual enterprises of the water borders had not taught the Deltans to fit easily to supervision and direction on the job. The natives charged that the company gave them only the lesser places and preferred the imported "Texans." Rousing battles have been fought at the bars and on the levees. This situation has improved. Yet even today, when trapping time comes, or a friend reports that the alligators are more plentiful than usual, some grow restless on the jobs. With high oyster prices, they can expect two months or more of bonanza pay on a lugger; an especially good season with the rats, and a man can bring home more in a day than a steady job will net in six months. Some of the companies have worked out a compromise. As trapping opens, for instance, a man takes a leave of absence. He returns satisfied, comparatively enriched, a happier Deltan. Deny him this, and he will fidget, swear at his Yankee overseer, and quit for the marsh.

Not all industries have adjusted themselves. I heard one superintendent fume, "I wish every damned muskrat in Louisiana would curl up and die! Then they'd have to come to us. What's the matter with these people? Is oil money poison?" And he took his cigar from his mouth and pitched it at the wall.

Another "industry" has been that of catering to city visitors—in the parlance of the natives, "the sports." Businessmen come here on week-end or vacation trips, for fishing, for hunting, for "rodeos" in pursuit of the fighting tarpon in the Gulf. To thousands the Delta is a place primarily of superb opportunities for such diversion; and an individual known as a guide, endowed with an amiable disposition and skill in finding good spots has been able to depend on a fair livelihood, or better, from this source. Joe Leiter, the wheat millionaire, set up extensive holdings with a Chateau Canard, Duck Castle, near the river passes, and lodges and clubhouses have appeared at many spots in both parishes.*

But recent years have limited the sport and the "sports." The early 1940's brought war close to the Delta, closer than to most parts of America. Old Forts St. Philip and Jackson had been abandoned, to sink gradually into the earth. Military needs now demanded advanced positions toward the Gulf in this area that

* About the river mouths federal agencies have set up a number of migratory waterfowl refuges, improving on nature by creating even more ideal conditions through special plantings, artificial water channels, and other methods. The naturalists have adopted a number of Eads' schemes to make the water behave as they desire, scouring here, building up new land there.

had again become a vital spot in the nation's scheme of defense. A great naval base rose near one river mouth, with underground storage tanks, headquarters for coastal patrol boats, mine-sweepers, and submarine chasers. Lugger operators were summoned for fingerprinting, for the issuance of mysterious numbers to be painted in letters that could be seen by planes overhead. Sometimes a shrimper watched excitedly and nudged his partner as an airship dived toward them. Tha's my boy, Louie. Look the lil' so-and-so waving. . . . But Maman did not like such goings-on, and the next time Louie came home, she lectured him. You stop that passing low over your Papa. You know what happen to duck' that fly that way!

Small hotels, auditoriums, and clubhouses were taken over by the government. Hundreds of men appeared in blue garb, to work over boats at the wharves; tall towers rose, and youths with telescopes kept guard upon the skies. Communication lines spread like spiderwebs, and strange-looking vessels chugged up the Mississippi. Silver balloons, their lights glittering, prowled about the edge of the river. It was not long before the Deltans knew the reasons for some of these protections.

The shrimpers along the Gulf saw black objects rising slowly near them, then the outlines of cigar-shaped vessels—Nazi submarines. Hearts pounding, the fishermen cut ropes, dropped trawls, and sped to shore. In a number of instances they were halted; uniformed Germans with wide smiles to denote "fellowship," handed them packages of food and asked questions through subordinate interpreters who spoke both English and French. The Deltans later sped to the Navy men with breathless stories, and seaplanes, dirigibles, and surface craft hurried to the spots. The United States knew now that the Gulf about the river mouths was alive with a pack of marauders.

New Orleans had emerged as a great center of military construction; plants overflowed into upper St. Bernard, and thousands worked with their machines on the sites of former plantations. The river below the city became one of the great veins of American troop transport and shipment of supplies. Guns of a power such as the Delta had never known were ready near the river mouth, and when they were used they sent tremors through the thin earth for long miles. I was at breakfast with a family when there came a sudden sound like thunder over the blue waters, and we felt the building shake slightly, then again and again. This was no mere drill; something was happening down there. I knew that one of the sons had left only a short time earlier on a ship headed for the Gulf. We fell silent; and only the younger children finished their meal.

That night we were told that the Nazis had taken the vessel, and that scores had died among the burning pools of oil over the water. We watched for hours as the star-spotted sky glowed about this point of death. Later I learned that the young man was listed among the missing; his body was never found. Now the Deltans woke frequently to hear trucks hurtling on the road toward the Gulf. Within sight of land, heavy ships were torpedoed, to burst into mountainous flame. Men died in agony under the serene white clouds; those who survived were hurried to the nearest landing spots, where trucks, busses, automobiles, station-wagons, and every other possible vehicle were pressed into service. Stretchers were carried out, emptied, filled again, and still the machines raced up and down. A new violence had come to this place that knew many varieties.

Amid the industrialism, and the implements of war that may be expected to remain during years to come, rise symbols of peace and of another kind of future livelihood for the Deltans. In the spring, within sound of the wash of the tankers against the levees, extend fields of close-packed white—not the usual Southern scene of cotton bolls, but of flowers. These are the Creole Easter lilies of Plaquemines, rich plants whose sudden development has been a phenomenon of the down-river region in modern times. For miles along the lower reaches, from Venice to Buras and beyond, stand columns of creamy-colored trumpets, bending and lifting, and a heavy aroma hangs over land and water.

Of all parts of America, the Delta has been found perhaps the best suited for production of this lily. Richly packed soil and high humidity, rain-fall and mild temperatures—these elements combine to nurture a special variety of the lilium longiflorum. Just how it came to Plaquemines is something of a mystery. Up the Mississippi, along Bayou des Allemands, visitors saw these lilies growing in small numbers during the late 1800's. The French and French-German settlers told them that they had been brought over by their grandfathers. In the early years of the present century, plantings were tried by florists along the lakes near New Orleans. A late freeze killed them; this latitude was too far north.

Down the Delta also the lilies had been spreading. According to some, a Chinese or Japanese farmer had left the nearby shrimp platforms and invested his savings in them. Perhaps he took plants already growing in Louisiana; or he may have brought them from the Orient. At any rate he set out small patches, propagating the growths by methods learned at home. Another freeze struck; though not killed, bulbs were spoiled for that year. The Oriental gave up; but other dwellers along the river had obtained odd lots from him. The women were pleased with the pretty things; the men smiled as their wives worked over the ornamental rows about their houses, and turned to more important matters.

Until about 1910, the United States obtained most of its Easter lilies from Bermuda. However, the island plants became heavily infected with parasites. By degrees Japan supplanted Bermuda, until the Japanese were sending this country twenty million bulbs every year. Florists meanwhile were looking to American sources. Orleanians took trips into Plaquemines, and what they saw astounded them. How long had these been here? Could the people guarantee so many every year? The Deltans and their wives gasped at the quantities mentioned, and wondered at the persistence of the strangers. We don' got that much; but maybe we could raise 'em if you say. . . . They quickly extended their plantings toward the rear levees and north and south along the river. When the Orleanians returned, they beheld many more lilies. Still the orders increased from many parts of the country, and the Deltans could not meet the demand.

It was not the cut flowers that were wanted, but the bulbs, to be kept in storage, then forced into early bloom for the Easter season. The Deltans learned to pinch off the buds, sending the sap back into the plant. The husband no longer spoke of the old woman's little field. They were his lilies. He squatted about the beds; he stored his seeds in river sand to keep them cool; he lifted the onionlike growths to see if parasites had attacked. He planted clover to prevent the sun from cooking the lilies; when the thermometer dropped he spent long hours of the night in covering the roots with burlap, with anything that would serve the purpose. The men, women, and children worked their way together along the rows, filling their hampers and covering them with palmetto leaves as a protection against the sun.

The florists hurried down at intervals, drew up contracts, and some Deltans sold their whole crop before they took their bulbs from the ground. Before long friction spread, and the lily growers formed an organization to deal directly with Northern operators. They suffered at first through painful experiences. Their bulbs, packed without skill, rotted on the way. In one instance they were stored too near the engineroom of the ship; on arrival in New York they were pronounced a total loss. But the Deltans learned new types of storage, using cork dust, sand, peat moss, and mixtures of these ingredients; and they were successful. By the late 1930's, more than a million bulbs lay in the ground. Taking advantage of the shade and soil in their orange orchards, the Deltans set out lilies there, to thrive among the trees, the pale blossoms luminous in the half-gloom. Packing quarters were set up in old dance halls; hands experienced with the skinning knife cut out grading strips with holes of varying size. The excited Deltans knew a windfall.

A wider vista opened. Pearl Harbor shut off Japanese lilies, and gave the Deltans an unparalleled chance. Only four percent of America's supply had heretofore come from native sources; the nation would take every plant that could be forced out of this rim of soil. Yet the Deltans missed the opportunity. Ever since large-scale cultivation of the lily began, blighting diseases had made progress. The Deltans suffered by the very richness of their region, in which everything thrived. Black rot darkened the bulbs; a mosaic disease mottled them. Today the Deltans labor over their fields, trying to "clean" them, experimenting, discarding bulbs; but production has dropped at the time of greatest demand. Yet leaders remember that their orange trees were once almost wiped out, and believe that they can conquer lily infestations as they did the others.

And each spring the Deltans nip off thousands of magnificent lily trumpets as they begin to bloom, and pile up the unwanted richness for removal. Recently at the river bank I watched several families as they brought basketfuls of soft-scented blossoms and cast them upon the water. The flowers clung to the edge for a time, then floated in long lines to the south. As far as the eye could follow, there stretched the lightly bobbing row of white over the brown current. Out of the Gulf steamed a gray vessel, and the wide waves at its prow cleaved the procession. For many years the Deltans will be turning this beauty to the sea.

In a number of respects, the twentieth century has not always been kind to Delta agriculture. The region lost some of its advantage in the production of pre-season crops, when improved transportation and refrigeration opened new markets to Florida, California and Texas produce. Mass production agriculture made it possible for these states to outstrip the Delta. A number of the crops in which Deltans specialized for the Chicago environs have since been supplied by other regions, and the Deltans have had to try substitutes. In citrus, Delta growers complain that the best fruit of Florida and Texas is sent to the midwestern and Atlantic seaboard cities while the culls are dumped on the New Orleans market to the injury of the Louisiana crop. Officials do not protect them, they say. In the language of one Frenchman, it is a matter of "Chacun pour soi, Dieu pour tous, et Diable prend le dernier"—"Each for himself, God for everybody, and the Devil take the hindmost." They shift their crops, they try to outguess their rivals, and they wait for improvement. Some think that they have been waiting a long time.

Rice has declined. The gradual lifting of the levees made it harder for the small growers to get their water from the river. More important, a fundamental modification of the state's agriculture was on its way. Men of the Middle West went to the dry prairies of Southwest Louisiana, to find there a soil with a clay base, admirably suited to large-scaled, mechanized cultivation of the crop, and this part of the state took over most of the rice culture from the Mississippi River. Several mills that once operated at Pointe à la Hache closed down one by one. Yet at some points the rice hangs on, and the wet fields sparkle cheerfully under the skies.

The world has moved closer to the Delta. The highway, part-paved, part-shelled, extends to Pointe à la Hache on the east bank and far down to Venice on the west. Until less than a decade ago, those below Buras still sent their vegetables and other produce by water to the outside world.* But now the truck has replaced the lugger, and most Deltans carry their goods to the edge of the road rather than to the wharf. Seafood in refrigerator trucks moves to New Orleans more quickly than in the old days; the river packets could not meet this competition. Schools have risen and improved. Newspapers arrive regularly from New Orleans; the busses make trips back and forth, and the radio is found in many houses and on oyster and shrimp boats, whose operators value it as much for the weather reports as for entertainment. Some who lived along the canals or lake edges have moved inside, to be "closer to things." The "things" include the beat of the nickel music machines in the stores and bars along the road. The old custom of attendance at the dances by all members of the family has died out. The younger ones, or Maman and Papa go; the old people stay home with the children. And those at the dance halls generally wear not the former home-sewn clothes, but costumes from the store, or from a mail-order house. (Sear', Roe-*buck* is a name with meaning here.)

The stores are providing more and more of the family's supplies. Maman is now inclined to buy canned soup because the children like it more than hers. "Store-bought" tends to imply quality, or at the least something out of the ordinary, not pulled off a bush or caught from the water. Many are giving up the small crops that once supplemented their trapping and fishing. Although the Delta can produce string beans of rich quality, they prefer to get them ready prepared. During a recent stay, I watched several families purchasing, strangely, canned sweet

* Oddly enough, while many acres of upper Delta land, sites of former plantations, are now idle—drainage abandoned, water creeping in from the back—present-day Deltans have opened up large areas toward the Gulf. New drainage districts, with heavy pumping machines, extend to the Jump, where the road ends—places that the older people said would never be used for agriculture. Oranges and lilies thrive here and the fishermen dispatch their produce to the Jump. The ground is so restricted that the river-edge roadway has been hoisted up along the levee itself, to save space.

potatoes. In this magnificently fertile territory, I caught sight of two vegetable trucks—making house to house stops along the winding road!

Yet by contrast, a man who drove me down the highway in the spring stopped three times to pick up snapping turtles, sunning themselves along the ditch. They were still so plentiful that by keeping his eyes open on his way to and from the sulphur plant, he could provide the family with as much turtle meat as it wanted.

Growing children are begining to dislike the old cypress shingle roofs; they are a sign of "country" custom. The younger group occasionally prevails on Papa and Maman to replace them with grim tin ones so that, as they say, the place "looks twenty years younger." Too many Delta houses, I think, are coming to look twenty years younger. One spruce adolescent asked my opinion of the tin roof. Hearing it, she could only shake her head; the next time I called, the picket fence that her grandmother had erected was also gone. And the girl and her sisters, as they "took the levee," wore red and pink cloth flowers in their hair. They could have picked real ones off the bushes. But in the city everybody was using replicas; and so the Delta girls also wanted them.

Part of the Delta is stratifying, to become more akin to other rural or semi-rural parts of America. The dollar sign emerges more and more as a standard of worth. This one, who has risen to a higher income, is disinclined to see so much of his shrimper friends; or his wife is trying to arrange it so. The man who used to hunt alligators with his cousins does not feel quite so welcome now that the other family has two boats. This, of course, is one phase of "progress." I prefer the older style, with the drying nets on the gallery, and let the city people think what they please.

Yet basically the Delta life continues much as it did during the last century. The individual who gets his news twice daily from the radio still turns to the remède-man to help with his sick child or his sick horse. The family that buys from the vegetable wagon yet enjoys such comparative exotica as frog-legs, marsh hen, snipe, an occasional eel and, if it is a Negro family, the flavorsome ripened tail of an alligator. (A day or so in the ground is said to add to the succulence.) And regardless of the ice-, slot- and other machines, almost everybody lives to the levee and watches it hard to see how the neighbors are behaving. It was on the levee that I recently met three small Deltans who convinced me that uniformity has not taken too firm root. They had Anglo-Saxon names, and a passerby might have accepted them as any "American" children. Between chatterings in French, they identified themselves. "I'm Sidné," said the oldest. "Me, I'm Gjonné (Johnny)," contributed his brother. "They call me Lil' Anné," their sister added. "And here comes Maman. Her, she's Big Anné!"

The father of Sidné, Gjonné, and Lil' Anné earns his living, as do most of his friends, by a succession of occupations, the old ones. They still spend more of their time on the water or about the wet grasses than on dry land. This Deltan understands well that he is most at home in the marsh, on the lakes and beaches. He has known bad years, and he will know others in the future; but he realizes that over a long period he can depend upon this place to support him as it always supported his people. He may take the new industrial jobs, but he is ready to return in a moment to the old methods and the old spots. Toward these newer means of earning a livelihood he maintains a skepticism. The plantations were once the great establishments; they went. So, he suspects, will the oil derricks and the rest of it. He will continue to trudge about the marsh and nose his boat through the canals, and when a good season is over he will play cards and drink with his friends at the bar; he will take his wife to the dance on Saturday and he will not mind spending his money. Didn' he work for it, ahn? He will stretch along the levee and enjoy the sun; and when the winds bring him the stir of the bird wings and the caress of the orange blossoms, he will know that his life is happy.

And toward the outer world the Deltan retains a quality of sharp truculence. He can hold his own against any city man, and he don' care who knows it, no. He hasn't been trimmed to New Orleans' size, he tells you. There is a saying along the west bank that sums up this attitude as well as any. The Deltan shoves out his chin and utters his challenge: *"I will and you can't stop me; I won't and you can't make me!"* He is, as ever, a direct actionist; yet he can combine his action with a bit of cunning. A dozen men and women have told with pride of the feat of a certain fisherman. He was pleased with the new road that the officials finally extended past his house; but he did not approve the way they failed to maintain it. One night he went out with a shovel and pick and struggled to enlarge the hole in the center. The next evening he did the same, and the next. Soon he had almost a crater, and one of the big-shot politicos broke an axle in it. The road was fixed.

Returning to the Delta last Christmas, on a day that seemed like green spring, I arrived during the morning at the home of my friends, a French family with Spanish and Tocko connections. It had not been an especially good year for them; they were in debt to the Anglo-Saxon storekeeper who lived next door. But it was the holiday, and what did a thing like that matter on such an occasion? The family had its fine orange wine; I brought some from New Orleans and, sitting around and watching Maman and the girls as they worked at the meal, we finished it. We went next door for more; proudly the merchant showed me a sign of his affluence—a large, prepared turkey, acquired at a specialty house in New Orleans. Unquestionably it was a fine fowl, thoroughly baked and decorated, though the filling seemed a bit pale and there was no gravy. Meanwhile I thought I detected a glimmer of disapproval in the storekeeper's eye, and I remembered my friend's bill at his place. He made the sale, wished us a Merry Christmas, locked the door with a precise gesture and went to his wife and his select, correct turkey.

We moved on to our adventure in dark meat, rice, and gravy—several pairs of magnificent wild ducks, shot the previous day, now gloriously metamorphosed with oysters, bayleaf, thyme, shallots, garlic, and other elements of Deep Delta virtuosity. We had no little bowl of cranberry sauce as the merchant did, and we did not miss it. The meal was long and strenuous and zestful. A Tocko aunt contributed a festive oyster salad, dripping with olive oil; the Spanish branch of the family brought over a redfish, seasoned to the last fin of its tail, of such a degree of delectability that one participant said "you want' keep it in your mouth all the time without swallowing."

Afterward the friends and relatives came. A Tocko cousin

produced an accordion, and a French grandfather sang an old peasant song. Over the wine I heard at least six languages in light-hearted conglomeration. The father, born French, had learned Spanish from his wife; he had picked up the Slavic tongue from others, and knew a little Italian, a Filipino dialect, and considerable English. An ancient neighbor used only French and his shoulders to express himself. Several visitors spoke fluently in Slavic, moderately well in French, and hesitantly in English. One robust oysterman seemed to comprehend every one of the tongues, but his remarks were always Tocko. A good-humored couple managed easily: he spoke to her only in French; she answered only in Italian. Their daughter listened to both of them and interjected comment—only in English; both knew what she said but neither essayed the speech that she chose. And when an acquaintance passed, everyone yelled at him, each in a different tongue. All told stories, on his friends and on himself; and one of the uncles broke out into such laughs that he fell off the gallery on top of a stray hog and lay there chuckling until the children helped him up. A pilot-cousin, passing on the river, blew his whistle, and some of us went to the levee to call to him.

Who wanted turkey and cranberries on a day like that?

Acknowledgments

As in the case of my previous book, "The Bayous of Louisiana," primarily again, to Eleonora Waldmann Wharton, for her intelligent and understanding assistance; and to Tess Crager, who suggested the present one; to Dr. Hewitt L. Ballowe, for his generosity and skilful aid; to the late E. P. (Pat) O'Donnell, who first introduced me to the richnesses of the Deep Delta; and to the Reverend Robert Wilken, O.F.M.

To Judge Albert Estopinal, Dr. Louis Ducros, Karl and Eunice Gille, and "Dad" Gille; to Roger Baudier; to Dr. Richard Joel Russell, Professor Fred B. Kniffen, and Professor Clair A. Brown; to Percy Viosca, Jr., Dr. James Nelson Gowanloch, and James N. McConnell; to Mrs. Roberta Green, Mrs. Ernest Roger, Jr., Urbane O. Hennen, Professor William T. Penfound, Ednard T. Waldo, and Florence Dymond.

To the Right Reverend Monsignor Joseph Langlois, P.A., V.G., for hitherto unpublished material regarding his uncle, Father Langlois, the botanist-priest of Plaquemines.

To the late Robert Usher, Librarian of the Howard-Tilton Memorial Library, Tulane University, and to Marguerite D. Renshaw, Mrs. Viola Andersen Perotti, Elsie Bing, Mrs. Mary Bell Herndon, Mrs. Elisabeth Shannon, and Mrs. F. H. Wilson of his staff.

To James A. McMillen, Director of Libraries, Louisiana State University, and to Mrs. Ruth Campbell, Curator of the Louisiana Room, Hill Memorial Library, Louisiana State University.

To Mrs. Cammie Garrett Henry of Melrose Plantation.

To Arthur W. Van Pelt, J. Ben Meyer, Alvar Hudson, Peter Kopanica, Victor Baker, Nick Bubrig, Jacinto E. Esmele, John C. De Armas, Jr., Angegard Buras, Anna and Nora Bannon, Mr. and Mrs. J. C. Ballay, Justice Omer Perez, Colonel C. Robert

Churchill, André Olivier, Florence and Anna Marie Kane, Margaret Dixon, Frances Bryson, Helen Gilkison, and to Miss Essae M. Culver of the Louisiana Library Commission.

To the Reverend Ambrose Kroger, O.F.M.; to the Reverend Jerome Haynes, S.V.D.; to the Reverend Peter Oswald, S.V.D.; the Reverend James Finnegan, and the Reverend Peter Boerding, S.V.D.

Selected Bibliography

Books

Anthony, Irvin. *Paddle Wheels and Pistols.* Philadelphia, 1929.

Arthur, Stanley C., and Kernion, George C. H. de. *Old Families of Louisiana.* New Orleans, 1931.

Basso, Hamilton. *Beauregard, the Great Creole.* New York and London, 1933.

Baudier, Roger. *The Catholic Church in Louisiana.* New Orleans, 1931.

Berquin-Duvallon. *Vue de la Colonie Espagnole du Mississippi.* Paris, 1802.

Brower, J. V. *The Mississippi River and Its Source.* Minneapolis, 1893.

Butler, Pierce. *Judah P. Benjamin.* Philadelphia, 1906.

Butler, Ruth L. (Tr.) *Journal of Paul du Ru.* Chicago and Crawfordsville, Ind., 1934.

Cable, George W. *The Creoles of Louisiana.* New York, 1884.

Castellanos, Henry C. *New Orleans As It Was.* New Orleans, 1895.

Chambers, Henry E. *History of Louisiana.* Chicago and New York, 1925.

———. *Mississippi Valley Beginnings.* New York, 1922.

Chambers, Julius. *The Mississippi and Its Wonderful Valley.* New York and London, 1910.

Charlevoix, Francois X. de. *Journal of a Voyage to North America.* London, 1761.

Cline, Isaac M. *Tropical Cyclones.* New York, 1926.

Corthell, E. S. *A History of the Jetties at the Mouth of the Mississippi River.* New York, 1881.

Cox, Isaac J. (Ed.) *The Journeys of René Robert Cavelier, Sieur de La Salle.* New York, 1905.

Cramer, Zadok. *The Navigator*. Pittsburg, 1806.

Creecy, J. R. *Scenes in the South*. Washington, 1860.

Cummings, Samuel. *The Western Pilot*. Cincinnati, 1848.

Darby, William. *A Geographical Description of the State of Louisiana*. Philadelphia, 1816.

———. *The Emigrant's Guide*. New York, 1818.

Daubeny, Charles. *Journal of a Tour through the United States and in Canada*. Oxford, 1843.

Dayton, Fred E. *Steamboat Days*. New York, 1939.

Dennett, Daniel. *Louisiana As It Is*. New Orleans, 1876.

Desdunes, Rodolphe L. *Nos Hommes et Nôtre Histoire*. Montreal, 1911.

Dictionary of American Biography. New York, 1928-37.

Dixon, Frank H. *A Traffic History of the Mississippi River*. Washington, 1909.

Du Bois, William E. B. *Black Reconstruction*. New York, 1933.

Ficklen, John Rose. *History of Reconstruction in Louisiana (Through 1868)*. Baltimore, 1910.

Fiske, John. *The Mississippi Valley in the Civil War*. Boston and New York, 1900.

Fortier, Alcée. *History of Louisiana*. New York, 1904.

———. (Ed.) *Louisiana: Comprising Sketches of Parishes, Towns, Persons, Arranged in Cyclopedic Form*. Atlanta, 1909.

———. *Louisiana Studies*. New York, 1894.

French, B. F. *Historical Collections of Louisiana*. New York, 1853.

Gayarré, Charles. *History of Louisiana*. New Orleans, 1903.

Goodspeed Publishing Company. *Biographical and Historical Memoirs of Louisiana*. Chicago, 1892.

Gould, Emerson W. *Fifty Years on the Mississippi*. St. Louis, 1889.

Hall, James. *Notes on the Western States*. Philadelphia, 1838.

Hammond, John Martin. *Quaint and Historic Forts of North America*. Philadelphia and London, 1915.

Historical Sketch Book and Guide to New Orleans and Environs. New York, 1885.

Hulbert, Archer B. *The Paths of Inland Commerce*. New Haven, 1920.

Hutchins, Thomas. *An Historical Narrative and Topographical Description of Louisiana and West Florida.* Philadelphia, 1784.

Ingraham, J. H. *The Sunny South.* Philadelphia, 1860.

James, Marquis. *Andrew Jackson: The Border Captain.* Indianapolis, 1933.

Kammer, Edward J. *A Socio-Economic Survey of the Marsh-dwellers of Four Southeastern Louisiana Parishes.* Catholic University of America Press, Washington, D.C., 1941.

Kendall, John S. *History of New Orleans.* Chicago, 1922.

King, Grace. *Creole Families of New Orleans.* New York, 1921.

———. *De Soto in the Land of Florida.* New York, 1898.

———. *Jean Baptiste le Moyne, Sieur de Bienville.* New York, 1892.

Latour, Major A. LaCarrière. *Memoirs of the War in West Florida and Louisiana.* Philadelphia, 1816.

Le Page du Pratz, Antoine S. *The History of Louisiana.* London, 1763.

Lonn, Ella. *Reconstruction in Louisiana.* (*After 1868*). New York, 1918.

Louisiana: A Guide to the State. American Guide Series. New York, 1941.

Lyell, Sir Charles. *A Second Visit to the United States of North America.* New York, 1849.

———. *Travels in the United States.* London, 1845.

Margry, Pierre. (Ed.) *Mémoires et documents pour servir à l'histoire des origines françaises des pays d'outre-mer, 1614-1754.* Paris, 1879-88.

Martin, François-Xavier. *The History of Louisiana from the Earliest Period.* New Orleans, 1829.

Mathews, John Lathrop. *Remaking the Mississippi.* New York, 1909.

McCaleb, Thomas. *The Louisiana Book.* New Orleans, 1894.

Meade, Robert Douthat. *Judah P. Benjamin, Confederate Statesman.* New York, 1943.

Murphy, Edmund Robert. *Henry de Tonty, Fur Trader of the Mississippi Valley.* Baltimore, 1941.

Nolte, Vincent. *Fifty Years in Both Hemispheres.* New York, 1854.

Nordhoff, Charles. *The Cotton States in the Spring and Summer of 1875.* New York, 1876.

Ogg, Frederic Austin. *The Opening of the Mississippi.* New York, 1904.

Parkman, Francis. *La Salle and the Discovery of the West.* Boston, 1907.

Parton, James. *General Butler in New Orleans.* Boston, 1866.

———. *Life of Andrew Jackson.* Boston, 1870.

Perrin du Lac, F. M. *Voyage dans les Deux Louisianes.* Paris, 1805.

Phelps, Albert. *Louisiana: A Record of Expansion.* Boston, 1905.

Phillips, Ulrich B. *Life and Labor in the Old South.* New York, 1929.

Pittman, Philip. *The Present State of the European Settlements on the Mississippi.* London, 1770.

Read, William A. *Louisiana French.* Baton Rouge, 1931.

Rightor, Edward. (Ed.) *Standard History of New Orleans.* Chicago, 1900.

Robertson, James Alexander. *Louisiana under the Rule of Spain, France and the United States.* Cleveland, 1911.

Robin, C. C. *Voyages dans l'Interieur de la Louisiane.* Paris, 1807.

Rowland, Mrs. Dunbar. *Andrew Jackson's Campaign Against the British, or The Mississippi Valley in the War of 1812.* New York, 1926.

Rowland, Dunbar. (Ed.) *Official Letterbooks of William C. C. Claiborne.* Jackson, Miss., 1917.

Saxon, Lyle, *Father Mississippi.* New York, 1927.

Scroggs, William Oscar. *The Story of Louisiana.* Indianapolis, 1924.

Sears, L. M. *John Slidell.* Durham, N. C., 1925.

Shea, John D. G. *Early Voyages Up and Down the Mississippi.* Albany, 1861.

Shugg, Roger W. *Origins of Class Struggle in Louisiana.* University, La., 1939.

Smith, Buckingham. (Trans.) *The Narrative of Alvar Núñez Cabeza de Vaca.* Washington, 1851.

Sparks, William H. *The Memories of Fifty Years.* Philadelphia, 1870.

Stanwood, Edward. *A History of the Presidency.* Boston and New York, 1898.

Stoddard, Amos. *Sketches of Louisiana.* Philadelphia, 1812.

Stubbs, William C. *A Handbook of Louisiana.* New Orleans, 1895.

Tannehill, I. R. *Hurricanes.* Princeton, N. J., 1938.

Trollope, Frances. *Domestic Manners of the Americans.* London, 1832.

Trowbridge, J. T. *The South.* Hartford, Conn., 1866.

Twain, Mark. (Samuel L. Clemens). *Life on the Mississippi.* New York and London, 1903.

Viosca, Percy, Jr. *Louisiana Out of Doors.* New Orleans, 1933.

Walker, Alexander. *The Life of Andrew Jackson.* New York, 1858.

Waring, George, and Cable, George W. *History and Present Condition of New Orleans.* Washington, 1881.

Warmoth, Henry C. *War, Politics and Reconstruction; Stormy Days in Louisiana.* New York, 1930.

Warren, Harris Gaylord. *The Sword Was Their Passport.* Baton Rouge, 1943.

Williamson, Frederick W. *Yesterday and Today in Louisiana Agriculture.* Baton Rouge, 1940.

Periodicals and Pamphlets

Browne, C. A. "The Development of the Sugar Cane Industry in Louisiana and the Southern United States." *Proceedings,* International Society Sugar Cane Technologists, Sixth Congress, Baton Rouge, La., Oct. 24–Nov. 4, 1938. (Reprint.)

Eads, James Buchanan. "Physics and Hydraulics of the Miss. River." New Orleans, 1876.

"The Election Frauds in Plaquemines Parish." *Louisiana Historical Quarterly,* July, 1927.

Faye, Stanley. "Privateersmen of the Gulf and their Prizes." *Louisiana Historical Quarterly,* October, 1939.

"Fishers of Men among Fishermen of Louisiana." *Report of the*

American Board of Catholic Missions, July 1, 1936–July 1, 1937. Chicago, 1937.

Fontaine, Edward. "Contributions to the Physical Geography of the Mississippi River and Its Delta." *Journal of American Geographical Society.* New York, 1872.

Greer, James Kimmins. "Louisiana Politics, 1845-1861." *Louisiana Historical Quarterly,* July, 1929.

Hearn, Lafcadio. "St. Malo." *Harper's Weekly,* March 3, 1883.

Kendall, John S. "The Huntsmen of Black Ivory." *Louisiana Historical Quarterly,* January, 1941.

———. "Piracy in the Gulf of Mexico, 1816-23." *Louisiana Historical Quarterly,* July, 1925.

———. "The Successors of Lafitte." *Louisiana Historical Quarterly,* April, 1941.

Marigny, Bernard Mandeville de. "Reflections on the Campaign of General Andrew Jackson." (Tr. by Grace King.) *Louisiana Historical Quarterly,* January, 1923.

McLure, Mary Lilla. "The Elections of 1860 in Louisiana." *Louisiana Historical Quarterly,* October, 1926.

Penfound, William, and Hathaway, Edward S. "Plant Communities in the Marshlands of Southeastern Louisiana." *Ecological Monographs,* January, 1938.

Prichard, Walter. "Some Interesting Glimpses of Louisiana a Century Ago." *Louisiana Historical Quarterly,* January, 1941.

Ries, Maurice. "The Mississippi Fort, Called Fort de la Boulaye." *Louisiana Historical Quarterly,* October, 1936.

Russell, Richard Joel; Howe, H. V.; and others. "Lower Mississippi River Delta." Louisiana Department of Conservation, *Geological Bulletin No. 8,* 1936.

Russell, Richard Joel. "Louisiana Stream Patterns." *Bulletins of American Association of Petroleum Geologists,* August, 1939.

Scribner, Frank Lamson. "Southern Botanists." *Torrey Botanical Club Bulletin,* Vol. 20, 1893. (Typewritten copy at Howard-Tilton Memorial Library, New Orleans.)

Scroggs, W. O. "Rural Life in the Mississippi Valley about 1803." *Proceedings of the Mississippi Valley Historical Association,* VIII, 1915.

Shugg, Roger W. "Survival of the Plantation System in Louisiana." *Journal of Southern History,* August, 1937.

Smith, T. Lynn. "The Population of Louisiana; Its Composition and Changes." Bulletin No. 293, Louisiana State University. University, La., 1937.

Souvenir Program of the St. Maurice Church Fair, St. Bernard Parish. New Orleans, 1912.

Stubbs, W. C. "Origin and Development of the Sugar Industry of Louisiana." *Louisiana Sugar Planter and Sugar Manufacturer,* June 2, 1923.

Wilken, Robert, O. F. M. "Crosses on the Delta." Historical Sketch Commemorating the Diamond Jubilee of Our Lady of Good Harbor Church. New Orleans, 1940.

Theses

Landry, Ernest Adam. The History of Forts Jackson and St. Philip. M. A., Louisiana State University, 1938.

Pharr, Jane. The Administration of Federal Relief in Plaquemines Parish. M. A., Tulane University, 1934.

Schneidau, John Donald, Jr. Plant Succession on a Drained Wetland Area in the Vicinity of New Orleans. M. S., Tulane University, 1940.

Miscellaneous

Inventory of the Parish Archives of Louisiana, No. 44, St. Bernard Parish; No. 38, Plaquemines Parish. Department of Archives, Louisiana State University. University, La., 1938.

Journal of the Special Committee, House of Representatives, to Investigate the Frauds Perpetrated in the State, During the Late Presidential Election. New Orleans, 1845.

Newspapers and Journals

Files of *De Bow's Review, Louisiana Sugar Planter and Sugar Manufacturer, New Orleans Item, New Orleans Times-*

Democrat, New Orleans Times-Picayune, New Orleans States; the *Rice Planter;* the *Plaquemines Protector of Pointe à la Hache; L'Observateur Louisianais* of New Orleans.

Index